(White)Washing
Our Sins Away

(White)Washing Our Sins Away

American Mainline Churches,
Music, Power, and Diversity

Deborah Justice

SUNY
PRESS

Published by State University of New York Press, Albany

© 2022 State University of New York

All rights reserved

Printed in the United States of America

No part of this book may be used or reproduced in any manner whatsoever without written permission. No part of this book may be stored in a retrieval system or transmitted in any form or by any means including electronic, electrostatic, magnetic tape, mechanical, photocopying, recording, or otherwise without the prior permission in writing of the publisher.

For information, contact State University of New York Press, Albany, NY
www.sunypress.edu

Library of Congress Cataloging-in-Publication Data

Names: Justice, Deborah, author.
Title: (White)washing our sins away : American mainline churches, music,
  power, and diversity / Deborah Justice.
Other titles: Whitewashing our sins away
Description: Albany : State University of New York Press, 2022. | Includes
  bibliographical references and index.
Identifiers: LCCN 2022005648 | ISBN 9781438489612 (hardcover : alk. paper) |
  ISBN 9781438489636 (ebook)
Subjects: LCSH: Church music—Protestant churches. | Church music—United
  States. | Public worship—Social aspects—United States.
Classification: LCC ML3111 .J87 2022 | DDC 781.71/0973—dc23
LC record available at https://lccn.loc.gov/2022005648

10 9 8 7 6 5 4 3 2 1

Contents

Acknowledgments		vii
Introduction: Academia, Presbyterians, and Me		1
Chapter 1	Using Sound to Reconfigure Mainline Protestant Sacred and Social Identity	13
Chapter 2	"The Least Puzzling or Flamboyant of Christians"	41
Chapter 3	Telling the Story of a Useable Past	57
Interlude		83
Chapter 4	Sonic Diversity: Deciding When to Hear Harmony	95
Chapter 5	"We're Only Medium Contemporary": Creating Identity Boundaries	131
Chapter 6	Spatial Diversity: Making Places for Traditional and Contemporary Worship	155
Chapter 7	Social Diversity: Defrosting the Frozen Chosen	181
Conclusion: Music, Faith, and Reconfiguring American Protestant Identities		215
Notes		225
Bibliography		239
Index		253

Acknowledgments

This project has been building for years—there are many people to thank.

Reaching deeply back, I want to thank some of my high school teachers who set me on a path of research and writing. Garrett Woznicki was my senior year English teacher, as well as the faculty supervisor for the school newspaper where I served as senior editor for two years. Woz taught me to write and critically engage the world. Victor Brutout ignited my interest in American history and contributed to that path of analytical writing.

I owe my mentors in the fields of ethnomusicology and related fields a debt of gratitude. Anne Rasmussen helped set me on the trajectory studying music and religion at the College of William and Mary. She provided a strong example of uncompromising scholarship and teaching, spending countless hours poring over thesis drafts, shepherding my first conference papers to fruition, and supporting initial ethnographic research. Mark Slobin, Neely Bruce, Eric Charry, Alec McLane, and Jody Cormack strengthened my scholarship at Wesleyan University. The Department of Folklore and Ethnomusicology at Indiana University continued to help me along the way; special thanks to Alan Burdette, Melonnee Burnim, Ruth Stone, Judah Cohen, John Kay, Portia Maultsby, John McDowell, and Daniel Reed. Our cadre of graduate students helped each other learn to write and research. Special thanks to Dave Lewis, Rebekah Moore, and Izlem Ozdegirmenci Bayraktar. I am also especially grateful to Fredara Hadley for her feedback on this manuscript.

Grant funding from the Louisville Institute supported early stages of this project's research, and generous support from the Yale Institute of Sacred Music in the form of a postdoctoral scholarship assisted formative years of this project. During my time there, conversations with Martin viii / Acknowledgments

Jean, Tisa Wagner, Chloe Starr, and Melanie Ross, and the 2012–2013 Postdoctoral and Visiting Fellows Harold Buchinger, Melvin Butler, Kathy Foley Andrew Irving, Ayla Lepine, and David Stowe were invaluable.

Thanks go to colleagues and mentors from Syracuse University's Department of Art and Music History who have supported my working through various iterations and aspects of this project: Theo Cateforis, Amanda Winkler, Romita Ray, Carol Babiracki, and Sydney Hutchinson.

Professional colleagues from the Society of Ethnomusicology (particularly the Religion, Music, and Sound section); Christian Congregational Music Conference in beautiful Rippon, England; International Society for the Study of Popular Music; and the International Society for Media Religion and Culture have helped hone my scholarship over years of conference presentations, shared meals, and late-nights drinks: Sarah Bereza, Danielle Brown, Joshua Busman, Florian Carl, Basil Considine (to whom I am also deeply indebted for his generous editing skills), Jonathan Dueck, Jeffers Engelhardt, Stewart Hoover, Tripp Hudgins, Bo kyung Blenda Im, Monique Ingalls, Birgitta Johnson, Alisha Lola Jones, Andrew Mall, Maren Haynes Marchesini, Nate Myrick, Anna Nekola, Adam Perez, Mark Porter, Lester Ruth, Tom Wagner, and Deborah Whitehead. Working with these scholars has improved my work and left me greatly enriched with friendship and comradery.

Thanks go to the worshipers, musicians, and clergy of many churches that I have called home, visited, and researched, from the First Presbyterian Churches of Williamsburg, Bloomington, New Haven, and Ithaca; Neffsville Mennonite in Lancaster; St. Paul's United Methodist Church in Ithaca; and beyond. Presbyterian Research Services has been wonderfully supportive in providing information and materials. Thanks go to First Presbyterian Church offices of Tucumcari, New Mexico, and New Haven, Connecticut, and to Pam Kidd for providing photos. The kind people of Hillsboro Presbyterian Church welcomed my multiyear research with open arms, honesty, and generosity: Thank you. David Kidd, Pam Kidd, Nancy McCurley, Tim Gmeiner, Sherry Kelly, Stephen Nix, and too many individual congregants to list shared their minds, hearts, time, and music.

Friends and family have generously, patiently supported this project, from early stages to final edits. Thanks to David Deacon, Rachel and Daegan Fox von Swearingen, Deb Shebish, and Jochen Wirsing: you have been much-appreciated sounding boards for years. My extended family on both the Justice and Bower sides have provided a loving network of care and support throughout my life: Thank you. In addition to giving me a strong foundation in the church, my parents, Robert and Ruth Justice, have provided inexhaustible love and endurance in listening to me talk about my research. Thank you. Finally, thanks to my dear son, Jonah Robert Justice, whose little in utero kicks kept me writing along and whose smiles now light up my world.

Introduction

Academia, Presbyterians, and Me

WHITE PRESBYTERIAN CONGREGANT IN HIS LATE FORTIES: It's so nice that you are here to study our church. So, you're getting your degree in what now?

ME: Ethnomusicology. It's—

WHITE PRESBYTERIAN CONGREGANT IN HIS LATE FORTIES: [*Interrupting*] So, the study of ethnic music?

ME: Well, it's more the study of music in culture, or culture in music, depending. Like musical anthropology.

WHITE PRESBYTERIAN CONGREGANT IN HIS LATE FORTIES: But you're here at a Presbyterian church? [*Pauses, considers*] Well, I guess if you think about it, we're all part of some ethnic group or another. Huh. I never thought about it. [*Grinning, he calls down the hallway to his wife*] Hey honey! We're ethnic!

It is indeed true that White American mainline Protestants are an unusual subject of study for an ethnomusicologist like myself. It is so strange that I am opening *(White)Washing Our Sins Away* by telling my own story— as a White person, a Presbyterian, a scholar, a musician—to situate this work within the broader study of American religion, music, and society. Mainline Protestantism still lies outside the expected and actualized arena of ethnomusicology as a discipline. This is because, as the congregant's preceding comments allude to, interconnected scaffolds of race, class, and

2 | (White)Washing Our Sins Away

power have structured the entwined historical development of both the academy and religious institutions in America. In other words, White Christians have normally studied the cultural practices of "Other" people rather than our own.

As a small child, some of my favorite memories involve the visceral experience of playing at church: stacking hymnals like play blocks, hiding in the closet of choir robes, pretending the long golden candle-lighter was a magic wand, smelling the pungent wax of old candles in the storage closet, and—perhaps best of all—pulling on the bell rope. My father was the pastor of a small Presbyterian congregation and quite often, when both my parents were busy during the week, I would get to go with him to work. Our northern Minnesota town so tiny that it did not have a traffic light. Life was pretty simple. Weekly schedules of Sunday worship and Christian education and Wednesday choir practices (my mother is an alto) shaped much of the ebb and flow of life.

In 1989, we moved from what was basically southern Canada to southern California. My father had decided to pursue a graduate degree in clinical psychology at Fuller Theological Seminary's School of Psychology and Marriage and Family Therapy. As a kid, my mind was blown by new-to-me racial and linguistic diversity of the Los Angeles suburbs. I had never thought about race much because everyone around me had been White. In Minnesota, I think I had seen one Black student in my whole school and foreign languages were not prevalent, aside from someone's Lutheran grandpa praying a Swedish blessing or foodie discussions of *lutefisk* (a traditional Nordic delicacy of dried, aged fish pickled in lye) and *potica* (an Eastern European dessert bread). In my new California school, I was one of only three White students in my class, my new best friend was an Argentinian immigrant kid from across the apartment courtyard, and the biracial clerks at the local grocery store were multilingual. I did not have a lot to express about my own identity besides "White"—my parents had some vague details about our European-rooted family histories, but they were among increasing numbers of White Americans who were not thinking of themselves as coming from specific European-descended ethnic groups, but rather as simply "American."[1]

As we settled into our new environment, our family did what most pastors' families do once they have left full-time pulpit service: We went "church shopping." In our tiny rural Minnesota town, the idea of "shopping" for church options would have been fairly laughable due to the small size of the community (there were only four churches in town), but in the

California suburbs, our family's worship choices were reflecting broader societal shifts in living patterns and religious consumption (see chapter 1).

We tried out so many churches. Combining my mother's heavily evangelical background, my father's higher church tendencies (despite a severe aversion to incense), and my own ten-year-old preferences, Sunday dinners became a "postgame" analysis that would put many sports analysts to shame. While the church facility, size, and architecture, preaching, and other aspects were heavily debated, music was always a central feature. Did they have a choir? If yes, how was the choir? If no, what did they have instead? How was the repertoire? How was the vocal quality? Did the musicians seem like they were worshiping or performing? Along those lines, how was the organist? If they didn't have an organist, what did they have? What were the songs that we sang as a congregation? Did the other people in the congregation actually sing, too? Overall, musically, was what we had just experienced any good? And on what criteria were we assigning a rating of "good"?

Just by the time our family had finally settled into an alternate Sunday compromise between a Nazarene church on odd Sundays and an Episcopalian congregation on even ones, we moved and had to start it all again.

This time, in 1992, we repeated the whole process with a heavy dose of local Mennonite subculture in Lancaster, Pennsylvania. Things were different then because the church music scene had evolved. More and more congregations were offering an informal Sunday morning service with modern, amplified praise band music in addition to their traditional organ-and-choir-based worship. These services were similar to the acoustic-guitar-toting Jesus People of the 1960s and '70s, but there was something different about this newer repertoire and its performance. Mainline Protestant traditionalists seemed to be suspicious of the music's secular sound and evangelical overtones. Although it was hard to see the bigger picture as it was emerging at the time, White Protestant congregations of both mainline and evangelical varieties were beginning to draw battle lines for a pervasive, sprawling aesthetic and theological conflict that came to be known as the Worship Wars. Now, not only did our family have to decide on a congregation, we had to pick between Traditional or Contemporary worship. Sunday dinner debates continued.

I left my parents to figure it out for themselves by going off to the College of William and Mary. I loved my new church in Williamsburg, Virginia. First Presbyterian had a historical brick façade that blended into the colonial town, solid preaching in which Pastor Wilson asked

4 | (White)Washing Our Sins Away

hard questions more often than he dispensed easy answers, and it was musically top-notch in my eighteen-year-old opinion. My family had never identified racial diversity as an important factor in our Sunday dinner postgame analyses, and I was only slowing coming to a greater awareness of the world, so I was not surprised or particularly bothered that First Presbyterian was overwhelmingly White (like most American Presbyterian congregations). To the contrary, I took it as a good, progressive sign that one of the paid section leaders in the choir was a dark-skinned Black man whose smiling face stood out in contrast to the congregation. The Sunday morning worshipers never did diversify significantly over the four years that I attended the church, and only years later would I read sociologist Gerardo Marti's work on White congregations hiring worship leaders and musicians of "conspicuous color" in efforts to diversify their faith communities.[2] At the time, I was just happy that the choir sounded great, the congregation sang enthusiastically, the organist was a university keyboard professor, and, on top of everything else, First Pres had a college handbell group that took practice as seriously as our Sunday brunch waffles.

I was not, however, at William and Mary primarily to find a place to worship. I was there to study ethnomusicology. Drawn by the excellent mentor that I found in Dr. Anne Rasmussen, I saw my entry into the field back in 1998 as a positive, diversity-advancing choice (this was before we would have used the term "woke"). I was initially attracted to the study of music "in culture,"[3] or "as culture,"[4] because of my personal fascination with unfamiliar genres of music and the societies that produce them. I had been playing hammered dulcimer since I was a kid and that had taken me on a winding road that led through all kinds of music, from American old-time to Irish, Balkan, Greek, Turkish, and more. The more exotic the music was, the better; *everything* seemed so much more interesting than the classical and Christian musics my conservative parents had allowed in their home when I was growing up. I dove into ethnomusicology head first. As an undergraduate student, I played in the Indonesian gamelan ensemble and fell in love with Middle Eastern music, so much so that I studied Arabic and double-majored in Middle Eastern studies. I even spent time volunteering with the Presbyterian church in Cairo following my graduation.

I thought I had traveled fairly extensively, but working and living in Egypt was a culture shock that threw my own previous touristic experiences into sharp relief for me. The Sunday dinner points of difference my parents and I used to identify as marking American churches dramatically different from each other seemed almost insignificant now. Everything in Egypt felt so different, from the minutia of daily life to worship music and church culture to broader social norms and beliefs. It took endless hours to explain my usual American way of life to the local Egyptians, and equal amounts of time to explain their ways of life and music to the people at home. I started becoming disturbed by the unevenness of it—I was acting as a representative of Egyptian music and culture to my people at home in the United States. They thought I was an expert in it; I had specialized in this area at a nationally renowned university, after all, and I had been living in Cairo for about six months. On paper, this looked good, and I did have more experience with Egypt than the average American, but every day in Cairo, new surprises showed me how unprepared and unqualified I was for this interpretative role.

The slowly dawning awareness that was hitting twenty-two-year-old me resonates with broader dynamics within the Western academy and, in particular, the field of ethnomusicology and the related discipline of anthropology. These disciplines have a troublesome history that parallels my Egyptian experience: White Westerners studying and analytically explaining the "foreign" to people "at home." Overall, Western explorers and scholars were "discovering" things, places, and lifeways that were new to them but already well known to the "Other" peoples who had invented them. In the West, these novel foreign elements needed to be explained, interpreted, and classified, so anthropologists and ethnomusicologists developed scientific systems and methodologies for doing so. It would take me years after I got back from Cairo to understand two things: first, how the concept of ethnomusicology as a colonialist enterprise could help to explain why White mainline Protestants in America have never been a major subject of ethnomusicological, or by extension anthropological study; and, second, how important it is to American society as a whole that White mainline Protestants *do* become the subject of ethnomusicological and anthropological study.

The first step of wisdom is said to be recognizing that there are things that one does not know, and by the time I returned from Egypt to begin my master's degree in ethnomusicology, I was beginning to understand how much I did not grasp. I had started feeling subtly uncomfortable presenting myself as an expert on music cultures that were not mine. On the other hand, the apparent counter solution of somehow only allowing people to research their own traditions also seemed like a dangerous tactic that would probably increase racism. I had been taught that being

6 | (White)Washing Our Sins Away

an outsider to a tradition could sometimes bring types of distance that might be helpful in mitigating an insider's inherently biased views, but an outsider may not understand nuances and cultural details that take a lifetime to sense and understand. Any objectivity was a myth, I decided, as I went off to graduate school.

"The cardinal, the mightiest of the songbirds!" proclaimed the 2003 orientation leader at Wesleyan University in Middletown, Connecticut, as the school's mascot flew past. The beautiful New England campus offered natural areas full of gorgeous autumn trees that set off a wild mix of architectural styles. To me, though, one of the most striking things about Wesleyan was how the school's secularism and ultraliberal policies (e.g., gender-neutral housing) seemed to contrast with the religious roots reflected in its name. Wesleyan University was named for John Wesley, the father of Methodism, and is among the oldest of the originally Methodist-founded institutions of higher education in the United States. Even in its earliest days, though, Wesleyan was making itself unique: while the Methodist movement under-girded the university's early emphasis on social service and education so much so that Wesleyan's first president, Willbur Fisk, used his inaugural address to declare that education advanced two purposes: "the good of the individual educated and the good of the world," Wesleyan stood apart from many of its historical American peer colleges and universities by offering a liberal arts program rather than theological training.

In contrast, most of America's oldest institutions of higher education were founded to advance Christianity. Colonial-era universities were most frequently founded with motivations similar to those that began my undergraduate alma mater; in 1693, an English royal charter aimed to establish the College of William and Mary as a "perpetual College of Divinity, Philosophy, Languages, and other good Arts and Sciences."[5] In their primary goal of cultivating a learned clergy of White men, colonial educational institutions sought to transfer European values of Christian literacy and learning into the New World. While the distinct focus on training pastors softened over time, the connection between church and academy did not. By 1854, evangelistic Disciples of Christ leader Alexander Campbell was advancing an increasingly popular national view that "colleges and churches go hand in hand in the progress of Christian civilization."[6] Many agreed, and by 1881, 80 percent of the colleges and universities in the United States were church-related private institutions.[7] Over time, higher education has secularized, but those early connections had an impact through much of the twentieth century and continue to the present day.

By the time I attended, the secular campus culture made it quite clear that Wesleyan University was not church affiliated. I loved the modern hippie vibe and settled into a rigorous MA program. I continued my involvement with Arabic by serving as a teaching assistant for a language course. I worked in the World Music Archives and took classes in South Indian music and Ghanaian drumming. But, I wrote my master's thesis on "my" world: hammered dulcimer communities in the Eastern United States. At the end of my thesis defense, senior ethnomusicologist Mark Slobin (who after a variety of earlier research areas had turned his own scholarly sights on klezmer and Yiddish music) said, "Yes, yes, excellent work. I think we've covered every aspect. Now, I want to know: what is going on in churches? In class, you keep writing about worship conflict in churches. It's very similar to what we are having in our synagogues . . ." We talked for an hour. At the end, he walked over to his bookshelf and pulled down a slim blue book, Charles Etherington's 1962 *Protestant Worship Music: Its History and Practice*. "Take this," he said. "It's the only book I've seen that tries to talk about the lived experience of Christian music in mainline worship from an anthropological perspective. At Indiana, you could start with that, you know, if you wanted to."

Floating out of Slobin's office in 2005 on a cloud of graduate school success, I wondered how this little book could be so unique. I had never formally researched church music, but over forty eventful years had passed since *Protestant Worship Music*'s publication. The Catholic Church had undergone rigorous cultural and intellectual introspection during Vatican II. From personal experience, I knew that in Protestant circles, rising evangelicalism and the continuing turn-of-the-millennium Worship Wars had seen Christian publishers spawn scores of books, revised hymnals, expanded worship materials addressing multiculturalism, and countless articles by worship authorities debating music, culture, and the institutionalized church. Between this activity by Christian practitioners and, sometimes overlapping, scholarly productions from musicologists, ethnomusicologists, anthropologists, and sociologists, I could hardly imagine a dearth of academic coverage considering North American mainline Protestant church music within cultural and historical contexts. However, when I started looking for ethnographic resources on mainline Protestantism in the United States, I discovered that Slobin was right: there was nothing.

8 | (White)Washing Our Sins Away

For my doctoral work at Indiana University, I had planned to write about phenomenology and old-time string band music, but Slobin's questions kept swirling in my head instead. The musical controversies we had discussed at my thesis defense were intensifying. Back in Pennsylvania, the Mennonite church that my parents had finally decided upon suddenly fired both the senior pastor and the music minister over worship style issues. My own Presbyterian church in Indiana had made a series of musically based choices that resulted in their longtime organist quitting under duress. These churches were not unique in their experiences. The Worship Wars were not resolving themselves. Rather, conflicts ostensibly over musical style were flaming smoldering embers that were rooted in far deeper issues than mere sonic tensions. I decided to refocus my dissertation on the Worship Wars in American mainline Protestantism.

The oddity of middle-class White Christianity, and especially mainline Protestantism, as an ethnomusicological topic was quickly made clear to me. I had known that mainline worship was not going to be an exotic doctoral topic (American Presbyterians are so renowned for their staid worship that we are sometimes called "the frozen chosen"), but Indiana's Department of Ethnomusicology and Folklore seemed to be right in line with disciplines that loved studying "vanishing" music cultures. Presbyterianism in the United States was shrinking from being one of the nation's most influential religious cultures to becoming a small minority within the nation's religious landscape. I was hearing guitars (electric and acoustic) displacing pipe organs every Sunday. Projected lyrics were replacing denominational hymnals. Sanctuaries and crosses were being rejected for neutrally decorated fellowship halls and warehouse spaces. My preliminary research had demonstrated that no one had yet ethnographically documented mainline Protestant worship and I wanted to before it was, frankly, too late. I remembered reading a pivotal anthropological paper back when I was an undergraduate at William and Mary. In 1956, Horace Minor had described the Nacirema, an unfamiliar tribe living in North America, "as an example of the extremes to which human behavior can go."[8] Minor analyzed the Nacirema as an anthropologist of the time would have analyzed any newly discovered tribal group, but, in a satirical indictment of the academy's exoticism of "Other" cultures, he had actually subversively described contemporary Americans of the mid-1950s. Nacirema is American spelled backward. Fifty years later, it was time, I thought, to bring a serious ethnographic study of musical conflicts in mainline Protestantism, or rather, of a major transition in American religious and musical life, to the academic table.

I was, again, wrong. My class cohort was studying "exotic" topics from around the world, from Bali to Nepal to Cuba. In a Music and Religion class where we were supposed to present audio examples from our research, when I played excerpts of Contemporary worship music, the other students and the professor burst into laughter. "Oh, wow, it's like '80s pop karaoke, but somehow even worse!" As my colleagues made fun of both the music and the people making it, I was balancing a sense of personal insult (after all these months of talking about our projects, how didn't they respect that this was my immediate family's religious tradition?) and shock that the guise of professional objectivity could fall off so quickly when faced with something "at home." In his study of evangelical Christian music, Jewish sociologist Ari Kelman writes about encountering a similar disconnect within the academy:

> My academic colleagues, who were not concerned with my faith, as they assumed that I did not have much . . . were concerned with the withering effects they believed that worship music might have on it. Working primarily in secular, research universities, some of my colleagues are scholars of music and others are scholars of religion, and their inquiries betrayed some shared assumptions . . .[9]

My classmates seemed to share similar assumptions about musical and spiritual quality with both Kelman's colleagues and scholars at most Western colleges and universities: studying modern, White middle-class Christian worship music in America was at best unnecessary for—and at worst subversive to—the goals of an objective, secular, diverse, and liberal academy.

Opposition to analyzing mainline Protestants' lived experience of sacred musicking[10] extended into the all-important realm of graduate funding. My department's director of graduate studies told me that securing external sources for my dissertation research and writing would likely be nearly impossible: "Good luck, but no one is interested in funding the study of sacred or religious music, especially church music." He was a scholar of myth, so I wrote off his comments as ironically funny until they seemed to prove true. With the exception of one generous grant from the

10 | (White)Washing Our Sins Away

Presbyterian-linked Louisville Foundation, I could not get external funding. In terms of quality, my work was on par with my cohort of fellow students, but as I hit paywall after paywall, I started to understand the centuries of academic history that had built this funding infrastructure. My work was attempting to analyze—not advance—Christianity, so most religiously based funding sources were not suitable. Ethnomusicological and anthropological sources balked at the seeming establishmentarianism of the study. These disciplines, often rightly, tend to lambast the harm that Western colonialist and missionary interventions have done to local cultures around the world. How, they asked me, could I want to study the religious communities who were responsible for this history of colonialism and oppression without vilifying Presbyterians as cultural destroyers? Was I trying to glorify this cultural meddling? Wasn't I a Presbyterian myself? Was my work self-servingly promoting White supremacy?

No, absolutely not.

White mainline Protestants in America have generally not been the subject of ethnographic research because their practices have been considered the normal default to which the "ethnic" is compared. "If you were in charge of something big before 1960," notes religious historian David Hollinger, "chances are you grew up in a white Protestant milieu."[11] Just as comparative musicology and early ethnomusicology compared the "Others" to the West, and even as the academy has secularized, underlying assumptions of WASP (White Anglo-Saxon Protestant) normalcy and cultural hegemony have prevailed. "We," the liberalized WASPs of the Western academy, have been studied through qualitative sociological means (which assume levels of cultural familiarity with the subjects of study) but have not been subjected to the substantive ethnographic methods that we have been applying to the rest of the world. This is because "we" have been operating from the assumption of "us" as the racial, religious, and cultural default. "We" have been so normal that "we" are well understood and do not need to be studied.

But this is not true.

A lack of understanding about how the long-hegemonic racial and religious majority of the United States experiences itself—and particularly how it experiences itself while slowing slipping from that dominant position—holds broad implications for American society. As I write this in the summer of 2020, the nation is undergoing an unprecedented period of progressive change. Historian Ibram Kendi has recently asserted that "the only way to undo racism is to consistently identify and describe it—

and then dismantle it."[12] I am not alleging that mainline Protestantism or the academy have been purposefully racist . . . but, as one of the White Presbyterians in my dissertation research said about her predominantly White church, "it sure would be nice if we had more Black people." By studying White mainline Protestants through the same lenses normally applied to "Other" people, *(White)Washing Our Sins Away* contributes to an antiracist cultural shift. It has taken over ten years, expanded research, more international experience, and this cultural shift in America until, finally, this book's time has come.

(White)Washing Our Sins Away certainly aims to provide White mainline Protestants' insight of ourselves, but the book also reaches much farther. *(White)Washing* holds relevance for anyone who has involvement with such Christianity—both as manifested in individuals and in the cultural and education systems central to the United States.

Chapter 1

Using Sound to Reconfigure Mainline Protestant Sacred and Social Identity

Shortly after I moved to Syracuse, New York, in 2012, I did an internet search for local Presbyterian churches. One result caught my attention. Underneath the headline of "First Presbyterian Church United: A community of faith in downtown and greater Syracuse NY," the website had a simple message: THE END **THE CHURCH IS CLOSED.**

The congregation had been one of the oldest in the city, with prominent Syracuse families as fixtures of the majority White congregation. The complex featured three historical buildings, stained glass windows by the elite Tiffany and Keck studios, and an ornate pipe organ. However, losing about 95 percent of its membership over the previous half century (dropping from one thousand to eighty-five faithful) had decimated the congregation financially and socially. After 178 years of service, the church closed after final services on Easter Sunday of 2012.

Local church leadership had called on the Presbyterian denomination for help in closing the congregation. Such terminations were becoming so common that an experienced "transitional Presbyter," the Reverend Doctor Marianne Rhebergen, was assigned to the case. The remaining church members voted to create a small soup kitchen and adopt a new mission of nontraditional worship outside their old building. The ornate pipe organ and the choral music from the church's large collection were put up for sale.[1] Drawing on her previous experience in Poughkeepsie and Philadelphia in closing old congregations, Rhebergen tried to put a positive face on the historic closure: "This is a story of a phoenix rising out of the ashes," she told reporters from Syracuse.com. "This is a time of

14 / (White)Washing Our Sins Away

tremendous change, challenge, and opportunity for urban churches. This congregation is leading the way to what it means to be a modern urban congregation . . . [to] give up life so that something new will be born."

∾

After living in Syracuse for a while, I had been struck by the architectural beauty of one of its old churches. Every Wednesday as I biked downtown, I would pass a massive, brick gothic revival church with ivy crawling up asymmetrical towers on either side of its rose window. The founder of the architectural school at Syracuse University had designed the building in 1876 and when the evening sunset hit the west-facing stained glass, the effect was remarkable.

One Sunday in 2014, I decided to visit the congregation for worship. Pulling open the tall, heavy front door, I was greeted by a space that could easily hold hundreds. There were, however, about twenty people in the congregation. Most of them were elderly and White. Ushers enthusiastically did their duty of greeting me, giving me a bulletin, and helping me find a seat. An older woman was playing the organ as the pastor began the service. Worshipers sang the hymns, but the beautiful lofty space built for magnitudes of voices swallowed the sound.

After the service, the gray-haired woman sitting in the pew in front of me turned around and said, smiling, "You must be new here, welcome. You have such a lovely voice. I do wish we still had a choir you could join, but it was so nice to sit in front of you." As we all left the sanctuary, the pastor was standing at the door to greet participants. He grasped my hand heartily, asking if I was new in town, and making sure that I had left my contact information on the friendship registry.

Park Central was an active faith community, but it was only an echo of its former vibrant congregational self. As the beautiful building evidenced, the church was once a hub of worship in Syracuse. Yet, according to Presbyterian Research Services, by 2014, Park Central Presbyterian membership had shrunk to 144 members. Average Sunday attendance was sixty-five worshipers. Two-thirds of the members were White congregants over the age of fifty-five. Nearly 50 percent of them were over sixty-five years old. Still, remnants of Park Central's prominent, affluent past remained; by 2017, the annual congregational budget was averaging around $500,000, more than triple national Presbyterian norms. The church was holding on through surviving financial resources, rather than growing with new members.

~

While I was in Nashville, Tennessee, in 2009, I sat down with the executive presbyter of the Presbytery of Middle Tennessee, Phil Leftwich. I had just returned from a trip to Presbyterian Research Services in the national denominational headquarters in Louisville, Kentucky. The researchers had been forthcoming with national congregational statistics. For mainline Protestants in general and Presbyterians specifically, the overall numbers were—frankly—grim. Statistical projections suggested unsustainable denominational membership losses in the relatively near future.

My personal experience, however, left me confused. The Indiana church I had been worshiping in most recently and the Tennessee church I was now studying were growing in leaps and bounds. I wanted to talk to Leftwich about how he saw his own congregation and the expanding Presbytery of Middle Tennessee in light of these national statistics. Luckily for me, he was an analytical sort who mixed optimism and realism:

> We can be pleased about that comparative to the other 163 presbyteries nationwide . . . [there are only] seven others that are consistently growing . . . Now, I am pleased that that is happening rather than loss, but when I look at the real demographics of Middle Tennessee . . . demographically, the growth in this area far outruns our church growth . . . About 60 percent of the population in Middle Tennessee are unchurched.

The Presbytery of Middle Tennessee was one of the 4 percent of presbyteries that were growing. But Leftwich raised significant questions: The Nashville urban area was growing far faster—why was Presbyterian growth not keeping pace with Music City's overall expansion? How was it that more than half the people in the region remained unaffiliated with a church community? And the hardest question to answer, when would national statistics of so-called "mainline decline" catch up with the local situation?

~

16 / (White)Washing Our Sins Away

In spring of 2015, I flew from New York to Austin, Texas, to interview for a job at a Presbyterian seminary. The institution was taking a unique route; despite music being so central to worship, hardly any Presbyterian ministerial education focuses on it. This seminary wanted to address that issue. After a long day of interviewing, the committee took me for dinner and drinks at a fine dining restaurant situated in one of the downtown high-rise buildings with amazing views. Our private room had large glass windows that provided a stunning perspective on the state capitol building and rapidly growing city.

As the evening wound down over dessert and after-dinner drinks, someone asked, "Megachurches have those electric guitars and drums and all, but why are so many Presbyterian churches jumping on this noisy Contemporary music bandwagon?" I started answering on a systemic level, saying that many mainline churches are frightened because they can see their membership aging and shrinking. They can see national racial demographics shifting around them. They aren't sure what to do to stay culturally relevant, but they see clearly that they need to do something. Breaking in, the White, male, middle-aged chair of the search committee loudly declared, "The church is strong in Texas!"

I saw the writing on the wall in terms of my getting the job, but said, "That does seem to be true, judging from the number of steeples I can see from up here. But that is not true everywhere in the US."

"Well, I don't know what you're doing wrong up North," he set his glass down on the table with authority, "but we know what we're doing down here. The church is strong."

❧

Historic congregations closing their doors. Churches barely staying afloat. Faith communities struggling to keep pace with urban expansion. Local successes masking national trends. And musical controversy that embodies all of it.

Mainline Diversity: Sonic, Sacred, and Social

On the broadest level, *(White)Washing Our Sins Away* analyzes how individuals within communities perceive difference, value it, and then develop institutional responses to it. On a more specifically contextual level, this book analyzes race, power, and spirituality in the United States by exploring how White American mainline Protestants have used the internal musical controversies of the turn-of-the-millennium Worship Wars to negotiate their shifting position within the nation's diversifying religious and sociopolitical ecosystems.

By the early 1990s, many White American churches had started hearing newer spiritual musics centered around guitars, praise bands, and choruses in competition with historical musics featuring pipe organs, chancel choirs, and hymns. Worshipers and leaders started talking about Contemporary music and Traditional music. Mainline Protestants were noting generally decreasing Christian prominence within the United States' religious landscape, but they also saw their own membership numbers dropping the most sharply. Demographically, mainline Protestants were trending Whiter and older than America's overall trajectory. Neighboring evangelicals, who had been quicker to adopt Contemporary musical forms with ties to popular music were faring better. Perhaps, thought mainline Protestants, adding Contemporary music would help them retain their historically central sociocultural position. Motivated by self-preservation and a desire to spread their faith, they started debating the merits of both musical styles as cultural tools. The debates intensified, spawning aesthetic and theological controversies that came to be known as the Worship Wars. Concrete beginning and ending dates for the Worship Wars do not exist (and they are still going on for some churches), but by the early 2000s, particularly from around 2005 to 2010, the embers of conflict had burst into flame.

When mainline churches were able to harmoniously sustain both Traditional and Contemporary services, they often felt that they had triumphed over polarization and strife to achieve an admirable compromise, reporting an increased sense of pride in their tolerance and diversity. In reality, the "opportunity for diversity" was often more highly valued than the personal experience of diversity, as most individual congregants only ever went to the style of service they preferred. Still, mainline Protestants celebrated the diversity they heard resonating in their musical choices:

> "I love our congregation because we are so DIVERSE!" a middle-aged Presbyterian told me, her blue eyes and blonde hair shining in the Tennessee sun.
>
> I took a sip of tea to gather my thoughts. In my months of doing ethnographic fieldwork at her church, I had never

18 / (White)Washing Our Sins Away

seen a Black person or more than a handful of People of Color.

"Tell me more about that!" I said.

"Well," she folded her hands demurely and smiled, "The church did some surveys. We have people from every zip code in the city, and different economic levels. We have very liberal people and very conservative people. And, you can hear it every Sunday morning! The music—that's why you're here to study us! We have both Contemporary and Traditional. We support different styles, even if everyone personally doesn't like everything equally. Supporting diversity and tolerance is so important to us."

She was radiating sincere love for her congregation. I took another sip of tea.

She paused, looked at her garden flowers, and said, "It would be nice if we had more Black people, though."

The Worship Wars tensions peaked around the time that I interviewed this woman in 2010, but they are still going on in many churches today. Although—or perhaps because—they remain overwhelmingly White,[2] mainline Protestant congregations have been feeling a continual need to participate in America's national conversations about diversity and tolerance, and they know the stakes of the conversations are high. Yet, despite their avowed desire for greater diversity, particularly racial diversity, even churches that supported the Traditional–Contemporary divide have tended to embody diversity in musical style rather than race. *(White)Washing* explores how, through the dynamics of the Worship Wars, predominantly White faith communities have often been striving to be allies and advocates of diversity, yet their inclusive musical aspirations often struggle to create the types of congregational diversity they say that they would like to have.

(White)Washing analyzes overlapping relationships between music, religious identity, political belief, historical context, and race by drawing on over a decade of ethnographic fieldwork and relevant literature across multiple academic fields. One of the first sustained, culturally contextualized investigations of American mainline Protestantism, this book explores how mainline Protestants in the United States came to hear values through music, and then used internal musical controversies about those values to negotiate the externally shifting sands of the American religious ecosystem.

Religion in the United States:
Decreasing Christianity and Mainline Decline

"After a long life spanning nearly two hundred and forty years," eulogizes sociologist Robert P. Jones:

> White Christian America—a prominent cultural force in the nation's history—has died. . . . WCA first began to exhibit troubling symptoms in the 1960s when white mainline Protestant denominations began to shrink. . . . The cause of death was determined to be a combination of environmental and internal factors—complications stemming from major demographic changes in the country, along with religious disaffiliation as many of its younger members began to doubt WCA's continued relevance in a shifting cultural environment.[3]

Once an overwhelmingly Protestant nation, the United States recently crossed a major threshold: the country no longer has a Protestant majority. In 2007, when the Pew Research Center conducted its first Religious Landscape Study, more than half of adults (51.3%) identified as Protestants.[4] By 2015, however, the Pew study found that only 46.5 percent of adults described themselves as Protestants.

This decrease encompasses all subtypes of Protestantism, but as captured in the buzzword "mainline decline," the most striking blow has been to mainline Protestantism. After enjoying centuries of cultural pre-eminence, by 1970, mainline Protestants were down to being 30 percent of the population.[5] By 2014, they only made up 15 percent of the American religious landscape.[6] As a particular case in point, although the largest Presbyterian denomination, the Presbyterian Church (U.S.A.),[7] remained relatively affluent and well educated into the twenty-first century,[8] the group lost nearly 50 percent of its membership between 1965 and 2005 (as detailed in the illustrated chart from PC[USA] Research Services, see figure 1.1).

These changing national demographics and culture have seen postmillennial rhetoric emphasizing the general anachronism of the "old colonial mainline,"[9] but who are America's mainline Protestants? The term carries social, political, and theological connotations, with the usage and meaning of the label often shifting depending on who is using it and why.

Figure 1.1. Membership in the Presbyterian Church (U.S.A.), 1965–2005. Source: Presbyterian Church (U.S.A.).

Major demographic surveys identify mainline Protestants as a substantive population group. For sociologists and politicians, "mainline Protestant" conveys concrete demographics and ballot-box ethics. For theologians and worshipers, the term clarifies doctrinal beliefs and denominational communities.

While mainline Protestant is, as sociologists Roof and McKinney summarize, a "vague and somewhat value-laden term,"[10] there is general agreement on its central features. In the United States, mainline Protestantism encompasses the largely White, historically established Christian churches descended from European institutional roots. For most of US history, mainline Protestants were the dominant cultural and religious group. They tend to be moderate on issues such as theology and personal lifestyle. Since the early twentieth century, these churches' sense of ethical responsibility toward the public sphere has shown increasing concern for social justice over individual morality.[11] Mainline Protestants tend to exhibit "high faith in institutional structures . . . reasonable tolerance of ethical differences, a thoroughgoing commitment to ecumenical cooperation, and an all-embracing conception of the church's public role."[12] This definition of mainline encompasses a range of denominations, including the approximately twenty-two million members of the so-called Seven Sisters of American Protestantism: American Baptist Churches, the Episcopal Church, the United Church of Christ, the Disciples of Christ, the Evangelical Lutheran Church in America, United Methodist Church, and Presbyterian Church (USA) are generally agreed upon by scholars as constituting the vast majority of mainline Protestants in the United States.[13]

Within the North American Christian landscape, the label "mainline" takes on specific connotations and negotiates specific relationships. By the end of the twentieth century, various Protestant groups—mainliners, evangelicals, charismatics, Pentecostals, fundamentalists, and more—had emerged. While there has been some degree of overlap between these groups, in processes described by ethnomusicologist Timothy Rommen as *disidentification* and the negotiation of proximity,[14] these religious groups have worked to establish their own unique identities in relation to their cultural and theological neighbors. For cultural insiders, subtle differences from their nearest neighbors often require the strongest disidentification. For example, American Presbyterians may more vigorously highlight their differences to Southern Baptists than to Japanese Zen Buddhists.

Within US Christianity, mainline Protestantism has generally come to be positioned in sharpest counterdistinction against its closest cousin: evangelical Protestantism.[15] Emphasizing differences to create a clear-cut mainline-evangelical dichotomy does illuminate theological, aesthetic, and political divisions within American Protestantism, but that approach also errs in favor of (over)simplification to obscure affinities between individuals and communities across institutional structures. As ethnomusicologist Monique Ingalls notes, "Many individuals and groups within mainline Protestant denominations (e.g., Lutherans, Episcopalians, and Presbyterians) and the Catholic Church share priorities, theological beliefs, and worship practices with denominations and church fellowships more commonly assigned the label "evangelical" (e.g., Baptists, Pentecostals, and non-denominational churches)."[16] For example, *Christianity Today* identifies as "a magazine of evangelical conviction" but also reports that over a third of its readers belong to mainline churches.[17]

When speaking theologically, mainline Protestants affirm what the biblical gospels call the *evangel* or "good news" that defines Christianity, yet the same believers often culturally and politically distance themselves from the conservativism of American evangelical Protestantism. As the polemically dubbed Worship Wars (discussed in the following section) developed over the late twentieth century, musical practices and worship styles served as vehicles for mainline-evangelical disidentification. Mainline congregants often linguistically distanced themselves from *those*

22 / (White)Washing Our Sins Away

evangelicals, *their* loud Sunday morning "performances," and *their* rhetoric of "being saved," "born again," and "washed in the blood of the Lamb." By often dismissing evangelical worship as entertainment-focused performance, mainline congregants would contrast it to their own more "authentic" and "spiritually focused" worship. Although familiar with phrases like "born again" and largely affirming the theology behind them, many mainline Protestants members generally chose not to use them.

The trajectory of the term "mainline" resonates with the fortunes of mainline Protestants. Initially, mainline meant railway main lines in general, then the Philadelphia main railway line specifically, then referenced elite high society in Philadelphia, and finally described established societal norms in general by the 1940s. Mainline churches ministered to the better educated, affluent circles of society. The similar term "mainstream" also came to refer to popular social norms, although the word comes from earth science hydro-current descriptions and does not carry the same specifically religious connotations as mainline. Both linguistically similar terms are relatively new, having taken off in popular usage after 1970.[18]

Over time, however, both mainline and mainstream developed negative connotations. Whereas cultural norms had once been seen as popular (particularly in WASP-y post–World War II White America), with the rise of 1960s and '70s counterculture, conformity began to be seen as negatively hegemonic. As popular music scholar Keir Keightley explains, "mainstream" came to imply mass-manufactured experiences, full of insincerity, manipulation, and lack of originality.[19] Ethnomusicologist Kiri Miller describes musical communities built around a "shared rejection by or rejection of the 'mainstream,' now essentialized in its turn as corrupt and culturally bankrupt."[20] As results from slang repository *Urban Dictionary* demonstrated in 2020, Americans now associate both mainline and mainstream with negative connotations, loss of identity, inauthenticity, and words such as "sell-out, poser, trend, average, and fake."[21]

These negative connotations have resonated with the history of mainline churches in the modern United States. In 2002, sociologists Robert Wuthnow and John Evans wrote:

> We recognize that "mainline" includes a certain irony, given the fact that these denominations comprise less than a tenth of the American population and that even among Protestants, more than half belong to other denominations. . . . "Historically old-line Protestant" is perhaps better in some respects,

although the backward-looking connotation of this phrase is unfortunate. And, while some scholars prefer "mainstream" to "mainline," the subtlety of this distinction has escaped us.[22]

Mainline Protestantism's current lexical woes have come hand-in-glove with broader social changes. Historically, mainline churches were able to depend on people's sense of civic and religious duty, social pressures, and geographic proximity to fill their pews. In recent decades, however, the American religious landscape has seen change in two contrary directions. Historical patterns of culturally obligatory attendance and institutional religious affiliation have decreased. Instead, spiritual practices of individually driven, affinity-based, optional activities have increased.[23] This shift has transformed American Christianity and the nation's broader sacred landscape.

Destination Diversity

On one smoldering summer afternoon in 2008, I was sitting in the plantation-house-turned-church offices of Hillsboro Presbyterian Church in Nashville, Tennessee. The property was in the southern suburbs of the city, surrounded by lush greenery. Bird songs and the smell of flowering trees wafted in through the window screen. I had asked the associate and senior pastors to describe the church:

> SENIOR PASTOR DAVID KIDD: If you were to ask either one of us, never minding the interest in music, "Why do people come here?" We would probably answer pretty quickly the same answer . . . Because it's a different kind of place.

> ASSOCIATE PASTOR NANCY McCURLEY: We're called—it's a good term—we're a destination church.

> JUSTICE: What does that mean?

> ASSOCIATE PASTOR NANCY McCURLEY: It means that we get people who live all over the city of Nashville and beyond who will drive past many Presbyterian churches, to come to this one, and many, many other types of churches to come to this

24 / (White)Washing Our Sins Away

one. It's out of their way. It's not in their back yard. But they *choose* to come here because it represents the values that they would say they hold most dear. It's a diverse congregation theologically, politically, economically, and racially. It represents to them what they see as what would be authentic to the call of Christ.

These two pastors were not the only people telling the story of Hillsboro as a destination church. Worshipers, clergy, and denominational officials repeatedly returned to the idea. In both externally focused publicity materials and internal congregational rhetoric, the faith community understood itself as a consciously chosen sacred destination.

Hillsboro is a unique destination, but the congregation was not unique in thinking of itself as a "destination church." When Pastor McCurley called out the phrase as an existing term, she demonstrated how Hillsboro's self-understanding came to exist within a broader discourse of American church identity. By the late twentieth century, "destination church" had become a common phrase within both mainline and evangelical circles. Beyond internal Christian discourse, sociologists, including Nancy Ammerman[24] (drawing on work from Joel Baum and Jitendra Singh[25]) and Robert Wuthnow,[26] were using a related term to describe the growing phenomenon. In their terms, "niche churches" across the United States were reasserting their identities on the basis of the unique social and spiritual niches they could fill in a religious landscape rife with choices.

This new niche church mentality contrasted existing models of church-going behavior.[27] Historically, first in Europe and then the United States, geographically defined "parish churches" had been the norm. Churches, like schools and many basic shops, had been designed to serve relatively compact local communities from within a walking-distance radius. Parish churches are "strongly identified with the people who inhabit a given locale and are therefore tied into the dense network of affiliation that is the local community."[28] While not compelled as strongly as some of their religious neighbors (like Catholics or Mormons) to stay within their neighborhood churches, historically, most mainline Protestants had also freely chosen to worship close to home.

By the end of the twentieth century, however, new social and economic dynamics were combining to change worship patterns. In *Sacred Subdivisions: The Postsuburban Transformation of American Evangelicalism*, cultural geographer Justin Wilford explains a national shift toward today's individualized, affinity-based church consumer culture.[29] Whereas people used to live in close proximity to their places of work and worship, during the post–World War II construction boom, more American families chose the benefit of suburban houses with yards at the cost of commuting into urban centers to work. As time went on, cheaper vehicles and new freeway networks created decentralized work and leisure patterns that were no longer anchored by urban centers. Suburban churches sprang up, but people interacted with them in new ways. Having become accustomed to driving places to meet their needs and wants, potential congregants would not necessarily select the closest church. Instead, they would "church shop" to assess faith communities on various factors.

As people were more geographically free, they were also becoming less institutionally connected. As Robert Putnam notes in his seminal *Bowling Alone: The Collapse and Revival of American Community*, as the twentieth century turned to the twenty-first, Americans were feeling increasingly disconnected and traditional social structures—from bowling leagues and bridge clubs to churches—were becoming decreasingly important. People felt less social pressure to attend their neighborhood church, or to attend church at all. As individual denominations faced both declining numbers and pressure from growing evangelicalism, mainline Protestants downplayed internecine differences to champion ecumenicalism.[30] For many mainline Protestants, previous expectations of denominational loyalty—for example, Presbyterians must worship at a Presbyterians church—gave way to more relaxed ecumenical "church shopping."[31] The Methodists might be a little farther away, but the distance and a few minor doctrinal differences paled in comparison to, for example, better child care, more parking, and their wonderful choir. As one Hillsboro Presbyterian member pointed out, "At this point in religious history, nearly every church is a destination church because you choose freely to go there."

By the turn of the millennium, American worshipers were increasingly church shopping to comparatively try out various houses of worship until they found one with their desired characteristics and offerings. Many were enjoying the "one-stop-shopping" that larger congregations' greater financial and human capital offered, overflowing with robust programming in state-of-the-art facilities. While megachurches—Protestant congregations with sustained average weekly attendance of two thousand people[32]—had been a feature of the United States' religious landscape since the 1800s, their new turn-of-the-millennium prevalence now dovetailed with increasingly affinity-based attendance choices. Congregant expectations of holistic parishioner care began to rise beyond the resources of average congregations:

Only large churches could offer the wide range of services necessary to meet the needs of various segments of the metropolitan population, such as counseling, Christian schools, and recreational and social activities, as well as homes or treatment facilities for unwed mothers, alcoholics, and drug addicts.[33]

By 1998 and again in 2006–2007, the National Congregations Study found that the largest 10 percent of American congregations contained about half of the nation's churchgoers. By 2015, the latest version of the survey found that the trend had intensified; half of the churchgoers in the United States could be found in 7 percent of the congregations.

Where did this prognosis leave modestly sized mainline congregations? How could a congregation of a few hundred faithful hope to thrive and minister in this religious marketplace? In some ways, the situation looked grim, but—and this remains true up to this book's publication— while most US Christians are in congregations that are large, most congregations remain small. In 1998, 2006–2007, and 2015, the National Congregations Survey consistently confirmed that even as more Americans were worshiping in larger congregations, the average attendee continued to worship in a congregation with about four hundred regular participants. When the 2006–2007 report showed that the average congregation only had seventy-five regular participants, the report analysis noted a logical and ethical difficulty:

> It [the fact that most people attend large congregations, but that most congregations are small] means that denominational officials can serve the most people by concentrating their attention on just the largest churches. But that strategy can leave most congregations out of the picture. When confronted with a policy decision, should you ask what the impact might be on most churches, or what the impact might be on most churchgoers? That is a tough question.[34]

While most Christians enjoy feeling like they are part of the global body of Christ, many of them do not want to literally embody that abstraction by worshiping with thousands of others every Sunday.

Smaller and midsize congregations, hoping to survive well into the twenty-first century within this new religious ecosystem, knew they needed to strategize. Due to their size-proportionate resources, these churches would be unable to offer services at the scale of large churches in ministering to a wider variety of parishioners with a wide variety of needs. Yet, the shift away from local parish attendance and the growing prevalence of church shopping meant that congregants were exercising freedom of choice as never before. As Sherry Kelly, a Baptist-turned-Presbyterian music director from Tennessee, explained in 2008, "There's a church on every corner. And so if they can't find it in one church, they'll find it in another."

To survive and thrive, many average-sized congregations like Nashville's Hillsboro Presbyterian worked to become niche, or destination, churches. The pastor of neighboring First Presbyterian of Nashville explained, "I think churches need to understand that we have a niche, and that's about all we have! [*Laughs loudly*] You need to know what it is, and who you are." Looking to develop their niche,[35] congregations purposefully engaged in "specialized religious sorting"[36] designed to identify and serve a specialized "culturally or theologically defined constituency."[37] Churches took their survival seriously, engaging denominational strategic counselors or hiring external consultancy firms.

In his 2007 *The Megachurch and Mainline*, sociologist Stephen Ellingson observed that the average mainline church needed to "evade the social or demographic changes within the immediate environment that challenge[ed] the saliency or appeal of a particular tradition."[38] Noting evolving United States demographics, many mainline Protestant churches identified tolerance and diversity as a key component of their niche. Mainline Protestants have a history of falling on the moderate to liberal side of the American religious landscape, so emphasizing that identity was in keeping with longstanding strengths. While most Americans strongly associate diversity with race,[39] diversity also encompasses various other aspects of identity, too, from age and sex, to economic background, physical ability, and more. Changing contexts help individuals and institutions to be aware of their relative status as minority or majority members of a group. Hillsboro Presbyterian's associate pastor smiled as she explained:

> We have a student intern who's coming over from another church, and she says the interesting thing is they're so liberal that they're intolerant of the conservatives. And what blows her mind is how that can be integrated here.

Mainline Protestant congregations were diverse in many ways, but many conversations that I had with worshipers resembled this one:

28 / (White)Washing Our Sins Away

JUSTICE: Well, I was a little confused at first, because people would talk about it as being diverse, and I would look and have no clue! I'd just think—

CONGREGANT: [*Laughing*] "What are they talking about!?!?"

JUSTICE: Yeah, obviously "diversity" is something different than what I'm expecting!

CONGREGANT: Yeah, I agree. In a certain sense we're diverse, but in a certain sense we're really not. I think we're diverse, we don't have a lot of different cultural backgrounds, certainly not! And probably most of the people are mid-income, mid-level income. Or maybe not but it seems like it, at least middle. So, it is kind of weird to say we're diverse, but yet we're accepting of people.

That "certain sense," the caveat that "Hillsboro is diverse, but . . ." reveals a specific category of diversity that Hillsboro and many other White American churches felt (and still feel) they are lacking: racial diversity. This theme continually resurfaced during my fieldwork. After speaking at length about her church's demographics and use of the term "diversity" to denote largely theological and political differences, one middle-aged congregant summarized: "I do think it's diverse, although, you know, it would be nice if we had a few Black people or something! [*laughs*]."

Having predominantly White membership within increasingly diversifying American society was frustrating for many mainline congregations because, as Chicago pastor David Swanson observes, "most mainline denominations have intentionally pursued racial diversity for decades, yet . . . segregation remains the norm in these congregations."[40] In an increasingly multicultural United States, White mainline congregations were becoming increasingly aware that their membership had not been keeping pace with their surrounding spiritual and social demographics.[41]

Diversity through Music to Retain Cultural Relevance

Creating a Dichotomy

In 2008, Jack Marcum, then head of Presbyterian Research Services, was reflecting on the frustrating conundrum facing many mainline churches.

Despite progressive ideology and historical prominence, membership trends and projections were not looking good. Increased diversity seemed to hold out the promise of increased cultural vitality, yet it remained largely elusive. Although these congregations would "like a better fix on why so few new people are joining . . . doing something is better than passively observing."[42] But what to do?

All American churches were facing generally decreasing social trends in religious affiliation, but some churches were growing. Some strategies did seem to be working. Both mainline and evangelical groups perceived correlation between musical style and church growth. Since the late 1960s, there had been a revolution in the music of evangelical Protestantism: a new musical pop-rock-style repertory for congregational singing had evolved. Dubbed Contemporary, it became the musical lingua franca for evangelical churches in North America and beyond.[43] Evangelical churches had also been faring better than their mainline cousins in terms of membership.[44] Perhaps, thought many mainline churches, doing "something" could be adopting more modern worship music?

Change would have to happen strategically. Since current mainline membership was largely happy with worship in its existing form (most of those who hadn't been satisfied had already migrated to other churches), retaining current members was a priority. Congregations aimed for a "both-and" scenario, creating new musical diversity without disturbing the existing sonic cornerstones of mainline Protestantism. Hoping to reverse steadily declining membership and regain numerical strength and cultural prominence though musical diversity, many mainline Protestant churches began offering Contemporary Sunday morning services alongside their Traditional services.

Clear stylistic labels—Traditional and Contemporary—that differentiated the services helped churches signal that they were implementing something distinctly new. Church music leaders, like Hillsboro Presbyterian's Stephen Nix, understood the importance of signaling diversity: "I like to think of music as being sort of like ice cream. You know? So you like chocolate ice cream, so I like vanilla ice cream. It's all ice cream. It's all great. . . . But I also realize that *niche* is being handled right now."[45] By 2011, mainline magazine *Christian Century* was noticing how pervasive the binary had become:

> Worship planners still find themselves talking about the relative merits of exactly two [styles]. There's either the densely theological hymn by Wesley or Luther (gobs of words sung

over gobs of chords) or the vapid pop-rock song by some cool young person (maybe five words over three chords).[46]

For many of Protestants, both mainline and evangelical alike, the labels Contemporary and Traditional channel musical diversity into two related, market-ready frames.[47]

How did dichotomizing worship music into the Traditional-Contemporary binary benefit America's White mainline Protestants churches? On one hand, the clear-cut Traditional-Contemporary binary allowed market-savvy churches to simplify musical options into a sleek, customer-friendly binary that appealed to potential church shoppers through product recognition.[48] Quick either-or choices hold a lot of power, such that a recent study from Cornell University concludes that indecision as "perceived indifference can generate feelings of dehumanization toward the noncommittal person."[49] The Traditional-Contemporary binary was also comforting because it was the newest iteration of many older dichotomies that have helped people make sense of the world.

Western discourse has tended to be framed in pairs: high culture and popular culture, sacred and secular, constraint and freedom.[50] Beyond the classic good versus evil, the study of religion and religious music has been structured through binary oppositions, including Weber's routinized-charismatic,[51] Niebuhr's church-sect,[52] Schneider's body-movement,[53] Douglas' ritualism-effervescence,[54] Turner's differentiated-liminal[55] and structure-communitas,[56] Ellwood's established-emergent,[57] and Alberoni's institutional-nascent.[58] With so many binaries presenting slightly different perspectives, sociologist R. Stephen Warner concludes, "Allowing for differences in emphasis, all of us were writing about the same thing:"[59] trying to talk about formality, structure, individualism, and community.

Binaries help us order the world, but they are not static. As cultural historian Lawrence Levine writes in his study of highbrow and lowbrow as cultural categories, dichotomies are not fixed constructions, but rather ways of seeing the world that develop in relation to culture.[60] People contextually shift and redefine binaries, notes anthropologist Talal Asad, to navigate specific scholarly, sacred, and social relationships.[61] Ethnomusicologist Jonathan Dueck suggests musical conflict as "a kind of cosmopolitanism pointed inward towards cohesion among subparts of a diverse social group . . . and outward toward mediating broader inter-group identity."[62] In other words, groups often interpret binaries with one set of meanings for themselves and a different, related meaning for outsiders. Mainline Protestants were hoping for just that; incorporating the Traditional-Contemporary binary might work both within their congregations and also to reposition those congregations within America's larger sacredscape.

The Worship Wars

You'd think I had just murdered Jesus again!

—Contemporary worship director Stephen Nix

Single churches offering multiple worship services defined largely by their musical content signified a critical shift within American Christianity. The premise of a single congregation worshiping through a single musical style has formed a one-congregation-one-worship-style model so strong that it underlies the work of most studies of religion.[63] Supporting both sides of a musical binary was uncharted territory for mainline Protestants. While White evangelical congregations had historically been more open to popular music in worship, they had never taken things to quite this level in supporting separate styles of worship. Trying to accommodate both Contemporary and Traditional worship challenged existing Christian worship paradigms. As ethnomusicologist Monique Ingalls explains, Contemporary worship music is simultaneously a popular music, a vernacular music, and a sacred music. It engages worshipers in a variety of performance spaces that were once distinct. Adopting this mass-mediated body of song has inaugurated widespread changes in the sounds of worship, but also in how congregations socially structure their music-making, experience worship, and, ultimately, understand themselves as a religious group.[64] This new musically based departure from previous models of congregational unity was redefining the limits of group identity.

For many congregations, departure from the traditional group limits proved to be a bit too much. Liturgical historian Lester Ruth writes:

American Protestants declared war on each other . . . over worship. . . . Bitter disagreements, angry arguments, and political machinations spilled across the church. Pastors and musicians were fired or sometimes left on their own, shaking the dust off of their feet. Congregants voted with their feet, or their wallets, or with raised hands if the question of which worship style was right was brought to a vote.[65]

By the turn of the millennium, the so-called Worship Wars[66] were blazing across American Christianity. Ethnomusicologist Jonathan Dueck offers a concise definition of the Worship Wars as a "mediated set of aesthetic conflicts in the Christian world between adherents of hymnody rooted in Western art music, on the one hand, and adherents of Christian popular music, on the other."[67] Dubbed Traditional and Contemporary, these musical styles were positioned as a polemic opposition to each other. This binary Worship Wars frame came to predominate White Christian music in America over the latter third of the twentieth century and into the twenty-first.

How and why did the rich, varied musics of so many of America's churches get channeled into a two-part dichotomy? For White mainline Protestants, a number of factors—fear, aspiration, evolving sense of belonging, and belief—combined to make a perfect cocktail. As I discuss further in chapter 4, deep-seated difference over *musical immanence* and *musical transcendence*—how similar worship music should sound to everyday music—were dovetailing with related issues of theological immanence and transcendence.

Historians Loveland and Wheeler note that congregational leaders and worship experts have been instrumental in using "broader shifts in the American religious landscape as resources from which they construct crises of meaning and membership."[68] Sociologist Stephen Ellingson suggests a similar "public-arena model," in which professional claims makers recast social conditions into problems and then mobilize public support to solve them.[69] As churches were beginning to experience early skirmishes, influential worship experts from across evangelical and mainline denominations quickly penned a new body of literature. Titles like *Putting an End to the Worship Wars*,[70] *Beyond the Worship Wars: Building Vital and Faithful Worship*,[71] and *The Future of Protestant Worship: Beyond the Worship Wars*[72] reinforced the crisis's existence and intensity. Following Worship Wars rhetoric, all churches in America, it seemed, were caught up in these conflicts.

Yet, while the Worship Wars literature addressed "The Church," not all segments of American Protestantism were engaging with the Contemporary-Traditional binary. For example, similar genre tensions between Saturday night and Sunday morning—when musical influences and musicians mixed across sacred and secular venues—had seen many popular secular entertainers get their start in the Black church. Musical tensions about modernization and secular music have long existed within Black Christian worship, as evidenced in the work of ethnomusicologists like Birgitta Johnson[73] and Alisha Lola Jones.[74] But, Johnson clarifies, the specific labels and rhetoric of the Worship Wars have not been central to Black churches. Gospel scholar Melva Costen also asserts, "Some of the terms used to express the existing tensions between various styles of Euro-American worship—such as 'worship wars,' 'cultural wars,' 'dumbing down,' and 'blended worship'—are not relative to the soulful evolution of African American worship."[75] Black churches draw from a variety of African diaspora musical and ethnic traditions,[76] but none of these were dominated by—or included within—the Worship Wars' Traditional-Contemporary binary.[77]

Still, mainstream Worship Wars rhetoric ostensibly addressed "The Church" as a whole. Whites did make up the majority of Christians in the United States at the turn-of-the-millennium height of the Worship Wars (and still do), but the color-blind approach extended Traditional and Contemporary beyond the primarily White churches involved with the genres. As Reynolds Chapman of the Duke Center for Reconciliation noted in the widely read magazine *Christianity Today*, "I began to realize that ['contemporary'] songs that I knew . . . were written primarily by and for a white audience."[78] It was ironic that as mainline Protestants were looking to music to help them with diversity in America, Worship Wars discourse addressing "The Church" unintentionally inscribed White Christian cultural and theological values of groups as normative.

In the worst cases, on the conservative, nonmainline fringes, Worship Wars discourse did connect White Contemporary worship with Black music. Drawing on hackneyed noble savage tropes or ideas of non-Western music as spontaneous and round in comparison to the squared-off limits of music of the Western church,[79] Contemporary music was derided as a slippery slope bringing the "rhythmic, pelvic-thrusting" "horizontal desire embodied in the vertical" of African-derived music[80] into White worship spaces. This strain of discourse had little to do with Black churches, but used racist grounds to decry popular music unfit for White Christian worship.[81] While instances of overtly racial grounds for dismissing Contemporary music were fairly isolated, underlying White concern over popular music

34 / (White)Washing Our Sins Away

in worship—often based on implicit longstanding relationships between popular music and race in America[82]—was not (see chapters 5 and 7).

While these trends appear clear in hindsight, at the time that the Worship Wars were most intense, worshipers, clergy, musicians, and scholars were simply doing their best to deal with rapidly evolving conditions. Applying the public-area model or similar theories does not mean that Christian worship experts intentionally manufactured the Worship Wars, or that musical controversies were covert vehicles for consciously race-based agendas to be carried out. The body of literature written by Christians and for Christians about the Worship Wars did, however, grow with stunning speed. There was urgency, they believed, because Traditional and Contemporary worship expressed different theologies.[83] "All Christians should understand their own theology and express it as fully as possible in their worship,"[84] wrote organist and professor Donald Hustad. If congregations adopted Contemporary music without due consideration, they were risking not only their cultural traditions, but also their core theological convictions. "What worries me," wrote theologian Marva Dawn, "is that many congregations are hurriedly switching their worship practices (throwing out hymnbooks, for example, in favor of music that is overly self-conscious) in order to 'grow' their churches—without adequate consideration of the long-term, negative results in the character of worship participants."[85] Ethnomusicologist Anna Nekola summarized the situation: if Christians did not believe music had the power to move people, then music could not be dangerous, but it is precisely because they understand music as having such power that it has been a key site of dispute within the church.[86]

The people writing and talking about the music were, not surprisingly, those with the strongest opinions about it. They tended to paint Contemporary music as the binary opposite of Traditional music. Contemporary worship was either a panacea for imbuing new life and the Spirit of God back into failing churches or, alternately, a sacrilegious abandonment of centuries of theologically sound religious heritage. Controversies over worship music were aesthetic arguments in and of themselves, but the conflicts also embodied deeper issues. Picking a side in the Worship Wars staked claims about the role of institutionalized religion in society and human-divine relations.

Fueled by Worship Wars discourse and word-of-mouth cautionary tales, alarm about the dangers of musical controversy infiltrated local congregations. Everyone knew of horror stories:

PASTOR IN TENNESSEE (2009): The church tried to support both Contemporary and Traditional Sunday morning services. It was your classic nightmarish case. Feelings were hurt. Hundreds of congregants left. My predecessor (as senior pastor) resigned under pressure.

ORGANIST IN INDIANA (2008): The church wanted to add a new Contemporary service, so the [pastor] told me that since I was going to only be providing half the music, now I would be getting paid half as much. But I wasn't going to be working any less! Playing is a service to God, but it's also my only income. After decades with that church, I quit. They got some pianist to pretend to play the organ for cheap and it didn't sound so great. People stopped going to that service then.

DEACON IN PENNSYLVANIA (2010): The pastor thought the music minister wanted too much control; the music minister said the pastor was interfering in worship. People started leaving. Finally, the church got tired of it and fired both of them.

The truly terrible tales spread. When congregants and leadership service talked to other churches and read the widely circulating topical literature, there was a general fear that musical diversity might also bring dangerously divisive Worship Wars dynamics. As ethnomusicologist Monique Ingalls observes, "the word 'contemporary' invokes a history of widespread conflict over worship style."[87]

For most faith communities, however, the Worship Wars were as imagined as they were experienced. The Barna Group's research found that concerns about potential crisis exceeded actual conflicts:

Drawing on national surveys among church-goers, Senior Pastors of Protestant churches and worship leaders from those churches, Barna revealed that while there are definitely battles being waged within Protestant churches regarding music, the battle is not widespread. One-quarter (24%) of Senior Pastors say their church has music-related tensions, but only 5% of them claim that those tensions are "severe"—which amounts to just 1% of the Protestant congregations in the U.S. About three out of ten pastors at the music-conflicted churches say

> the tensions are "somewhat serious." All together, then, only 7% of Protestant churches have "severe" or "somewhat serious" music issues rattling their congregation.[88]

Nonetheless, congregations experienced the danger of the conflicts as real. People's worry manifested in concrete form through local decisions and actions. Sociologist Robert Wuthnow cautions, "It is important to consider how mainline members *perceive* their churches. Indeed, perceptions may be more important than reality."[89] For mainline Protestants, the Worship Wars were a very real feature within the North American religious landscape.

Still, potential benefits outweighed potential dangers. Increasing numbers of mainline Protestant churches began offering both Traditional and Contemporary worship services. *(White)Washing Our Sins Away* is about what happened next. How did churches balance these new musical tensions? How did their musical endeavors relate to the broader diversity they wanted? How have mainline Protestants, among the oldest Christian denominations in America, used sonic change to renegotiate their social and sacred trajectory within the twenty-first-century United States?

Organization and Stylistic Notes

The introduction and chapter 1 have brought in *(White)Washing*'s major themes, but a few stylistic notes should be clarified before moving forward. In order to counter historical gaps in scholarly method (discussed in chapter 2), this book is based in large part on long-term ethnographic fieldwork. In choosing research locations, I focused on demographics and dynamics that reflect mainline Protestant norms. As I cast my net for a main field site, I was looking for a statistically average mainline Protestant congregation. I wanted to study the *whys* and *hows* behind churches breaking with historical precedent to embrace both sides of the Traditional-Contemporary dichotomy. A congregation of unusual size, or one that was in the initial phases of Traditional-Contemporary implementation, would have more outliers and questions than answers. When I contacted Hillsboro Presbyterian and explained my research, the pastors responded enthusiastically to my inquiries. "We are a teaching parish, after all!" they declared as they encouraged the congregation to welcome my research with open arms.

People at Hillsboro and in other locations were generous and forthcoming in sharing their experiences and offering their opinions. I am forever indebted to their welcome and candor. Sometimes people shared sensitive materials, even asking that their names not be used or clarifying that they were just telling me something so *I* would understand a situation better and then asking me not to include what they said verbatim or to attribute it to them. I have honored those wishes. Overall, to protect people's privacy, unless the speaker was a leadership figure—like a pastor or music director—I have left names out of this book. I conducted the bulk of the fieldwork at Hillsboro between 2007 and 2011, but for readability, I have not listed specific interview dates for the anonymized interviews. Unless otherwise specified, interviews and experiences date from this time period at the height of the Worship Wars.

This book employs a few other stylistic interventions. I use capitalization to indicate when certain common words label specific social categories above the words' general usage. I capitalize Black and White because I am using these labels as social constructs, not colors. I capitalize West when it serves as a sociopolitical label, but not when it means the cardinal direction opposite of east. I capitalize Traditional and Contemporary when indicating worship styles. I have tried to avoid using these two words as lower-case general adjectives. For the sake of better writing style, I sometimes use the terms "America" and "United States" interchangeably to refer to the geopolitical entity that is the United States of America.

After the introduction brings in the book's main themes and questions, chapter 1 positions mainline Protestants within the broader social and sacred landscape of the United States at the turn of the millennium. This chapter explores why and how so many mainline Protestants and other Christians came to adopt the Traditional-Contemporary dichotomy of the Worship Wars.

Chapter 2 situates the ethnographic study of mainline Protestant church music in the United States as part of contemporary antiracist work correcting historical trends in the Western academy. Anthropology and similar ethnographic fields have historically shunned Western Christianity as too normal to study in favor of exploring and explaining the exotic to Westerners at home. Examining cultures unevenly through different research methodologies has resulted in self-perpetuating, colonialist practices in academia. This chapter explores how studying the sacred

38 / (White)Washing Our Sins Away

music-making of White Western Christians both provides new topical content and helps reshape the social sciences.

Chapter 3 explores how a church can tell the story of its history to create a "useable past" that serves its present and future identities. By following one Presbyterian church in Nashville, Tennessee, we see how their representative story weaves threads of schisms and mergers, European heritage and local history, economics and race, personalities and presbyteries, demographics and denominations, and Traditional and Contemporary musical choices into a portrait of the faith community today.

Next, an interlude, sketches of worship, brings readers into Traditional and Contemporary worship. From stained glass windows, organs, and hymnals to a praise band, electric guitar, and folding chairs, rich ethnographic descriptions and photos illustrate how Traditional and Contemporary styles manifest in an average Presbyterian congregation.

Chapter 4 analyzes how worshipers were hearing sonic diversity in the Traditional-Contemporary binary. Exploring the nuts and bolts of the music, this chapter follows the three major questions mainline Protestants were asking as their congregations adopted Contemporary music: What instruments to play? What music to play and sing? How to sing? Ultimately, I suggest that, rather than only pitting electric guitars versus organs, congregants are choosing between musical transcendence and musical immanence.

Continuing to explore musical elements, chapter 5 asks questions about hymnody as a bridging strategy between Traditional and Contemporary worship. How have mainline Protestants have been experimenting with the musical heritage of American evangelicalism—however broadly construed—to create a useable past that promises to build a sustainable future? How are Contemporary musical leaders changing Traditional hymns for use in Contemporary worship? What do average congregants think about new settings of old music?

Chapter 6 analyzes the spatial elements of Contemporary and Traditional worship. When mainline Protestant churches began adopting Contemporary music, they had to create physical spaces for it. From "secular" spaces to church fellowship halls to sanctuaries, this chapter traces the locations of Contemporary worship in modern mainline congregations.

Next, chapter 7 analyzes the social dimensions of Contemporary and Traditional worship musics. Along with sonic changes, Contemporary music impacted historical patterns of mainline Protestant authority and agency. Contemporary music also challenged mainline White Anglo-Saxon

Protestant expressive social conventions and behaviors. As they implemented Contemporary worship, mainline churches have had to reassess longstanding constructs of their social roles.

The conclusion looks to the future, beginning conversations about where we as a nation can go from here. Ethnographically based studies of White Christianity like this one provide concrete data to combat systemic problems that Pastor David W. Swanson describes: "When white Christianity has attempted to affect change on racial segregation and injustice, our own deeply held assumptions have undermined our best strategies and models. So rather than knocking down the racial barriers that trouble us, we unwittingly end up reinforcing them."[90]

Chapter 2

"The Least Puzzling or Flamboyant of Christians"

The Tennessee sun was slowly setting over the regional presbytery offices when I sat down to talk with Executive Presbyter Phil Leftwich. We had both just seen the latest study from Presbyterian Research Services up in Louisville, Kentucky. *What* had been happening was clear, both for Presbyterians and other mainline Protestant communities around the United States. Major sociological surveys—including the Pew Research Center, Public Religion Research Institute, Hartford Institute for Religion Research, and Duke's National Congregations Study—had been steadily documenting how the oldest religious institutions in America were changing. As they faced unprecedented national demographic and social shifts, mainline Protestants were renegotiating their identities to try to survive and remain culturally and spiritually vibrant. These congregations had frequently articulated goals of greater diversity and increased cultural relevance, and had often commissioned studies to find paths forward. These faith communities nevertheless tended to retain their historically typical demographic characteristics—predominantly middle class and White—but mainline Protestant congregations were going through intense change.

"It's almost a joke to refer to this as the Worship Wars," said Leftwich, "but I get these phone calls, from some pastor in some church saying, 'Help, all hell has broken loose! We're having a war!' And I'll say, 'What's going on in the music program?' And the pastor says, 'How did you know it was the music program?'"

I was conducting fieldwork at a church in Leftwich's presbytery, interviewing worshipers and clergy, and analyzing the music—all in order

41

42 / (White)Washing Our Sins Away

to understand *how* mainline Protestants were experiencing, creating, and renegotiating their identities in the postmillennial United States. Musical controversies were pervading American churches nationwide, but we knew more about *what* was happening than *why* and *how*. *Why* were America's oldest religious institutions devoting so much time and energy to their music programs? *How* were mainline Protestants using musical controversy as a tool for diversity and social relevance? Leftwich nearly jumped out of his chair:

> Well, you've very plainly just identified the significant difference of what we know about Presbyterians and what we don't!
>
> Sociologically, we can profile Presbyterianism. We can track the history of it. My goodness, back better than ten years ago John Mulder Louis Weeks and Jim Coulter at Louisville Seminary went through an extensive Lilly Study that eventually ended up in a seven-volume study that went through two hundred years of Presbyterianism on this continent.[1] It's full of not just church history, but sociology on the nature of who we are. Our identity as a denomination. So we've got the sociological stuff. On general church life stuff that applies to us, Alban Institute has been a master of sociologically profiling church sizes, denominations, differences, how we worship, how we do missions. And that's all sociological stuff.
>
> But the anthropology you're talking about? *Nobody's* doing anything with that! And you're right, gosh, we could walk around the corner to the outreach foundation and we could find out more about what's going on with Presbyterians and anthropology in Zimbabwe than we could about what's going on here, because we have not dealt with that at all. Not at all. And I can tell you that, in my lifetime, and my seminary training, that we have never dealt with it in that period of time, in the sixty-four years that I have occupied the planet, and being raised literally from the cradle as Presbyterian, I don't think we've ever looked at ourselves that way. If we are going to learn from them, we've got to be able to compare ourselves to them, apples to apples.

Why would Presbyterians in the United States know more about Presbyterians and music in Zimbabwe than in their own neighborhoods? How could so little be known about the lived worship experience of mainline

"The Least Puzzling or Flamboyant of Christians" / 43

Protestants, historically the largest, most powerful demographic in the United States? What were the societal effects of such a large blind spot?

Deciding who and what is worthy of being studied rests on familiarity. If a thing or cultural pattern is too familiar, people often do not study it carefully because they believe it is already understood. If people see something as very unusual, they study it as a novelty (whether curious or dangerous). Majority cultures and their people with power decide who and what are normal, novel, and worthy of study. For the last few centuries, mainline Protestants have held considerable amounts of power. They have studied themselves in some ways, but not in others. Their current position—and understanding of it—in the United States results from deeply rooted history, specifically in the European Christian heritage of Western academia and society.

European Roots

As Christianity emerged as the dominant religion in Europe, its spiritual truths became pervasive social truths. By the time the Renaissance was ending, varieties of Christianity had long been established as the overwhelmingly dominant state religions of Europe. Christianity influenced truth-claims that shaped how people thought about the world and structured society. Religious differences laid the groundwork for major military campaigns. Sacred beliefs often overshadowed scientific methods. Everyone in Europe was not Christian, but everyone in Europe was affected by Christianity.

When Europeans turned their sights to expanding their empires globally, they took their worldviews with them. An ambitious series of fifteenth-century papal bulls had clarified that lands inhabited by non-Christians were not really inhabited. Such empty lands were free for the taking—in fact, Christians would be ungrateful to God not to occupy them—held the culturally pervasive European "Doctrine of Discovery."[2] While "White" was not (and still is not) a clearly defined racial category, the darker the non-Christians were, the more likely they were to be seen as subhuman "heathens," and thus moral obligations against their enslavement or exploitation need not apply. European practices were seen as normative and non-Western practices as aberrations.

For some European Christians, however, close readings of the biblical gospels complicated slavery and conquest. In the 1611 King James translation of Mark 16:15, Jesus instructs his followers, "Go you into all

44 / (White)Washing Our Sins Away

the world, and preach the gospel to every creature." In the book of Matthew, Jesus gives what became known as Christianity's Great Commission: "Go and make disciples of all nations, baptizing them in the name of the Father and of the Son and of the Holy Spirit, and teaching them to obey everything I have commanded you."[3] If Christians were supposed to spread the gospel message to all nations, Europeans in the Age of Discovery had to weigh an ethical question: Was it worse to convert dark-skinned people to Christianity and then enslave them or to enslave them because they were not converted to Christianity? Customs varied regionally, but pervasive British traditions holding that Christians could not enslave other Christians threatened to clash with the lucratively expanding human trade. These reservations were quickly countered with strategically applied Old Testament prescriptions about slavery (and a healthy dose of systemic racism) to easily hold most abolitionist resistance at bay for centuries. Europeans began to validate their colonial expansion through the patina of mission work. As historian Jemar Tisby notes:

> Europeans evaluated the people they encountered . . . based on how similar they were to themselves. This is a common human response when interacting with other groups . . . indigenous people were not considered intellectual or social equals but were valued based on their ability to do the will of Europeans . . . blank slates on which Christian missionaries could write the gospel.[4]

Then-contemporary interpretations helped position Christianity as "the cultural tent pole holding up the very ideal of white supremacy."[5] Converting non-Whites and then enslaving them could be understood as elevating their natural state.

> While it may seem obvious to mainstream white Christians today that slavery, segregation, and overt declarations of white supremacy are antithetical to the teachings of Jesus, such a conviction is, in fact, recent and only partially conscious for most white American Christians and churches. The unsettling truth is that, for nearly all of American history, the Jesus conjured by most white congregations was not merely indifferent to the status quo of racial inequality; he demanded its defense

and preservation as part of the natural, divinely ordained order of things.[6]

Western Christian interpretations of Christianity became self-fulfilling prophecies that divinely validated European supremacy. The power of European Christian colonization spread this belief far and wide. As theology professor Willie Jennings notes, "The lie is that in order to know the world, one must know the European world. The truth is that in order to know the world that has come to be, one must know the European world."[7]

In America, White European colonists prioritized education to further their own spiritual and social understanding of Christianity. In trying to continue familiar Old World bases of authority in the New World, higher education in the American colonies intertwined Christianity, truth, knowledge, and power. Most early universities in what became the United States were founded to educate clergy, as Khyati Joshi notes in *White Christian Privilege: The Illusion of Religious Equality in America*: "At the time of the nation's founding, most of its major universities were affiliated with the church, from Puritan Harvard and Calvinist Yale to Anglican Columbia, Presbyterian Princeton, and Baptist Brown."[8] As these schools expanded beyond educating clergy, the discourses, logics, and truths of their Christian foundations provided the underlying structure for American higher education.

Studying the "Other"

Western education and influence grew. At the head of global colonial empires, by the Victorian era, Western scholars and curiosity-seekers were becoming increasingly enthralled with collecting and categorizing the world. Centuries of travel writings about non-Western cultures by explorers, soldiers, and missionaries were being joined by organized research that was taking description and analysis of the exotic to new levels. Museums and taxonomies were springing up as colonial powers collected specimens of every sort from around the world to bring home for comparative analysis. Scientific fields of social research focusing on the non-Western world began to develop. Researchers like Johann Gottfried von Herder (1744–1803) began writing about pastoral folk cultures in contrast to urbanized populations. Anthropology and comparative musicology (founded in nineteenth-century Germany as *vergleichende Musikwissenschaft*) wanted to compare and rank the folk cultures of different peoples. In all this analysis, there was little emphasis on culturally analyzing the already-familiar European content. The Western materials were the experimental controls, whereas the focus was on the exciting, exotic variables brought back from afar.

Part of the turn-of-the-century Western fascination with folk cultures related to perceived danger. In addition to colonialism abroad, as the Industrial Revolution and technological innovations like electricity, automobiles, and audio recording were transforming Western urban life, people rightfully believed that these inventions would impact cultures the world over. Many observers began to worry that rapid modernization and Westernization threatened to overwhelm the pastoral, natural folk. Soon, scores of song-catchers, folklorists, musicologists, and fairytale collectors were scouring the countryside around the globe. Western musical scholars from Frances Densmore, Cecil Sharp, and Béla Bartók to Alan Lomax took genuine interest in preserving cultural materials, but they also often began to "correct" or impose external scholarly organization on the materials they collected. Urbanized, modernized Western collector-scholars were coming from a powerfully hegemonic system, as Willie James Jennings, associate professor of systematic theology and Africana studies at Yale University Divinity School notes:

> Western education is designed within a forced affection, shaped to take all of us on a journey of cultural addition—add to the great European master other thinkers who are not white or male but who approximate them, add to the great European artists other artists who are also great like they are, add to the eternal wisdom and universal insights of Europe the wisdom of other peoples that resemble them. Add these nonwhite others as embroidery to frame a picture, or spices to season a dish.[9]

Potentially vanishing lifeways and exotic cultures seemed like marginal curiosities that could supplement the Western push for progress, manifest destiny, colonialism, and missionary work.

Yet, as ethnographic scholars spent more time doing fieldwork, they often came to see themselves and their research subjects in a tense relationship with the mainstream culture and the colonialist, capitalist hegemony of Western society. On one hand, the ethnographers benefited from the impending cultural destruction. The very existence of their scientific fields that preserved folk materials or explained "foreign" cultures in the face of modern Western homogenization was predicated on the impending progress of exactly that urban Western expansion. As folklorists Bauman and Briggs note, studying tradition "continues to provide useful means of producing and legitimizing new modernist projects."[10] On the other hand, the ethnographers often also resented the perceived loss of lifeways and cultures. As a result, studying societies that resisted modernist Western expansion generated particular ethnographic interest.

Global Christian communities often came to provide rich foundations for studies of such resistance. Initially, anthropologists and ethnomusicologists had generally been less inclined to study the work of Western missionaries because such activities were seen as endangering native soundscapes and music cultures. As ethnomusicologists Jonathan Dueck and Suzel Reily explain:

> Ethnomusicological researchers in the United States have been relatively uninterested in (and sometimes even hostile toward) the cross-cultural study of Christian musics. One reason for this is surely that, in many of the canonical areas explored by the discipline, it is nearly impossible to dissociate Christianity from a history of missionizing projects, which have often been understood (across the disciplines) as modes of cultural imperialism and as threats to the integrity of local music and cultures.[11]

However, Christianity and its musics *did* become interesting to anthropologists and ethnomusicologists in what anthropologist George Marcus termed "accommodation and resistance" studies, in which scholars side with smaller groups resisting the hegemonic power of larger ones.[12] Viewing the world through this lens, anthropologists became "fascinated by the missionary and the syncretic."[13] For example, African Christianity became interesting to more scholars when Africans asserted their own cultural identities, explains ethnomusicologist Clara Henderson:

> There was a call by historians, missiologists, and others in the academy for scholarship that unearths the innovations of local African Christians to Africanise their liturgy, theology, and music from within these historical mission churches and

48 / (White)Washing Our Sins Away

to examine from different perspectives the encounters and exchanges shared by missionaries and Africans.[14]

In her work with BaAka tribes in Africa, ethnomusicologist Michelle Kisliuk celebrates how "missionized people reinterpret the lore of the missionaries, resulting in a spirited resistance to the 'colonization of consciousness.'"[15] The musics of Western Christianity came to serve as a bland, unstudied background that illuminated indigenous ingenuity and innovation as the real objects of scholarly interest.

Outside of such resistance studies, however, Western Christianity and its music has generally been seen as unworthy of attracting ethnographic academic interest. As recently as 2007, anthropologist Webb Keane commented on his own work among Indonesian Calvinists (a Reformed Christian group that shares common roots with the Presbyterians in this study):

> I cannot say, as did F. R. Williams about his own pioneering work on Melanesian Christians, that, "[i]n eighteen years of anthropologizing, I have never been so bored." . . . But members of the Reformed Churches, whether Dutch or Indonesian, are among the least puzzling or flamboyant of Christians. They are not millenarian or even revivalist. The state does not view them as dangerous subversives . . . nor can one make any strong claims that they are a well-spring of political resistance. . . . They have not elaborated an alternative cosmology or created new rituals, and do not commonly undergo demonic possession or take part in exorcisms or even, usually, listen to fire-and-brimstone preaching. The hymns of the Reformed Churches sound like those one might hear in a mainstream Protestant service in the United States. Despite the theological importance of original sin and the possibility of damnation, these do not figure prominently in their sensibilities. Even the doctrines of election and predestination have, in practice, become muted.[16]

The very similarity to North American or Western European mainstream Protestant practice renders Melanesian, Indonesian, or African Christianities anthropologically lackluster.[17] White Presbyterians from North America—like ethnomusicologists Martha Roy[18] and Clara Henderson[19]—have

"The Least Puzzling or Flamboyant of Christians" / 49

been much more likely to be involved in fieldwork as ethnographers than as the subjects of the ethnographies themselves.

Historically, in the United States, mainstream Christianity and its musics have rarely been studied anthropologically. After working on religious music in rural Appalachia for over twenty years, ethnomusicologist Jeff Titon came to conclude that Christianity, and especially Protestantism, was an "academically unglamorous subject,"[20] and that "scholarship in religious music has suffered from neglect"[21] due in large part to disciplinary bias. American mainline Protestants have historically been the most culturally pervasive—and thereby the least attractive to ethnographers.

In the United States, most ethnographic studies of church music have focused on ethnic minorities or "certain subsets of the nebulous American category called 'white people' [which] are stereotyped and fetishized in much the same way as racially marked groups."[22] The music of White Christianity has tended to be investigated when it conformed to disciplinary expectations of exoticism, often through links to rural heritage or idiosyncratic, extreme traditions such as snake handling or speaking in tongues.[23, 24] Such fundamentalist Protestants and even ritualistic Catholics have been seen as "exotic—and increasingly foreign to the everyday lives of non-Christians and mainline Protestants alike."[25]

Thus, while "Christianity played a critical role in fashioning the broad comparativist theories that founded sociology and anthropology,"[26] as anthropologist Fenella Cannell notes, the historical trajectories of social science disciplines have *not* positioned the lived experience of Christianity as a central object of study. Rather, Whiteness and Christianity have been pervasive in shaping the Western educational and cultural canon. The lack of anthropological attention to Christianity—and in particular to mainstream White Christianity—has quietly reinforced patterns of Judeo-Christian Eurocentric cultural dominance.

Turning the Lens

In 1956, anthropologist Horace Mitchell Miner published "Body Ritual among the Nacirema" in the flagship *American Anthropologist* journal. His article applied standard anthropological technique to analyze a complex social system involving medicine men, magic-mouth-men, and secretive personal shrines. The article became foundational in anthropology textbooks because it was actually a satirical description of contemporary

North American society as a critique of anthropological approaches to "Other" cultures. Nacirema is American spelled backward; medicine men are doctors, magic-mouth-men are dentists, and the secret shrines are bathrooms. Miner's goal was to highlight how anthropologically exoticizing certain cultures while ignoring middle-class Americans skewed Western understandings of the world (including themselves). While anthropology and ethnomusicology were slow to transform their demographic focus, scholars from around the world had been growing increasingly uncomfortable with the data disparities created by analyzing the world as "the West versus the rest."

Historically, ethnographers had been harvesting information from global communities for a Western audience. As grandfather of the field Bruno Nettl noted before his passing in 2020, ethnomusicologists have been largely "members of Western society who study non-Western music, members of affluent nations who study the music of the poor."[27] As fellow ethnomusicologist Andrew Mall writes:

> The ethnomusicological scholarly and pedagogical canons reflect this [bias], with an abundance of publications and courses on non-Western music that reveal the discipline's colonialist heritage, such as the music of Africa and the African diaspora, the Middle East, South Asia and Southeast Asia, and many other regions and cultures around the world. But there are comparatively fewer studies of, say, Nordic folk music, freely improvised music in Germany, Western art music, or even Western art music in non-Western cultural contexts. . . . Students of ethnomusicology are then mostly exposed to only these musics in their courses . . . members are less suited to advise research projects, communicate with non-academic audiences, or evaluate new scholarship. . . . The canons of ethnomusicology are self-perpetuating.[28]

The canons came to be so self-perpetuating that the subjects of ethnographies increasingly wanted to read and critique the finished scholarly products. By 1996, anthropologist Caroline Brettell had written *When They Read What We Write*. She explains:

> Native (and sometimes nativist) scholars—these readers are different from one's professional colleagues at home because

they often define themselves as both insiders and outsiders with respect to a specific cultural context.

The number of so-called native or indigenous anthropologists is increasing and, aside from ethnographic work that they produce, they are writing about their particular problems and perspectives on fieldwork in their own society and of their relationship with the larger global anthropological community.[29]

Acknowledging this shift meant that anthropologists and ethnomusicologists had to start contending with the structural disparities of their disciplinary roots.

Just as increasing numbers of "so-called native or indigenous" scholars had started writing about their own worlds, middle-class White scholars began looking at their own communities. Reconsidering Western Christianity as a viable object of ethnographic inquiry has become increasingly central to this disciplinary repair. By 2006, anthropologist Joel Robbins was asserting that *The Limits of Meaning* was the "first of such collections to my knowledge built around the assertion that anthropological studies of Christianity can contribute to questions of general theoretical import, such as the place of meaning and meaninglessness in human cultures."[30] In the same year, anthropologist Fanella Cannell could write:

These insights [about Christianity] have remained marginal to mainstream anthropology and sociology for a long period and indeed have come to be more widely read again only relatively recently. With a more recent wave of prestigious commentators, including most famously two brilliant contributions by Talal Asad[31] and Marshall Sahlins,[32] the topic of Christianity has started to move to a more central place again on the disciplinary agenda.[33]

New voices began pushing to position the lived experience of White, middle-class Christians in the United States as a viable object of ethnographic study.[34]

As anthropology and ethnomusicology began to engage with American Christianity, they joined three perspectives, according to ethnomusicologist Philip Bohlman, that were already forming a "discursive counterpoint" representing sacred music in the United States: 1) Scholars of religious musics, most of which is "sectarian and denominationalist";

2) musical scholars who, "in contrast, have more often employed scholarly approaches that effectively separated religious music from religious experience, thereby secularizing sacred music and redeploying it in a secular rather than sectarian history"; and 3) worshipers "who perform the sacred music of the United States and locate the music in their everyday practices." Bohlman highlights the difficulties that occur when religious practitioners "read what we write" and anthropological lines between "us" and "them" blur:

> Methodologically, the third set of voices poses a special problem for musical and religious scholars, for it further challenges the tendency to objectify music as either text or context, musical or ritual practice. . . . The third set of voices illuminates a neglected middle ground, the borderlands between sectarianism and the unstable territories opened by the pragmatic insistence on separating church from state.[35]

Western Christian music had been studied in particular ways. Through the "long tradition of art music composed for the church and through the sublimation of sacrality into the romantic image of the composer as genius, as inspired,"[36] historical masterworks of the Western canon, like Mozart's *Requiem* or Bach's cantatas, had been cast as high culture/art in contrast to the low culture/craft of everyday sacred music practices. Historically, much of the latter was often dismissed as unworthy of serious Western musicological study along the lines of E. Eugene Helm's 1970s aphorism: "All art is not the same . . . a Gothic cathedral is, pure and simple, superior to an igloo."[37] Igloos and Inuit hymns had been assigned to anthropology or ethnomusicology,[38] while musicology departments and music schools have focused on cathedral-filling Western sacred musical works.

Music schools had elevated the practical study of church music to degree-granting programs on the applied side of their curricula. However, following the general focus of Western music schools and conservatories,[39] these programs tended to approach church music as Western classical art music rather than considering its function in worshipers' everyday spiritual and cultural practice. As representative examples, Yale's prestigious Institute of Sacred Music opens their list of sample courses in the subfield of history of sacred music or religion and the arts with J. S. Bach's First Year in Leipzig and Mozart's Sacred Music. At Indiana University's Jacob's School of Music, The History of Christian Worship and Sacred Music is a pipe organ master class. Although these programs may incorporate courses on practices of various ethnic groups and Christian confessions, sacred music based in the Western classical tradition has generally formed the core of such educational institutions.

By the 1990s, however, many musicologists were beginning to acknowledge a tendency to "*systematically* undervalue certain periods, composers and works and privilege others because of the very nature of the conceptual and narrative tools that we apply."[40] As disciplinary and cultural lines began to blur, many scholars found themselves in a similar position to music historian Stephen A. Marini, who had noted that addressing "the public expression of religion and music in contemporary America" pushed him "to master new research methods, explore entirely new fields of scholarship, and learn how to write about a notoriously difficult subject."[41]

The predominantly White ethnographers of American academia faced a new challenge in studying mainstream Christianity in the United States; they would have to turn their scholarly lenses inward toward their own nation's historically predominant sacred music culture. Studying mainline Protestant congregations adapting to postmillennial culture shifts, sociologist Stephen Ellingson notes, "We have few sustained investigations of the processes by which congregations rework or fundamentally transform the historic traditions that provide meaning and identity for the organization and its members."[42] Writing from a perspective of liturgical ethnography, Catholic scholar Mary McGann noted in 2004:

> Ethnography is just emerging as a source of insight into contemporary worship and theology. . . . Scholars have yet to formulate models for such liturgical ethnography—forms that remain faithful to the complex, ambiguous modes of a community's ritual action and true to the polyvocality of local interpretations.[43]

By 2005, the editors of *Music in American Religious Experience* announced, "This book on music and America and religion acquires its distinctiveness by focusing on *experience*. . . . What the authors and editors here aspire to do is to hear religious music in the United States and locate it in the experience of citizens who sing and pray, worship and march."[44] By 2018, specialist on evangelical music Monique Ingalls was observing that "for many years, scholars largely ignored contemporary worship music. However, beginning in the mid-2000s, there has been an upsurge of academic interest in the music."[45] With cross-disciplinary scholarly interest increasing, studies of everyday Christian congregational music-making—including of White, middle-class Americans—have been growing.

Attention as Equity

"If we are going to learn from them, we've got to be able to compare ourselves to them, apples to apples," Executive Presbyter Phil Leftwich had exclaimed. Sending cultural researchers to Zimbabwe but *not* to White, middle-class mainline Protestant churches in the United States had been echoing bias within Western social sciences. Average worshiping Christians in America had not been exotic or endangered enough to be the subjects of anthropological inquiry. Mainstream White Christianity had been seen as normative, with other iterations of Christianity cast as derivative or underdeveloped. As a result, at the height of the Worship Wars in the early 2000s as mainline Protestants were trying to use music to address their slipping centrality in American society, there was a basic lack of information on the lived experience of worship and music within this historically predominant demographic of American Christianity.

In the second millennium, White mainline Protestants in America and the West can no longer assume that their social and sacred world can serve as cultural ground against which all other religious expressions are measured. In his award-winning book, *The End of White Christian America*, Robert P. Jones, head of the Public Religion Research Institute, notes how problematic such transitions can be: "When a social world succeeds in being taken for granted—as white Protestant Christianity was at the height of its powers—cultural meanings merge with 'what are considered to be the fundamental meanings inherent in the universe.'"[46] Whereas White Christianity shaped Western academia and the high art music canon, now it is one of many voices in an increasingly diverse American social and religious landscape. Turning the anthropological lens toward mainstream White Christianity in the United States plays an important role in their social transition:

> Mainline Protestants will need to choose between sectarian retreat and a new kind of engagement. It seems highly unlikely that the descendants of WCA [White Christian America], having

seen themselves at the American center for so long, will find a self-imposed retreat comfortable. . . . The only other course is a different social arrangement in which white evangelical and white mainline Protestants find their seats at the table alongside Catholics, Jews, Muslims, Hindus, Buddhists, and the religiously unaffiliated. This time, they will be guests rather than hosts.[47]

Studying White Christian music-making from an anthropological perspective indeed switches historical positions of power. Doing so helps include mainline Protestants and other White Christians at the table, combating the divisive dangers of sectarian retreat and concerns that disempowered Whites may have no place in America's new diversity (see chapters 3, 7, and 8). Considering the everyday sacred music-making of middle-class White mainline Protestants in the United States ultimately contributes to growing antiracist social discourse in the United States and beyond.

Chapter 3

Telling the Story of a Useable Past

> We always tend to look at things in the parameter of where we're living and the span of our short life. We don't look back into history and say, "Hey, let's look back, you know, fifty years, or one hundred years." You know? We would get better perspective.
>
> —Sherry Kelly, choir director, Hillsboro Presbyterian

Stories are powerful. They help us relate to each other. They convey facts; they also create facts. When we listen, we understand how the teller sees the world—how they see the past, the present, and how they may hope the future unfolds.

As an ethnographer, it is my job to collect many stories: to get people to tell *their* truths. Looking at something through all of its different lenses helps bring it into better focus. This approach is, in many ways, not "optimally efficient." Like most human pursuits, it can get messy and go down rabbit holes––I spend hours talking to people and being in community with people to understand their realities. Along the way, I have learned how to ask questions to help people tell their stories, even if we did not fully know what the story was when we began. Many times, the fullness of the story emerges in the telling.

Social science has technical terms for the anthropological listening and interviewing techniques I use. There are even more terms from the fields of ethnomusicology and communication studies for the parts that involve music. Still, stories remain central because their warm details (the *why?* and *how?*) complement the cold numbers (the *what?*) of quantitative

58 / (White)Washing Our Sins Away

statistical approaches. Those quantitative measures are also important; national survey numbers help demonstrate how stories are part of cultural patterns that connect individual experiences to broader dynamics beyond their tellers.

This chapter focuses on one such story, using one church's experience to highlight and analyze broad social, economic, theological, and cultural shifts. The stories this mainline Protestant congregation tells about its history and worship music—in particular, their adoption of the Worship Wars Traditional-Contemporary binary—become a prism for examining how people use the past to create the present and the future.

By time I began working with this congregation, they had been sustaining both Traditional and Contemporary services for about fifteen years. During my years of participatory research, they told many wonderful stories about that turn-of-the-millennium process, but as theologian Terrence Tilley notes, all sacred music is "necessarily historically embodied and inculturated."[1] Truly understanding a church's recent musical choices requires longer stories that go back for years.

Looking at the past gives us perspective, but that perspective is subjective. The way that this church—and any other community—tells the story of their past describes how they want to see themselves today. As with any story, the narrative may change, based on the answers to a few core questions: Who is telling it? When are they telling it? Who is listening? What do they hope to accomplish in the telling?

Many scholars have studied how people tell stories about their communities. Political theorist Benedict Anderson writes about "imagined communities,"[2] historical materialists Hobsbawm and Ranger describe "invention,"[3] phenomenologist Victor Turner analyzes "felt reality,"[4] and literary theorist Phillip Wegner suggests "imaginary community" built around a "narrative utopia."[5] Wegner's narrative utopia emphasizes the future potential held in "material, pedagogical, and ultimately political effects, shaping the ways people understand and, as a consequence, act in their worlds."[6] Liturgical scholar Lawrence Hoffman adds a sacred element, describing continually rebalanced elements of communal identity to create an ideal "liturgical whole."[7] Collectively, these and other theories suggest that communities tell themselves stories about their past and present in order to build an idealized future. However, constructing a narrative of communal identity through layers of ideology, culture, history, and subjective personal experience is no simple process.

The task, as ethnomusicologist Judah Cohen notes, "requires a great deal of nuance and imagination."[8] It is exactly this reworking, or reimagining, that provides communities with what literary theorist Lois Parkinson Zamora describes as a "usable past":

> "Usable" implies the active engagement of a user or users, through whose agency collective and personal histories are constituted. The term thus obviates the possibility of innocent history, but not the possibility of authentic history when it is actively imagined by its users(s). What is deemed usable is valuable; what is valuable is constituted according to specific cultural and personal needs and desires.[9]

A usable past is both authentic and imagined, based on both past historical events and modern sensitivities. By invoking a usable past, communities envision their former contexts as motivating their present identities and future possibilities.

In the moral and sociopolitical climate of the twenty-first century, American congregations are reexamining the stories that make up their useable pasts. While no single element dominates these stories, White people are increasingly taking on the work of antiracism to dismantle systemic inequities—and many mainline Protestants are facing an unpleasant reality. As Robert P. Jones, head of the Public Religion Research Institute, writes in his national-survey-based *White Too Long: The Legacy of White Supremacy in American Christianity*:

> Underneath the glossy, self-congratulatory histories that white Christian churches have written about themselves is a thinly veiled, deeply troubling reality. White Christian churches have not just been complicit; rather, as the dominant cultural power in America, they have been responsible for constructing and sustaining a project to protect white supremacy and resist black equality. This project has framed the entire American story.[10]

Uncomfortable as it may be for White Christians to confront this past, it is important that they critically listen to the specific stories that their faith communities have told and continue to tell. These stories are what hold promise for the future—both for White Christians and the rest of American society. As the national religious landscape shifts as never before, collective stories become even more important "not only because it is morally right or politically prudent. . . . If we are going to under-

60 / (White)Washing Our Sins Away

stand the surging current of racism, anti-Semitism, Islamophobia, and our increasingly tribalistic politics . . . it's no exaggeration to say our very identities—our souls, to put it theologically—are at stake."[11]

At first, the choice of what to sing on Sunday morning might seem far removed from racial politics, identity narratives, and social history. However, music provides congregations with embodied experiences of connection to the divine, each other, and the wider world. As a result, the decisions that faith communities make about what to sing and play—and the stories they tell themselves and each other about those decisions—play significant roles in constructing society.

Let me share a story with you. On March 5, 1995, Hillsboro Presbyterian joined other American mainline Protestant churches in presenting their worship through the Traditional-Contemporary dichotomy. These congregations felt specific turn-of-the-millennium motivations, but the roots of their decisions go far deeper. This chapter positions this church's representative story about implementing the Traditional-Contemporary dichotomy to provide us with newly useable ways of relating to the past, negotiating the present, and imagining the future.

Strengthening Historical Roots

Americans like to point to the nation's historical roots; American Presbyterians like to point out Presbyterians' centrality within those roots. Presbyterians were among the earliest Europeans in the North American colonies, extricating themselves from fraught sociopolitical, economic, and religious situations in Scotland, Ireland, and surrounding areas. Historian Mark Noll notes that American colonial Presbyterians quickly outpaced other European denominations "at adjusting to the helter-skelter realities of the new nation" and grew to become one of the largest, best-established religious groups in the colonies.[12] This relative numeric strength soon translated into sociocultural power: nearly one-quarter of those who signed the Declaration of Independence were registered Presbyterians.[13] Following the institutional pride in their Scots-Irish forbears that has historically undergirded Presbyterianism in America, local Presbyterian churches often trace their own roots as far back as possible.

Certain areas of the American colonies attracted more Presbyterians than others. To insulate his pacifist Quakers from Native American and Catholic threats, William Penn helped the comparatively fiery Scots-Irish

Presbyterians settle in southern Pennsylvania. Some of my own eighteenth-century ancestors (apparently after being on the wrong side of a battle in the north of Ireland) joined groups of Presbyterians settling in North Carolina. Many of these Scots-Irish settlers soon pushed into the colonial western mountain frontier.

Hillsboro Presbyterian Church traces its roots to those early North Carolinians and Tennesseans. Founded less than fifty years after the city of Nashville itself, the church celebrates its "direct descent" from the 1828 First Cumberland Presbyterian Church,[14] "one of the oldest Presbyterian churches" in the Middle Tennessee region.[15] Internal church history records that the congregation expanded steadily after beginning with only "six ladies and gentleman."[16] The congregation values its long history as giving their community a sense of belonging, with this endurance pointing to continued spiritual authenticity and cultural relevance.

Hillsboro's ancestral version of itself was part of the then–recently founded Cumberland Presbyterian denomination, a regional offshoot that broke away from the national Presbyterian Church in 1810 to accommodate rapid revival growth. (See figure 3.1 for a summary chart of Presbyterian denominations in United States history.)

Among other contentious issues prompting the split, Presbyterian seminaries were not producing enough highly educated clergy to serve the Cumberland frontier, so this breakaway denomination relaxed formal education requirements for leadership until founding its own Cumberland College in 1826.[17] Today, rather than negatively interpreting these early roots, Cumberland Presbyterians and their offshoots present these foundational actions as practical responses that placed adherence to God's call over the formality of human institutional structures.

The early congregation of First Cumberland Presbyterian Church had a lot of moxie, which soon turned it into a local and regional leader. As Nashville grew into an urban hub and industry center for religious publishing and music, the burgeoning congregation relocated to the city center. During its nineteenth- and early twentieth-century growth, the congregation changed names many times as it weathered reorganizations to emerge and reemerge as a local leader. First Cumberland gained a broader prominence by 1906, when pastor Dr. James E. Clarke "was the main leader of a number of Cumberland Presbyterian ministers who spearheaded the movement which . . . brought the great majority of Cumberland Presbyterians back to the parent Church, the Presbyterian Church in the U.S.A."[18, 19]

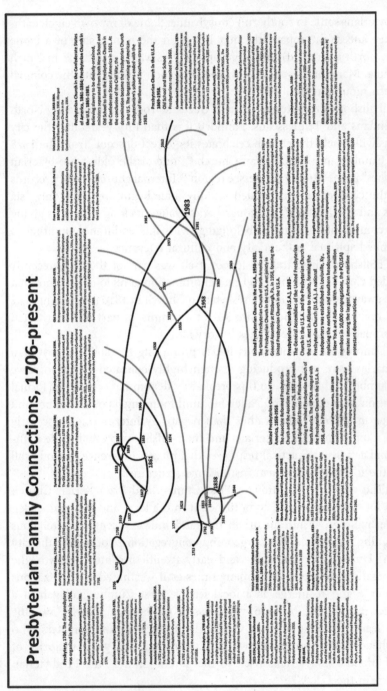

Figure 3.1. Presbyterian history in the United States. Source: Presbyterian Church (U.S.A.).

Establishing a Heritage of Progressive Inclusion

It is very significant that a Presbyterian Church in Nashville, Tennessee, pushed to join the PC(USA) in 1906. Hillsboro (née First Cumberland)'s leadership role in this history provided a prodigal son–like useable past for the turn-of-the-millennium congregation as it navigated its shifting position with a diverse, multicultural United States. Like a biblical narrative, the beginning of the story reveals sins that require redemption. As might be expected, given their relative affluence and social position during the early years of the Republic, many Presbyterians—including the "father" of American Presbyterianism, Francis Makemie—had owned chattel slaves or participated in the plantation system as traders, managers, and other beneficiaries.[20] Even in the North, White Presbyterians were not so progressive as to allow free Blacks to worship alongside them in their churches.

Over the late eighteenth and early nineteenth centuries, abolitionist sentiment grew within the Presbyterian Church, just as it rose across the United States. As a result, by the 1860s, the Civil War caused the Presbyterian Church—like most other American denominations—to schism over the slavery issue. Southern churches broke away from the national, more abolitionist PC(USA) to form the Presbyterian Church in the Confederate States of America. Cumberland Presbyterians were independent, having previously left the PC(USA) and never having joined the Confederate Presbyterians. However, when Tennessee, the home of Cumberland Presbyterianism, joined the Confederacy in 1861, Cumberland Presbyterians were placed sociogeographically in the South. After the South lost, the Presbyterian Church in the Confederate States of America renamed itself the Presbyterian Church in the United States, not rejoining the national PC(USA) until 1983.

This part of history is hard to acknowledge for many of today's White Christians in the United States––Presbyterian or otherwise. In 2016, the General Assembly of the Cumberland Presbyterian Church issued a statement of "Resolution of Repentance, Apology and Resolve." The section excerpted here speaks particularly to the years before many Cumberland churches rejoined the Northern PC(USA) in 1906:

> WHEREAS, the Cumberland Presbyterian Church was founded in 1810 in Dickson County, Tennessee, USA, and grew rapidly in a nation that endorsed, participated in, and benefited from the practice of enslaving African men, women and children

64 / (White)Washing Our Sins Away

who were brought to this nation through the brutal trans-Atlantic slave trade; and

WHEREAS, the Cumberland Presbyterian Church was inconsistent in its condemnation of American slavery as an institution—an institution that condoned the buying and selling of persons made in the image of God; an institution in which African American families were often separated, and individuals were beaten and abused in body and mind; and

WHEREAS, the Cumberland Presbyterian Church often condoned the segregation of its African American members into separate balconies, congregations, and classes because of the influence of cultural ideas of racial superiority and inferiority; and

WHEREAS, the Cumberland Presbyterian Church refused to allow its African American members full and equal membership following emancipation and the end of slavery; organizing instead separate congregations, presbyteries, and other judicatories that were denied representation in the General Assembly; and

WHEREAS, the Cumberland Presbyterian Church encouraged and supported the organization of the Cumberland Presbyterian Church in America (originally the Colored Cumberland Presbyterian Church) in 1874 in order to avoid the difficult work of integration, and to avoid offending its members who continued to hold fast to ideas of racial superiority; and

WHEREAS, the Cumberland Presbyterian Church was complicit in accepting Jim Crow segregation, lynching as a means of social control, economic oppression of freed slaves, and denial of educational opportunities; and

WHEREAS, the Cumberland Presbyterian Church and the Cumberland Presbyterian Church in America have both suffered from their separation, a separation that is harmful to the witness of the Church and a denial of our oneness in Christ; and

WHEREAS, the Cumberland Presbyterian Church laments the loss of friendship, gifts and graces from which our life, worship, witness and service would have been enriched had we not been separated all these years; and

WHEREAS, the Cumberland Presbyterian Church affirms the providence of God, whose purpose it is "that the whole creation be set free from its bondage to sin and death, and be renewed in Jesus Christ" (COF, 1.15); and

WHEREAS, the Cumberland Presbyterian Church acknowledges our ongoing need for repentance, so that "In response to God's initiative to restore relationships, (we) make honest confession of sins against God, (our) brothers and sisters, and all of creation, and amend the past so far as is in (our) power" (COF, 4.07); therefore, be it

RESOLVED, that the Cumberland Presbyterian Church repent and seek God's forgiveness for the many ways we have benefitted from, participated in, condoned, and been blind to our role in racism, oppression of our African American brothers and sisters, and all forms of brutality; and be it further

RESOLVED, that the Cumberland Presbyterian Church apologize to our African American brothers and sisters, seek their forgiveness, and work to restore the broken relationships our sin has caused; and be it further RESOLVED, that the Cumberland Presbyterian Church commit itself to preach the Word of God without compromise, and that we resolve to "oppose, resist, and seek to change all circumstances of oppression—political, economic, cultural, racial, by which persons are denied the essential dignity God intends for them in the work of creation (COF, 6.30). We seek to promote reconciliation, love and justice among all persons, classes, races, and nations: (COF, 6.32). (Quoted in the Resolution Marking the 50th year since the end of World War II, by Japan Presbytery of the CPC.)

—Adopted by the 186th General Assembly of the
Cumberland Presbyterian Church,
meeting in Nashville, Tennessee, on June 23, 2016[21]

66 / (White)Washing Our Sins Away

While Southern churches had clear reasons for issuing such statements of apology and reconciliation, most American mainline Protestant denominations have now issued similar statements as well. Even churches based in the North had often segregated their congregations, leaving Black churches denominationally unsupported and individual acts of racism uncensured.[22]

In 1906, four decades after the Civil War's end, roughly two-thirds of Cumberland Presbyterian congregations reunited with the Northern Presbyterian church. Rather than highlighting an overtly inclusive racial stance, the story that these churches have historically told attributes the merger to resolving a doctrinal question that had contributed to splitting the denominations in 1810. Nonetheless, the Cumberland Presbyterians chose to merge with Northern Presbyterians rather than pursue a similar union with their closer neighbors, the former Confederate Presbyterian Church.

While the details surrounding the denominational schism and reunion paled for most Hillsboro members with time, the idea of their congregation being a Northern church in Southern Nashville, Tennessee, did not. At the time of my field research in the early 2000s, Hillsboro congregants and clergy were still pointing to this heritage of progressive inclusion as evidence of the church's diverse niche. One longtime Hillsboro member––only eight years old when his family joined the congregation in the late 1950s––recalled the church's Northern identity being important in his parents' decision to join Hillsboro:

> My parents visited several of the Presbyterian churches. . . . And they were looking real hard at Harpeth [Presbyterian Church, one mile south of Hillsboro]. Back at that time, we had the Presbyterian US and the Presbyterian USA, and I guess the Presbyterian US was the old Southern version of the church, of which Harpeth was one, and this one [Hillsboro] was kind of the Northern branch, and they got down to Harpeth and my mom said that they were "not interested in growing their church" at that point in time. Which is kind of an unusual position! [*Chuckles*] But it was all kind of old families that had lived out in that part of the world forever. There was a lot of the north Williamson County people out in there. Didn't seem too vibrant. Anyway, she said they made the choice to come here instead.

The longtime congregant specifically equated Hillsboro's identity as a Northern church to the congregation being open and vibrant, a central factor in his parents' decision to attend it over neighboring Southern Presbyterian churches.

In the words of Pastor David Kidd, "A lot of this was back before the civil rights stuff really broke loose, but being a Northern church mattered." Once the civil rights era *did* get going, Hillsboro's identity as a Northern church meant that it acted differently than some of its neighbors. Many White churches across the South had formed Whites-only parochial schools in order to skirt desegregation rulings,[23] but Hillsboro began no such private school or day care. The church took small, progressive, but still locally risky steps; for example, while the congregants in the pews remained White, the church occasionally had Black musicians play.[24] Kidd's wife Pam recalled a Hillsboro session meeting during the 1970s:

> One of the men responsible for the church being alive . . . he had been raised in the Old South and was pretty much, probably in the kind way that Southerners have of being, racist. Not the redneck hate-hate racist, but the fine people who—it's just part of who they are, you know—went to a session meeting with David [the new-at-that-time senior pastor] and they were having some sort of a racial thing, and he stood up with David and stood for what was right, instead of what was [*pause*] you know.

While being racist in a "kind way" instead of a "hate-hate way" still creates harm, falling in line with Malcolm X's statement that "the white liberal is the worst enemy to America, and the worst enemy to the black man," the point of Pam's story was that Hillsboro was working within its local environment, trying to facilitate its members' successful, if sometimes imperfect, struggle to stand up for good. In Hillsboro's modern identity narrative, its past as a Northern Presbyterian church symbolizes institutional independence, theological conviction, and social progressiveness.

Midcentury Demographic Shifts: Adjusting to Suburbia

Following the Northern merger, First Cumberland relocated and changed its name to Hillsboro Presbyterian. Now directly across the street from Vanderbilt University, the parish became a prestigious university church. As Pastor James E. Clarke waxed eloquently in 1927, "It is a strategic location for service to students who come from and go to all parts of the world. Indeed, it is probably that no other Presbyterian church in the land is so situated in the very heart of a city's great learning center."[25] Proximity to Vanderbilt gave the church a strong sense of identity and mission, but the physical ties eventually proved to be too close. By the late 1950s, "the factor of economic growth in relocating Hillsboro, the 'din of market, whirl of wheels, and thrust of driving trade,' had to be reckoned with . . . a change of location for the Church had become necessary."[26] The congregation that had thrived on its proximity to Vanderbilt was then forced from its location by eminent domain,[27] to make way for Vanderbilt University's expanding medical complex.

Although its identity had always been as an urban church, Hillsboro was searching for a new location just as ripples of post-WWII suburban expansion were rolling across the nation. Around the country—and within the city of Nashville—many churches were being forced to navigate a similar, rapidly changing sociocultural geography.[28] The pastor from Nashville's First Presbyterian Church chuckled when he considered his congregation's stereotypical participation in the well-documented postwar pattern of church relocation:

> There was a sociologist who taught at the University of Chicago who wrote a book called *The Suburban Captivity of the Churches* and we probably were the illustration of that in the '50s! [*laughs*] . . . [At that time, they had] a pastor who couldn't see the value of maintaining a downtown presence, and, frankly, was probably losing lots of young families to more suburban churches . . . saw its future brighter out here, and like I say, we wouldn't be as large if we hadn't [moved].[29]

Hillsboro noticed First Presbyterian's suburban move––and that the congregation was "just exploding" with growth.[30] With this positive example to follow, national demographic projections, and its own eviction due to the Vanderbilt expansion, Hillsboro decided to find a new location that would serve the suburban population's projected growth around Nashville. As one congregant recalled, major suburban expansion for southern Nashville "wasn't in the foreseeable future, but you knew it was coming."

On a leap of faith, as the church history recounts, "Hillsboro United Presbyterian Church (U.S.A.), 5820 Hillsboro Road, began on June 4, 1954 when the property at this location, known as Singing Hills, was purchased from the R. E. Baulch estate for the sum of $80,000."[31, 32] The property sale went quickly due to the previous owner committing suicide on the premises. Hillsboro now owned a sprawling manor house and grounds where a White family and many of its Black servants had lived.[33]

> In September 1954, Hillsboro Church started regular Sunday School classes in the residence, later known as the Parish House, and a Sunday morning worship service in the solarium, which was named Singing Hills Chapel. A kindergarten was opened where the Baulch family servants had lived, and in the connected garages. Boy Scout Troop 40, which had long been sponsored by the Hillsboro Church, began regular meetings in the frame house which had been the home of the family caretaker.[34]

Hillsboro congregants felt "a tinge of nostalgia and perhaps a bit of sadness, especially among some of the older members, in leaving behind the beloved Church across from [Vanderbilt University's] Peabody College."[35] Hillsboro had been pushed out of its old identity as an urban university church, but the congregation decided that they had been called by God to reinvent themselves in modern suburbia, helping them to be open to new congregational possibilities.

Over the next five years before the eminent domain deadline, the congregation took conscious measures to smooth the urban-to-suburban transition. Hillsboro's rapidly growing neighbor, First Presbyterian, had eased its own 1949 move by temporarily maintaining two campuses—one downtown and one in the suburbs, so Hillsboro imitated this technique. As one longtime congregant remembered, "After they started building out here [in Singing Hills], it was probably a year and a half or so until they moved out." Half a century later, not many of the congregants at Hillsboro at the turn of the millennium could say that they *personally* experienced their church having two worship services in the mid-twentieth century, but the arrangement did provide an institutional precedent of sorts for separate Traditional and Contemporary services.

Despite Hillsboro's strategizing and intentionality, the relocation did not go smoothly. In the first place, the demographic promise of suburban sprawl took far longer to materialize than anticipated. "What happened was," exclaimed former Hillsboro pastor David Kidd, "when they came out here, oh man! [*Shaking his head*] They just hit the wall! I mean, the congregation just fell in a hole." A longtime Hillsboro member recalled that the area was "still on gravel roads back then . . . Town pretty well stopped up at Harding [about a mile north toward downtown Nashville

70 / (White)Washing Our Sins Away

from the new location]. I think there was a flashing light up at Harding, and that was pretty well the end of civilization as we knew it." Associate Pastor McCurley laughed as she remembered, "This really was the boonies!" Just like Hillsboro's new seventeen-acre acquisition of Singing Hills, much of the land in this area had been occupied by manor houses situated on rolling plantations. Even twenty years after the congregation's move, the area's transition from estates to suburbs remained more of a promise than reality.

As a result, by 1970, Hillsboro Presbyterian's attendance had dropped dramatically, down to about twenty-five worshipers per Sunday. The church history attributes the "dramatic drop in membership" to two main causes: "losing students and elderly members who were without transportation to the new location," and suburban zoning difficulties that resulted in delays and "compromising on a building plan that was far from ideal."[36] One congregational leader offered wider-sweeping analysis: "This [Forest Hills area] is, you know, a place of estates . . . You can look around and see that there's not the population density anywhere around us. It's enough to murder a congregation." Although an urban-to-suburban move had rung with initial promise, the congregational realities were grim. In 1972, things got even worse when the senior pastor resigned. Highly concerned, the Presbytery of Middle Tennessee saw the writing on the wall and called a young minister to Hillsboro who, barring a resurrection-style miracle, had "the mandate to be a chaplain in the hospice and close the church."[37]

As it happened, the new pastor's family—an outgoing, dynamic professional; energetic working wife; and nine-month-old son—precisely embodied the young adult demographic Hillsboro had hoped to attract by moving to the suburbs. David Kidd had been warned against taking this potentially career-killing position "astern a sinking ship," but the young idealist "believed that God would use me to give Hillsboro one more chance." His optimism flew in the face of national statistics showing steady declines in mainline church membership, already causing other churches like Hillsboro to close their doors for good. Although intimidated by the prospect of being part of a "failure of that magnitude," he vowed that if the congregation was to go down, "we would go down gloriously!"

The Centrality of Charismatic Leadership

This infusion of fresh leadership and a do-or-die sense of Hillsboro's last chance energized both human and financial capital. As Pam Kidd explained,

Telling the Story of a Useable Past / 71

"The only people who were left were the people who wanted that church to live so badly that they would do *anything*." Word of mouth became the primary method of inviting new members to the church, and Pastor Kidd was soon pursuing any and all recommendations from current Hillsboro members to invite more people to the church. Presbyterian culture does not often involve the unexpected, but Kidd was willing to try anything. He laughs as he remembers the struggle: "There's a whole block of hymns that just cascade out of the Church about the 'triumphant Church.' The Church is not triumphant . . . We hang on for dear life to the work of Christ in the world and throw ourselves at it as hard as we can. And then by God's grace, some of it is picked up and used."

Kidd's personal approach worked. As a woman who became a long-time Hillsboro member recounted, "He just showed up at our door one afternoon! I had my hair in curlers, the baby in the bed! I came to the door and we chatted for a little while. And so that's how we came to this church." Another member recalled visiting Hillsboro and being impressed that the young pastor "related to you on a one-to-one relationship. He invited us, me and my husband, to his home. He and Pam had us over for dinner. Neither of us had ever had that kind of experience in our lives with a church and a pastor." Thanks to this type of relational work, Hillsboro was soon growing by leaps and bounds.

Hillsboro's growth was leaping and bounding in particular directions. Demographically, like most Presbyterian churches that moved to the suburbs, Hillsboro was a predominantly White congregation. Unlike many newly suburban churches, Hillsboro had been forced out its old urban location, so its move did not share exactly the same White Flight motivations that were sweeping the nation as White residents and churches moved away from increasingly Black urban centers. However, the simple fact of the suburban relocation, aligning with Nashville's projected growth, put the church into the new midcentury American suburbs that catered to White families and institutions.

Because of this alignment, Hillsboro's energetic in-person outreach by the White clergy, White outreach committees, and White congregants tapped into a network of family, friends, and neighbors who were also mostly White. This homogenous network-building continues today for most White Americans: a 2013 national Public Religion Research Institute survey found that "social networks of white Americans are 91 percent white" and that "fully three-quarters (75 percent) of whites have entirely white social networks without any minority presence." As a result, as Beverly Tatum notes in her now-classic *Why Are All the Black Kids Sitting Together in the*

Cafeteria, "Of all racial groups, Whites are the most isolated. They are the most likely to live in racially homogenous communities and the least likely to come into contact with people racially different from themselves."[38] Without a specific strategy for intentional racial diversification, Hillsboro and other mainline churches were—and still are—using relational outreach strategies and inadvertently bringing in new congregants who mirror the existing ones.

By the mid-1970s, Hillsboro was busy triaging itself back into a healthy congregation. Given the congregation's critically small size after the move to the suburbs, almost any type of growth could be seen as diversification of some sort. Instead of focusing on any one specific area such as civil rights or poverty, Hillsboro decided to build engagement in a variety of areas. Like many Presbyterians, the few remaining members had financial capital. But, as Pam Kidd explained, they needed an infusion of energy:

> Some of them [the Hillsboro congregants] had a lot, well, had money. Like no zillionaires or anything! But they would just do whatever we came up with, and we knew they would be behind us. For a lot of the time, it was that way. It was like Mecca for somebody who wanted to just do things! We started all kinds of stuff. So, the church started growing and growing.

Once given concrete opportunities to apply their resources to enacting their faith, congregants launched themselves forward wholeheartedly. As a result, Hillsboro's outreach activities soon became a hallmark of the growing church that drew attention from—and attendance by—outsiders. According to Executive Presbyter Phil Leftwich, Pastor Kidd "pushed them out the door into mission and it has become a hallmark of not just internal recognition, but external observation by the wider community, and even the non-churched community." In 1994, these efforts were even honored nationally when Hillsboro was acclaimed as one of a hundred Protestant, Catholic, and Jewish "Congregations Making a Difference."[39] By 2010, the church had over thirty ongoing mission and community engagement programs in operation.

Over roughly forty years, Hillsboro's identity had changed dramatically. The thriving urban congregation's local property issues caused the church to embrace national currents of postwar suburban growth and move to the outskirts of Nashville. The relocation nearly resulted in Hillsboro's demise but, instead of folding, the congregation was revived by new leadership, energy, and growth. By the turn of the millennium, the demographics of both Hillsboro and its surroundings mirrored national

Telling the Story of a Useable Past / 73

demographic norms for the Presbyterian Church (U.S.A.): well-educated, well-to-do, and White (see figure 3.2). Nonetheless, the congregation also understood itself as having a heritage of activism, diversity, and conviction. In addition, at the turn-of-the-millennium, the congregation's success was

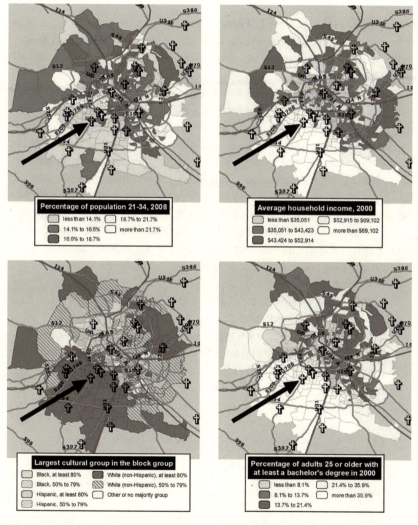

Figure 3.2. Demographic maps illustrating Hillsboro's location within Nashville in terms of race, age, income, and education. Crosses indicate locations of PC(USA) churches. The arrow points to Hillsboro Presbyterian Church. Source: Presbyterian Church (U.S.A.).

74 / (White)Washing Our Sins Away

defying national statistics of Presbyterian membership loss and rhetoric of overall "mainline decline."

Music as a Strategy for Survival, Diversity, and Cultural Vitality

By the mid-1990s, however, Hillsboro's now-booming growth actually presented the congregation with a new challenge. The church had nearly died out twenty years prior, but now there was not enough room for all the congregants who wanted to pack themselves into the pews on Sunday mornings. Church leadership saw two options: build a bigger worship space or offer multiple services in the existing space. Since the congregation had only recently finished construction on the existing facilities, further physical expansion was dismissed. Instead, in good Presbyterian fashion, multiple committees were formed to implement a second Sunday morning service.

Hillsboro's existing service—offering what would come to be labeled Traditional worship—was so successful that it would have been easy for the congregation to replicate it. However, the church did not do that. "It was just a trend everywhere," two elders explained, "that you would offer some kind of Contemporary service." The church leaders situated their decision-making process within Worship Wars rhetoric:

> ELDER #1: I was on the session at that time. It all came out of some reading and studying we were doing as a leadership team at that time . . . We were interested in increasing our membership. And we thought that the ripest segment of the population for appealing to were people who had no history of attending church before. But that we could not appeal to them with our eleven o'clock service.
>
> ELDER #2: Because they didn't have the framework of the hymns and scriptures . . .
>
> JUSTICE: Why go for unchurched?
>
> ELDER #1: Primarily because the people who have been at church have had so many appeals from so many different churches to come join. They've had a whole variety of experience. And

it's not like we were going to give up on that population, and not welcome people who had been lifelong churchgoers. But it was an opportunity in our mind to go after a group that was unexplored. Just out there and had no affiliation. Starting from scratch. Some people felt that had a lot of potential.

ELDER #2: And there had never been an effort to reach out to that segment of the population from our church.

ELDER #1: And this [was] really before there were very many nondenominational churches—

ELDER #2: Like there are now.

Another elder, who later became a member of the Contemporary praise band, remembered strategic motivation: "Our pastor was looking at other churches offering Contemporary services . . . . trying to reach out to people who won't darken the door of a Traditional church with stained glass windows, choir loft, organ, that sort of thing . . . and there were more and more of those sorts of churches cropping up." As the elders explained, Hillsboro's local decisions reflected the congregation's broader sociocultural environment.

Before implementing a Contemporary service, Hillsboro's worship leadership conducted both external and internal research. Pastors and lay leaders read extensively and visited other churches that already had both Traditional and Contemporary Sunday morning services. Church committees also conducted internal research on attitudes about adding a second service in general, and the possibility of Contemporary music specifically.

Like many mainline Protestant churches, as the steering committees studied potential growth plans, Hillsboro was becoming enmeshed in Worship Wars discourse that held that young people and the unchurched preferred to worship through popular music, finding Traditional services meaningless at best or negative at worst.[40] Many leading voices echoed opinions like that of *United Methodist Book of Worship* editor Andy Langford, who asserted that Traditional worship "is for many people anachronistic. It served past generations well and is a worship style that many still revere, but for a number of people in newer generations it reflects an alien culture that is rapidly disappearing."[41] In contrast, Contemporary music seemed to be socially relevant.

76 / (White)Washing Our Sins Away

Contemporary music was an outgrowth of the Christian youth culture kicked off by the Jesus People of the 1970s. Scholars have retrospectively classed the proliferation of musical activity into specific use-related subgenres so that descriptions like "Christian Contemporary Music," "Christian Worship Music," and "Praise and Worship Music" became category labels.[42] For most mainline congregations at the height of the Worship Wars, though, the basic content was sufficient to explain itself. Contemporary sounds held the promise of taking old congregations new places. To many mainline clergy and congregations, including Hillsboro senior pastor David Kidd and associate pastor Nancy McCurley, it seemed natural that Contemporary music would still attract a younger, twenty- or thirty-something demographic.

KIDD: My assumption was, well, this is going to be the young people.

McCURLEY: [*Laughs.*]

KIDD: In fact, I can remember sending material around to Tim [the organist] and to Sherry [the choir director] telling them, "Look, do we want these people to be a part of our church family, or do we want to send them somewhere else? Are they not welcome here?"

JUSTICE: When you say "young people," what age are you talking about?

KIDD: Anything, I suppose, thirty-five on down, something like that. I wouldn't want to put an arbitrary line—

McCURLEY: [*Breaking in*] Our youth, the college-age kids.

KIDD: [*Continuing*] Just the younger people. People who listen to a music that is totally different from [Western] classical church music. So, I remember this meeting, and . . . I kept emphasizing the importance of making sure it was for our young people, who are interested in this, and it's evident, you know, in what's happening throughout the church at large. And one of the "grand old dames" rose, very incensed, and had understood that what I was saying was, "This is for the young people, it is not for you." And she said, "What if we want to come?" Well, of course that's fine! [*Laughs*] I had no intention to exclude anybody, you know, but that was the pitch!

This "grand old dame" and other older worshipers might have surprised church leaders in their openness to Contemporary worship (see chapter 4), but Hillsboro and other mainline churches still approached their use of Contemporary music as signaling openness to newer, younger congregants.

The more churches had to work to adapt to new ways of worshiping, the more their congregations could take pride in their own openness to appealing to the perceived tastes of others. After all, the thought went, institutionally supporting these two opposing worship styles signaled a modern, cosmopolitan break from less-tolerant historical Presbyterian practice. For example, eighteenth-century worship tensions had grown so vicious that they split the entire Presbyterian Church, with one side deriding the opposing style as "Jarrs and Discords, which make the Singing (rather) resemble Howling" and "miserably tortured, and twisted, and quavered."[43] The then-future United States president John Adams leapt to this style's defense, countering that the first group's singing had "all the drawling, quavering, discord in the world."[44] This older conflict over musical styles intensified as a figurehead for deeper theological issues until American Presbyterians ultimately split into two opposing denominations—the New Side and Old Side—between 1741 and 1758.

By the early twenty-first century, however, congregants were lamenting the lack of choice instead of drawing group boundaries over musical styles. As one Hillsboro elder lamented, "We were offering congregants one type of worship service. If you didn't like the Traditional service, you didn't really have an option." Such exclusivity had previously been the goal of many churches' music programming, but Hillsboro hoped that supporting both Traditional and Contemporary would help them become an example of how modern congregations could demonstrate respect for diversity. The more effort that cultivating this tolerance took, the more churches could celebrate their diversity. Although there was some opposition, after much study, Hillsboro decided to add a Contemporary service.

Implementing Contemporary at Hillsboro

Hillsboro held their first Contemporary service March 5, 1995, on a trial basis. "Just by way of strategy, just in terms of getting it done, we all agreed

78 / (White)Washing Our Sins Away

that we would run it through the summer. Then, if it didn't provide what we were looking for, we could bag it with nothing being lost," explains Pastor David Kidd. The formula Hillsboro developed seemed simple: The new service was scheduled early "because we didn't want to run interference with the existing one," added Pastor Nancy McCurley. Sunday School for children and adults between the two services would function as a social bridge between the two services. The 11:00 a.m. Traditional service was to remain unchanged, and the same pastor would preach the same sermon at both services. Executive Presbyter Phil Leftwich explained that the time-limited trial period helped the congregation open up to Contemporary worship "without a whole lot of high anxiety. And it's usually the anxiety that drives the anger and conflict. It's not the anger that drives it; it's anxiety that drives it."

The Contemporary service also started simply. Aiming for a less formal atmosphere than the church's sanctuary, the Contemporary service began in the church library, a small, light-filled room with windows overlooking a courtyard rose garden. Hillsboro hoped that the nonliturgical space would communicate their targeted informality, group intimacy, and an ambiance that would not deter the unchurched.

Initially, just one Hillsboro musician was primarily responsible for musical programming and performance. People responded positively to his musical choices: a mix of popular praise and worship choruses and reworked hymns. One Traditional choir member who visited the new service remembers the strong impact of instrumentation during that initial Contemporary gathering:

> First Sunday, it was just synthesizer. I can't remember opening the song, but it had *bagpipes* on the synthesizer. As soon as it started, [Pastor] David [Kidd] sat right up and looked over, like "Oooh! We have bagpipes!" It was really kind of cool, like this is neat and different.

That choir member did not mention bagpipes as a particular throughline to Presbyterian Scottish heritage, but he soon quit the Traditional choir and brought his guitar to the Contemporary service. As an electric bassist recalled, a praise band formed "as more and more musicians, like me, invited ourselves to play along." As a result, the instrumentation soon diversified to include guitars (acoustic and electric), bass, and drums. The guitarist reminisced, "It was a great time! All of us musically had fun with it. In addition to being a worship thing, using music to lead people in worship with God, fun was the icing on the cake."

If the band was growing, the congregation was exploding. Worshipers lined chairs out the door and down the hallways. As a result, the church—which had earlier decided not to expand its physical presence—decided to refurbish their multipurpose fellowship hall to create a larger home for their Contemporary worship (discussed in chapter 6).

For some Traditional congregants, the new Contemporary service was a bittersweet development. Folklorist Dorothy Noyes notes that "the possibility and perhaps the attractiveness of alternative social arrangements"[45] can leave currently satisfied practitioners feeling disconnected. As a bass singer from Hillsboro's Traditional choir explained:

> We went from having a full church to having a less than half full congregation on Sunday morning, and the psychology of that is deadly. The new service would have felt all euphoria, because it was something new and exciting and different. I understand that, but the [Traditional] second service felt deflated and let-down. We felt like we'd been abandoned in a lot of ways.

The singer clarified that he agreed with Worship Wars logic suggesting Contemporary music as a solution to steadily decreasing national Presbyterian membership trends, but his comments also showed how intellectually understanding the demographic reasoning behind and excitement over the new Contemporary service has done little to mitigate some Traditionalists' feelings of loss, rejection, and being left behind.

Still, the Contemporary service continued to expand. Hillsboro soon hired a professional Contemporary music leader. The church's archives listed the position description:

> Hillsboro Presbyterian Church, a 700+ member PC(USA) church is seeking a part-time worship leader to lead our 8:30 AM Contemporary service which offers a blended diversity of musical styles, Hosanna, Integrity, etc. The position would lead this service and direct an 8-member praise and worship band.[46]

The announcement conveyed specific information using insider labels like "Contemporary" and "blended," as well as citing worship music publishers

80 / (White)Washing Our Sins Away

like Integrity and Hosanna. Hillsboro's temporary experiment had grown to fruition: the congregation was now embodying full-blown Traditional *and* Contemporary worship services.

One elder summed up the results: "Let's try it for six months and see how it goes. Nobody could object to that. And those six months, that's where it just grew like crazy. Once that ball had been started there was no way of stopping it. And, nobody wanted to at that point."

Conclusion

> People *choose* to come here because it represents the values that they would say they hold most dear . . . It represents to them what would be authentic to the call of Christ.
>
> —Nancy McCurley, associate pastor, Hillsboro Presbyterian Church

Churches always have fluctuating regular attendees and members. In any one congregation, some people will have attended for decades, whereas others will have just begun worshiping there. Overall, relatively few will have an interest in the detailed history of the congregation. Even fewer will be able to recite a congregational history dating back to the early 1800s. Nevertheless, the church's collective heritage will have contributed to each individual selecting this particular congregation from among many neighboring faith communities. Sociologist Mark Chaves explains that congregations, denominations, and religious traditions exist as

> institutionalized packages of worship elements forever carrying marks of their origins in a particular historical moment of collective religious practice, when they were trying to distinguish themselves, usually not by too much, from the traditions dominating the religious field at that time. They draw on the worship practices (and technologies) available at their time of origin to construct new kinds of collective worship events that, if they find enough people to practice them, retain their basic shape for a very long time.[47]

When Hillsboro tells its story of how it came to adopt Contemporary worship alongside its longstanding Traditional worship, the church creates

Telling the Story of a Useable Past / 81

a usable past that serves a yet-to-be-written future. The congregation does not fabricate untrue narratives, but rather subjectively weaves together perspectives and points in history. Through the story, the congregation emphasizes how different aspects of its identity—strong historical roots, a heritage of progressive inclusion, triumph over midcentury demographic shifts in adjusting to suburbia, and charismatic leadership—led to choices at the turn of the millennium to use music as a strategy for survival, diversity, and cultural vitality.

This chapter has used Hillsboro Presbyterian's story to demonstrate how a church's heritage shapes the congregation's current and future "ethics of style."[48] These convictions anchor the creation of worship styles, as well as impacting how participants understand the different styles helping them relate to each other, the Church, and the broader world. During the turn-of-the-millennium Worship Wars, congregants at Hillsboro and other mainline Protestant churches learned to hear and value Traditional and Contemporary musics as two halves of a dichotomy. The following chapters analyze that sonic process and the resultant social and spiritual ramifications.

Interlude

Traditional Worship, Hillsboro Presbyterian Church, 2009

At five minutes before 11:00 on a Sunday morning, the steeple bells were chiming the hour and calling people to worship (see figure I.1). Many congregants were only just then pulling into the parking lot (see figure I.2), but inside the church, the hallway was already abuzz with well-dressed congregants casually visiting over coffee. Nearly everyone was White. Older

Figure I.1. Hillsboro Presbyterian Church, Nashville, Tennessee. Photo by Deborah Justice.

84 / (White)Washing Our Sins Away

Figure I.2. View from Hillsboro Presbyterian's parking lot. Photo by Deborah Justice.

faces dominated, but children's laughter also rang out as young families arrived. A woman, wearing a dark red robe, stepped out of the sanctuary and rang a handbell loudly, interrupting the chatter. People quickly finished their drinks, smoothed their clothing, and moved toward the sanctuary. They had responded to a clear message: wrap up whatever else you are doing and come to worship.

Inside the sanctuary, the organist had just begun to play a contemplative classical prelude. The congregants' shoes clicked and squeaked in unintentional accompaniment as they walked quietly down the sanctuary's long aisles to sit in wooden pews. The organ and musician were hidden from view, tucked away behind a large wooden pulpit, but the music permeated the space, wafting around the altar with its simple golden cross, making its way up along stained glass windows to reverberate from high ceilings. Worshipers settled to sit in quiet musical contemplation as they prepared their hearts and minds for worship.

As the last tones of the prelude faded away, two children in flowing robes carefully walked to the front of the sanctuary (see figure I.3). These

Figure I.3. Acolytes entering the Traditional service, Hillsboro Presbyterian Church, Nashville, Tennessee, February 1, 2009. Photo by Pam Kidd.

acolytes carried long brass candle lighters with softly glowing flames to set the altar candles aglow.

Next, the church's senior and associate pastors took their places at the front of the sanctuary. Their long black liturgical robes made soft velvety swishing sounds as the senior pastor stepped up to the pulpit and the associate sat behind the wooden chancel railing at the side lectern. Although they did not have ceremonial robes, the worshipers had also dressed for the occasion—the congregants wore suits and blazers, skirts and heels rather than casual attire. The senior pastor smiled broadly and read the opening greeting from the morning's paper bulletin. Congregants followed along with the pastor's prayer, reading their own bulletins. Turning to the next page, they joined him in a responsive collective reading.

As the reading ended, the pipe organ rumbled to life, sounding an introduction to the morning's opening hymn (see figure I.4). Congregants took hymnals from the racks on the backs of the pews, and after consulting their bulletins for the page number, turned to #455. Worshipers looked down at their books to follow both the lyrics and four-part musical

Figure I.4. The organ and organist, Traditional service, Hillsboro Presbyterian Church, Nashville, Tennessee, February 1, 2009. Photo by Pam Kidd.

notation (see figure I.5). Attributed to thirteenth-century St. Francis of Assisi and set to a Reformation-era German tune, "All Creatures of Our God and King" was a well-known favorite both in this church and across

Figure I.5. Congregants singing, Traditional service, Hillsboro Presbyterian Church, Nashville, Tennessee, February 1, 2009. Photo by Pam Kidd.

many mainline Protestant denominations. As the congregation started singing the second verse, a grand piano joined the organ. The music kept escalating. On verse three, the chancel choir, which had been lined up against the back wall of the sanctuary, began processing into the worship space (see figure I.6). With magenta robes swaying, the thirty members sang as they walked, two-by-two, down the center aisle and into the choir loft where they assembled themselves to face the congregation.

After a reading and a prayer, a second congregational hymn filled the sanctuary (see figure I.7). Everyone who was physically able rose to their feet and raised their voices in #150, "Come Christians, Join to Sing," a Spanish traditional melody arranged by an American in 1824 and harmonized by a Scotsman in 1927 with 1843 lyrics from an English clergyman. The organ and piano played the song as it has been arranged for the Presbyterian hymnal, with the melody set to Western classical harmonies and voicings. At the end of the song, as the piano and organ cadenced, the congregants took their seats again.

The choir, however, remained standing attentively in their places for the anthem. The choir director, who had been sitting next to the associate pastor on the right side of the chancel, assumed her position at the front and center of the sanctuary to face her singers. She drew herself up, took

Figure I.6. Choir processing into the Traditional service, Hillsboro Presbyterian Church, Nashville, Tennessee, February 1, 2009. Photo by Pam Kidd.

88 / (White)Washing Our Sins Away

Figure I.7. A congregational hymn, Traditional service, Hillsboro Presbyterian Church, Nashville, Tennessee, February 1, 2009. Photo by Pam Kidd.

a breath, and cued the organist. Then, she turned to the choir to conduct the anthem, "One Faith, One Hope, One Lord" (see figure I.8). The choir's sopranos, altos, tenors, and basses interwove to execute the lush four-part arrangement. Congregants listened as the choral anthem musically articulated the service's theme. The lyrics spoke of unity, which the choir tried to embody in their uniform robes and well-blended sound. The singers had rehearsed for weeks, so they only glanced down at their black music folders occasionally for reference as they watched the director's cues. Her own robe flowed as she moved her arms vigorously to direct the vocalists. After the last strains of sound died away, the congregation responded to the anthem by nodding their heads affirmatively in a moment of silence. On the director's signal, the choir sat in unison.

The senior pastor stood behind the pulpit to read scripture, pray, and preach (see figure I.9). Nearly an hour after the service began, the midday sun was now bathing the sanctuary in colorful light from the stained glass windows. As the organ and piano struck up the final hymn, worshipers turned to #281, a congregational favorite, "Guide Me, O Thou Great Jehovah."[1] Reversing their entrance, the choir sang as they processed back down the pews' center aisle and out of the sanctuary. The pastors and

Figure I.8. The choir and director, Traditional service, Hillsboro Presbyterian Church, Nashville, Tennessee, February 1, 2009. Photo by Pam Kidd.

Figure I.9. Pastor Kidd preaching from the sanctuary pulpit in the Traditional service, February 1, 2009. Photo by Pam Kidd.

90 / (White)Washing Our Sins Away

acolytes, having rekindled their ceremonial lighters in the altar candles, followed the choir to the back of the sanctuary. The senior pastor's dark robe hung from his outstretched arms as he gave the closing benediction, seeming to form a temporary curtain between the ritual sacred space and the outside world. As he said "Amen," the acolytes walked past him, symbolically carrying the altar candles' light beyond the sanctuary's doors. The organ swelled to life, this time sounding Pachelbel's "Toccata in E Minor." A renewed hubbub of greeting and chatting erupted in the pews as congregants emerged from worship.

Contemporary Worship, Hillsboro Presbyterian Church, 2009

With only five minutes before the Sunday morning service started, many worshipers were just walking in the front door of the church. Bypassing the darkened sanctuary, they followed strains of music to the fellowship hall. "Come where we are," the lyrics called out. A few younger children ran down the hallway, but most of the families and older folks chatted and as they walked. This multipurpose space always saw a variety of activities during the week: the short carpeting had gymnasium markings for the basketball hoop that hung in the back above the kitchen service window, but across the room, a large rough-hewn cross stood to the left of a low platform and stained glass panels had been added to cover parts of the windows. On Sunday mornings, like this one, rows of folding chairs were waiting for worshipers. On the platform, the praise band welcomed congregants with tight vocal harmonies, electric guitar, electric bass, acoustic guitar, piano, and drum set.

Congregants brought their coffee and conversations with them as they gradually settled into their seats. By the time the last strains of the prelude were dying away, the rows of folding chairs were full and the people were quiet. The senior pastor stood up from his seat in the first row of folding chairs and walked up to a simple black music stand on the platform. Adjusting his suitcoat and tie, he smiled widely to open the service with a greeting and prayer (see figure I.10). The congregation's chinos, sweaters, and polo shirts echoed his business-casual attire. Their clothes were also basically the same styles that these White, white-collar professionals wore to work every day.

After the prayer, the worshipers looked down at their printed bulletins to find the next element of the service. The bulletin listed "Chorus

Figure I.10. Opening Welcome, Hillsboro Presbyterian Church, Contemporary service, February 1, 2009. Photo by Pam Kidd.

of Gathering," without providing a specific title. The congregation waited for the praise band leader to verbally cue the song, "Will everyone please stand and join us in singing 'Here I Am to Worship?' "[2] Worshipers rose to their feet as a projection screen descended on the wall behind the band. Congregants raised their eyes to the screen and read the lyrics to sing along (see figure I.11). "Thank you, you may be seated," the band leader gently queued the congregation quietly as the music faded away.

    The service flowed on as outlined in the bulletin, with music, prayers, and readings supporting the sermon's theme. The praise band mostly led congregational singing, but during the offering and a part of the service called "the special," the band played music and the congregation listened. These pieces had a wide range of content, from the latest popular Christian songs to secular titles with meaningful-if-not-overtly-spiritual content to popular hits reworked with Christian lyrics. This week's special, complete with conga drums, was a cover of the African-derived "Follow Jesus (Landa Jesu),"[3] originally recorded by the internationally renowned Christian band Selah. The praise band played enthusiastically, faces alive with emotion

92 / (White)Washing Our Sins Away

Figure I.11. Congregation singing in Hillsboro's Contemporary service, February 1, 2009. Photo by Pam Kidd.

(see figure I.12). The energy seemed contagious; congregants tapped their feet, bobbed their heads, and (quietly) clapped along. At the end of the piece, after about three seconds of laden silence, the congregation broke

Figure I.12. Praise band singers, February 1, 2009. Photo by Pam Kidd.

into loud applause. This was unusual, a few congregants later explained, because the pastoral staff had previously suggested that clapping in response to music might seem to inappropriately emphasize human musical skill, but "this time, the clapping was a *natural* response," like the foot-tapping and head-swaying "because 'Landa Jesu' was so incredibly moving."

The congregation calmed for the scripture reading, prayer, and the sermon. Saying a final, "Amen," the pastor stepped away from the music stand to return to his folding chair. In the band, all eyes were on the director. The bulletin had "Music" listed next. Although the band had rehearsed a specific piece for this slot, the band leader would sometimes spontaneously decide to deviate from the planned selection to better respond to the sermon's message. The director turned to his microphone and introduced the music with a few brief comments on how the "Outrageous Grace"[4] that formed the focus of the morning's sermon rang true especially for him personally and had moved him to choose this musical response. While the congregation rustled affirmatively and someone said, "Amen!" the band director began to play a slow version of the song's introduction (see figure I.13). The band and tech crew caught the director's cue and flipped past their planned selection to the "Outrageous Grace"

Figure I.13. Praise band leader Stephen Nix singing "Outrageous Grace" following the sermon, February 1, 2009. Photo by Pam Kidd.

chord charts and lyric sheets. Just in time for the congregation to join in singing, lyrics appeared on the projection screen. As people sang along strongly to this congregational favorite, more than a few congregants were moved with emotion and discreetly employed tissues to wipe away tears as the last notes faded out.

The pastor returned to the platform to deliver a closing benediction, ending with his arms outstretched and a sending invocation, "Go out into the world and fear nothing!" The band director silently counted off, "one, two, three, four" and the praise band launched into an up-tempo bluesy postlude that echoed the pastor's words. Taking a cue from the music's tone, the congregation erupted into chatter and activity over the band. Now-empty coffee mugs were refilled, bulletins recycled, and cell phones unsilenced as congregants spilled out into the sunny hallway.

Chapter 4

Sonic Diversity

Deciding When to Hear Harmony

Contemporary band musician: The pop instruments, like the electric guitar, the synthesizers, and all that, it's partly a surface sheen. But I think that has to do with—has *a lot* to do with—how the music makes you feel during the service.

Praise band director at a mainline Protestant church: Music is sort of like the end all and break all, you know. [*Dramatically*] Lord knows, we cannot have us sing a hymn like that! Oh, you put a guitar on that? That's awful, you've desecrated the holy temple. When it's not really a holy temple. It's in their minds.

Temples in the mind. Surface sheens and feelings—on an abstract level, this chapter explores *how* people make musical value judgments and *why* those choices matter. The ways that people think about sonic details spark decisions with resultant social and sacred effects. Musical value judgments matter on both small and large scales, from personal taste to cultural identity to economic realms and visions of the divine. Nowhere do the connections and implications play out more clearly than in large organizations—like American faith communities—which spend millions of dollars and countless hours on making music in hopes of connecting the faithful with the divine and each other. Understanding how *individuals* connect music to belief and action is one thing; understanding how

96 / (White)Washing Our Sins Away

multiple individuals and then *communities* have musical experiences that result in shared beliefs and actions takes us to another level. What we explore in this chapter is exactly that.

In their *Lovin' on Jesus: A Concise History of Contemporary Worship*, Swee Hong Lim and Lester Ruth offer an analytical summary of Contemporary worship: This music uses nonarchaic English, has a dedication to relevance regarding current concerns and issues in worshipers' lives, and adapts to match contemporary people, sometimes to the level of strategic targeting. Contemporary music also uses musical styles from current popular music, features extended times of uninterrupted congregational singing, and positions musicians centrally in both the liturgical space and in the leadership of the service. Finally, Contemporary worship has greater levels of physical expressiveness, informality, and a greater reliance upon electronic technology than Traditional worship.[1] Just as copious survey data told mainline Protestants and other American Christians *what* was happening in the nation's churches, worshipers could point to examples of what Contemporary worship *was*. But their complex feelings about the music brought the tensions of the Worship Wars to life.

As churches grappled with adding Contemporary music, mainline Protestants intuitively knew something that scholarship was beginning to demonstrate: if the music changed, congregational identity would change, too. By 2004, sociologist Mark Chaves had released the landmark study *Congregations in America*, the first systematic study to harness National Congregations Study data to provide a comprehensive overview of faith communities in the United States. Chaves found that the arts, and especially music, were central to congregational identity. He also found that the type of music congregations used correlated with other aspects of their identities. Testing for education, income, musical style, and expressive freedom, Chaves's study concluded, "The less poor and more educated a congregation is, the more formal is its worship, containing elements such as written programs, reading together, organ music, or silent prayer."[2] Traditional mainline congregations tended to be well-educated and affluent, and their worship features all of those elements. Using electric guitar and drums were, however, correlated with younger, less educated, less affluent congregations closer to the Pentecostal side of the theological spectrum. Chaves also concluded that worship practices that are closer together in social space tend to be closer together in sacred space such that "congregations' social homogeneity forges links between worship elements."[3] Mainline leaders took note: musical content matters.

Sonic Diversity / 97

This chapter turns directly to the nuts and bolts of Traditional and Contemporary music in order to understand how the abstract values of the Worship Wars developed and played out in local churches and individual lives. How did so many turn-of-the-millennium Christians come to *hear* worship musics within a dichotomy, which then encouraged them to *value* those musics unequally?

As many congregants told me, "Really, the difference between the Contemporary and the Traditional services is the music." Analyzing the content of Traditional and Contemporary worship, this chapter looks into fundamental questions: What instruments to use? What music to use? What words to sing? The ways that people answered these questions demonstrate how worshipers were choosing to hear similarities and differences. The human mind is not always aware of the strategies it deploys, but creating clear contrasts allows people to find meaning and order in their worlds. Supporting both sides of such a contrast demonstrates tolerance and diversity. For White mainline Protestants, highlighting Traditional and Contemporary as dramatically opposing musical genres proved a useful strategy. After the dramatic differences were established, the similarities could be carefully acknowledged to build delicate bridges of tolerance and compromise.

What to Play: Organs versus Guitars

> A large part of it [what differentiates the services] is the music, you know, drums, guitar, people being miked up.
>
> —A Presbyterian usher

Most Americans listen to a wide variety of musics. Most of those musics feature some style of guitar. Yet, in late twentieth-century churches, many White mainline Protestants suddenly developed very strong feelings about guitars. Painting in rapid, broad strokes, people took sides, either for guitars or for the instrument that guitars were replacing in their churches: the pipe organ.

Worshipers, clergy, and pundits were quick to position organs and guitars in binary opposition. Both instruments were playing Western music—no specialized tuning systems would have prevented them from playing together—but the conversations were not about togetherness.

Instead, worship experts were asking, "Should we use organs and pianos, *or* guitars, synthesizers, and drums?"[4] Popular Christian magazines featured polarizing stories like "The Triumph of the Praise Songs: How Guitars Beat Out the Organ in the Worship Wars."[5] By the late 1990s, the Christian worship industry—spanning worship magazines and books to blogs and denominational structures across mainline Protestantism, evangelicalism, and beyond—was using "organs versus guitars" as a symbolic figurehead opposition for the whole complicated aesthetic, theological, and sociocultural snarl of the Worship Wars.[6]

In local churches, when worshipers started talking about Traditional and Contemporary worship music, they were pointing out the contrasting instrumentation as a key point of comparison. Practically speaking, guitars and organs are simply two types of instruments, one using strings and the other air to create sound. People who study musical instruments can go into great detail about the physical differences, but mainline Protestants were establishing another level of sociocultural difference as well because they experience their Sunday morning music through the same set of sociocultural, historical, theological, and institutional lenses they wear the rest of the week. When people talk about instruments, they are also talking about cultural context, class, and race. It became useful for American Christianity, and for mainline Protestants in particular, to hear organs and guitars as very different from each other (similar to cultivating a "useable past," as discussed in chapter 3). This meaning creation was not a consciously implemented, coordinated strategy. Rather, for turn-of-the-millennium White mainline Protestants, it was an unconscious participation in the polarized Worship Wars dichotomy of "organs versus guitars" as part of a broader effort to secure their social and spiritual future.

Organs

> So, anything being played in the sanctuary with the organ must be old. I know that's not true, but that's the connection that I have.
>
> —Presbyterian in his late thirties

In the twenty-first-century American soundscape, pipe organs have become relatively uncommon. Flipping through radio dials or Spotify playlists, pipe organ music does not dominate. Pipe organs themselves—with rows of tall pipes and bass registers that make you feel the sound as much as hear it—are not easy to find; generally, only houses of worship, universities, and a few sports venues can afford their purchase and maintenance cost. Because the instruments have become so far removed from everyday life, pipe organs take on new significance as "forms of symbolic expression rather than media through which actions are performed; they become more representation than practice."[7] As one Traditional worshiper exclaimed, "Mentally and in your heart, you just kind of associate that type of [Traditional organ] music with the archangels and, you know, the angelic and the clouds, and things like that."

American Christians who associate organ music with the heavens are hearing the instrument's relationship to Western European Christian heritage. Dating back to ancient Rome, organs traveled with Christianity to the princedoms and parishes of Europe, and then to the colonized shores of America. Pipe organ traditions in most US churches were initially developed as continuations of White Christians' European practices (although some Reform Jewish congregations later adopted them as well). But as instruments, organs themselves are neutral machines, often also historically used in secular environments, like baseball and hockey stadiums and concert halls. The instruments are complex masterworks of wood, metal, and air that allow the player to interact with two consoles (keyboards), foot pedals that require podiatric dexterity that would put rock climbers to shame, and rows of "stops" that control how the keyboards sound (like a flute, a clarinet, bass, or everything all together by "pulling out all the stops"). Only positioning the resultant sounds within strong cultural contexts allows people like theologian Marva Dawn to exclaim that "the organ ushers us into the presence of God and an awareness of various divine attributes by means of its diverse sounds—majestic, mysterious, massive, ethereal, thundering, pastoral, trumpeting, meditative, plaintive, jubilant."[8]

While organs have some people hearing angels and seeing heavenly clouds, they conjure up "boring sermons, slow music, clerical domination, stained-glass windows, hard pews, racial segregation, long anthems in Latin, people dressing up, verbose prayers, a cold atmosphere, and institutional self-concern (always asking for money)" for others. Thus did the general editor of the *United Methodist Book of Worship* list these interconnected, entrenched, only-sometimes-stereotypical ills of mainline Protestantism that can be symbolized by Traditional organ music.[9] Traditional musical elements often code as "backward-looking," explains a Contemporary bass player: "Even if they have new music, you're limited by the very nature

100 / (White)Washing Our Sins Away

of it. With that instrumentation, it gets difficult to get the 'now' feeling from the service." Although an organist himself, Donald Hustad has also noted the organ's potential to have a negative symbolic role for modern Christians: "In the contemporary effort to attract delinquent [Baby] Boomers who have rejected the church, this [the organ] is another of the church's holy symbols which some people have decided 'must go.'"[10] Interviews with members at Hillsboro Presbyterian in Nashville, Tennessee, corroborated similar associations of organ music with previous personal negative religious experiences:

> ELDER #1: It is *that* instrument that turns them off, with which they have the most problems. It *is* the organ. It is an instrument that causes an emotional response in some people that they don't like.

> ELDER #2: It brings back memories of their childhood church that aren't necessarily good.

> ELDER #1: Whereas for some of us, it is inspirational.

A Catholic-turned-Presbyterian explains that hearing the organ in church "harkens me back to a time when in my spiritual life that seemed more inflexible. And so I enjoy hearing it, but it is not quite as spiritually fulfilling." Hillsboro's associate pastor confirmed that many of the Contemporary worshipers "are not seeking at all the church of their youth. They're trying to disassociate with that."

When people react to Traditional church organ music, they are responding to more than the sound alone. For most Americans, pipe organs resonate with ties to historical White, European Christian heritage, yet America is rapidly becoming less predominately White and Christian. The historical roots of most church pipe organ music in the United States today by no means prohibit people from all backgrounds from enjoying pipe organs or finding spiritual fulfilment through organ music. Sometimes, people are individually, idiosyncratically drawn to certain sounds; Debussy was fascinated by Indonesian gamelans and George Harrison fell in love with Indian music. Just as there are popular symphony orchestras around the world, there are beloved pipe organs playing J. S. Bach and more in churches around the world. However, the global presence of Western classical and church musics extends beyond individual proclivities. Questions of where, how, and why Western configurations and instruments—like orchestras and organs—have achieved status as art musics and become so globally pervasive reveal a homogenizing history of colonization, missionaries, and Western classical music elitism. While organ music in the average, modestly sized American mainline Protestant congregation does not necessarily continue that history, it does exist within the broader cultural context that this history created.

Guitars

> I don't have a pipe organ running around with me every day. But there's a guitar nearby me. I can turn on my radio and hear music; I can't hear a pipe organ on the radio all the time, but I can hear a guitar.
>
> —Stephen Nix, praise band director

Like organs, early guitars came to American shores with European colonizers. The instrument slowly developed over centuries; Arabic ouds inspired European lutes, which in turn prompted people to create various idiosyncratic versions before professional luthiers and companies developed the familiar six-string configuration we know today.[11] In contrast to pipe organs, however, guitars have become increasingly central to the most widely consumed musics in the United States since gaining wide commercial availability in the beginning of the twentieth century. In the United States, guitars transcended racial lines to become the cornerstones of blues and country, jazz and folk, rock and R&B, and most genres following those. The instrument became a symbol of accessible, anti-elitist music-making in America and around the world.

By the 1960s, the pervasive influence of American youth counterculture and the folk revival was pushing guitars into the center of the national soundscape. In many Christian circles, related energy was bringing guitars to the forefront of worship. Young people loved the folksy, unpretentious feeling of singing with a guitar. They often related the simplicity to a return to the early church: "Considering that Jesus was an itinerant teacher and healer who mostly walked from one ministry opportunity to the next . . . a first-century version of a stringed instrument would have served him well in accompanying any singing his

102 / (White)Washing Our Sins Away

disciples wanted to do."[12] The Jesus People movement and new informal churches like the Anaheim Vineyard sparked a creative outpouring of new guitar-based worship music.[13] Over the next few decades, this new music became known as Contemporary.

How people feel about guitars in worship has a lot to with how they have been accustomed to experiencing both guitars and church. When we humans encounter new experiences, we try to relate them to something familiar. We fill in unknown pieces with what we logically assume would be there. Researchers call this apperception. Every time we encounter something, we position it, at least to some extent, within our own preexisting frames of reference. As with most aspects of the Traditional-Contemporary binary, opinion was divided into two contrasting camps. People who had been familiar with Traditional music (regardless of their opinion about it) tended to understand that genre as the historical norm for mainline Protestantism (and thus, by extension, of American Christianity overall). If people had been less enthusiastic about Traditional worship but more enthusiastic about guitar-based musics, they were more likely to proactively apperceive positive effects of adding guitars. If people liked how Traditional worship had been, but had negative associations with guitar-based musics, they were less likely to support adding guitars to worship.

On the most extreme sides of the Worship Wars, if turn-of-the-millennium worshipers apperceived guitars and their accompanying musics negatively, then the instruments were not only "too loud," "shallow," or "annoying," they were actually "tools of Satan" or "evil."[14] This was the viewpoint of most fundamentalist and conservative evangelical circles that had earlier rejected twentieth-century rock and roll as "a radically and inherently *dangerous* music . . . sonically bad and innately immoral."[15] In contrast, more moderate modern mainline Protestants understood musical instruments as neutral, at most, as figureheads rather than active spiritual agents. Still, many mainline congregants who preferred Traditional worship often felt less comfortable with guitars, acoustic or electric, *in worship*.

CONGREGANT #1: I mean, I'm going to hear Celine Dion next week. I obviously don't hate guitars. It's not in general, it's just something about churches.

CONGREGANT #2: I'm a rock and roll fan. I certainly don't mind amplified music and singing. In its proper place.

CONGREGANT #3: It's something about the electronics involved. I mean I have an e-book, I read from an electronic device. But there is something about church.

CONGREGANT #4: The Contemporary service is a little bit Kum-ba-yah-ish for me. I'm always afraid somebody is going to break out the guitars and granola and some Birkenstocks, you know. Hippies will congregate.

Rather than expressing an overall distaste for guitars and amplified music, these congregants emphasize that they *do* value the technologies and musical genres. However, for them, worship is not the time for such sounds.

Overall, the younger congregants who had grown up with some form of Contemporary worship were more tolerant of guitars. As one woman in her early thirties explained, "I was brought up in a nondenominational church that has the exact same style as the Contemporary service. So that's what I was most comfortable with. It just sounds normal to me."For congregants like these, the instrumentation of worship had never sounded drastically different than something they could dial up on popular radio. As ethnomusicologist Monique Ingalls notes, increasing numbers of younger worshipers never knew Traditional worship, so "this musical repertory is normative."[16] Whereas these worshipers have trouble relating to organ music, they tend to hear guitar as "upbeat," "relevant to my everyday life," and "energizing."

Even Contemporary worshipers can have their limits. During much of my fieldwork at Hillsboro Presbyterian, congregants were unphased that the praise band guitarist was using a Les Paul guitar—the model recognized as standard for rock bands and used by groups from Guns N' Roses to Kiss. During one Contemporary service around the Fourth of July, however, he added a distortion pedal to play a Jimi Hendrix–style rendition of "America" as an offertory. Presbyterians often include patriotic music for the holiday, but the musical reference to Woodstock sent a murmur through the congregation. Interviews clarified that the reaction was decidedly mixed. In sum, for both Traditional and Contemporary congregants, the secular connotations of guitars and electronic music can reach a tipping point that overwhelms their ability to worship.

The desire to compartmentalize musical instruments and sounds as appropriate or inappropriate for worship evidences deeper preferences

104 / (White)Washing Our Sins Away

for *musical immanence* and *musical transcendence*. This chapter's conclusion addresses these preferences further, but the divisions of "sacred" or "secular" instrumentation analyzed here highlight how important sounds are in conveying theology. Does instrumentation, like a pipe organ, make worship and the divine seem set aside for Sunday morning, or does an electric guitar help incorporate worship and the divine into everyday life?

Beyond Organs versus Guitars

> I like the variety with the piano, guitars, and all. Even though the organist does a great job, also. I mean, the organ has great capabilities with music. It's not that I don't like the organ. It's fine. But we like a little bit of variety.
>
> —An elderly Contemporary congregant

Worship Wars rhetoric essentialized Traditional versus Contemporary instrumentation as organs versus guitars. The comparison is catchy and, as discussed earlier, it helpfully summarizes layers of musical and cultural comparison. Yet, while the binary provides a useful, iconic contrast, the reality of worship in many local congregations is more complex. Praise bands are just that—bands. Their instrumentation can vary, and they generally involve more instruments than the average Traditional service. As a Worship Wars rallying cry, a slogan like "Organs versus Guitars" packs a lot more punch than "Organs versus Everything," "Organs versus Pianos," or "Organs versus Keyboards" (particularly because organs have keyboards themselves). While "Organs versus Guitars" creates a useful talking point, "Organs versus Variety" offers another way to think about it.

A young, White male guitar player as a Contemporary worship leader (e.g., Tim Hughes and Chris Tomlin) has been a more pervasive trope than Contemporary worship leaders on keyboards (e.g., Kelly Carpenter and Michael Neale).[17] Yet while most worship leaders played guitar, many other Contemporary musical leaders of national repute, from Keith Green to Bob Kauflin, played keyboard instruments or incorporated them heavily into their arrangements. As one keyboard player explained, "I'm convinced that my being a pianist and thus being able to bridge classical/pop aesthetics is why I was hired as the music director to bring 'contemporary worship' to a church in Toronto. And I can't be the only one with this experience." At my primary field site, Hillsboro Presbyterian, the Contemporary band leader played keyboard instead of guitar. To understand the relationship between Traditional and Contemporary instrumentation, I statistically analyzed the musical content of thirty average Sundays (not holidays, not Sundays the choir was on a break) at Hillsboro Presbyterian between mid-2008 and early 2009. How would Traditional-Contemporary instrumentation stereotypes play out in a real congregation?

On the Traditional side, the organ indeed predominated the music, featured in 94 percent of music under analysis. For preludes and post-ludes, the organ played alone. On offertories, congregational hymns, and anthems, piano often accompanied the organ. Aside from the pipe organ, a grand piano was the only other instrument used regularly in Traditional worship at Hillsboro, playing in 58 percent of the musical selections. In contrast to the pipe organ, though, the piano always accompanied singers or other instruments (including the pipe organ) rather than playing solo. Some other instruments like handbells or strings were featured very occasionally. Overall, the pipe organ lived up to its Worship Wars reputation of thoroughly permeating Traditional worship music.

On the Contemporary side, overall, the instrumentation was far more varied. Piano dominated, due to the praise band leader being a keyboard player rather than a guitarist. From preludes to postludes and everything in between, piano played in 97 percent of the music under analysis in Hillsboro's Contemporary service. Drums, electric guitar, acoustic guitar, and electric wind were also present in over 50 percent of services' music. The electric wind instrument was slightly idiosyncratic to Hillsboro, but the musician was so talented that people reported "really enjoying the texture." The electric bass only played 21 percent of the time, due largely to that musician's busy schedule. The praise director explained:

> I have a core group, and then I have what I call ancillary musicians that will come in and out . . . Basically, I like the core praise band to be a bass guitarist, a rhythm guitar/lead, as well as another rhythm guitar, which can also be acoustic of course, piano, and then four singers. And then we have a woodwind instrument. And of course the drum set.[18]

Due to this genre-typical band design, the instrumentation in the Contemporary services varied more than that in the Traditional service. Additional changes increased the variation, such as the director arranging for a subgroup to play a duet or trio or someone appearing as a special guest.

106 / (White)Washing Our Sins Away

Compared to the consistent, acoustic sound of the Traditional service's organ and piano, the Contemporary service was plugged-in and varied.

What to Sing: Hymns versus Praise Choruses

> Martin Luther hymns are considered "traditional," but think about when they were brought about. Just like Franz Liszt is now considered to be the height of Romantic music, which is considered classical, in his day, he was thought to be almost a rock and roll artist! In any sort of culture, a rising genre in music always sort of takes this bipartisan faction, and they keep going over the same problem that has existed years and centuries prior to them.
>
> —Stephen Nix, Hillsboro Presbyterian praise band director

Repertoire involves complex issues of heritage, institutional authority, denominational identity, and local congregational values (discussed further in chapter 6), but within the charged atmosphere of the Worship Wars, mainline Protestants came to position the newer Contemporary repertoire in opposition to Traditional worship music. Just as Worship Wars discourse simplified instrumentation into "organs versus guitars," for many White Christians, repertoire settled into "praise choruses versus hymns." Only after differences were established could similarities be acknowledged to build "useable" bridges to express institutional tolerance and diversity.

Repertoire Sources: Hymnody

Hillsboro band leader Stephen Nix was only half joking when he said, "You know what makes it a hymn? Put it in a hardback edition and it's a hymn . . . We've always laughed that you can put a ZZ Top song in a hymnal, and it will become a hymn." For most mainline Protestant churches, congregational music has historically revolved around worshipers singing hymns. While Traditional worship continues this practice, Contemporary worship music draws repertoire from broader sources. Most Contemporary worship music consists of either reworked hymns or popular praise and worship repertoire, although a smaller percentage draws from secular pop songs that can crossover for sacred use (e.g., "Lean on Me" by Bill Withers).

Worshipers agree that Traditional worship music relies on hymns, but what exactly is a hymn? Academic definitions are vague: "a song of praise to the deity or a saint" or "a sacred lyric of original content for use in worship."[19] In the latest version of their denominational song book, the Presbyterian Hymnal Committee defined hymnals rather than hymns as "a collection of songs that reflects the full extent of the biblical narrative and also the full array of biblical language used for God."[20] This definition works well for the content in most mainline Protestant hymnals: songs for congregational use that span time periods, geographical regions, and, to a certain extent, musical genres.

For mainline Protestants and many other Christian groups, denominational hymnals act as institutional theological and musical filters. By creating musical and theological canons, the books offer music that conforms to a particular set of beliefs and is articulated within a particular cultural framework.[21] The content of hymnals has often helped denominations "negotiate proximity"[22] to their religious neighbors by identifying unique points of theology and heritage: Lutherans sing from this book; Episcopalians sing from that book. The hymns that mainline Protestant congregants sing date back centuries (e.g., Hillsboro Presbyterian's Traditional hymnody averages composition dates of 1710 for the music and 1830 for the lyrics). Worshipers explained that holding hymnals in their hands every Sunday brought this abstract past into the concrete present, helping them feel ownership and belonging. The familiar feel of the books and the familiar sound of the repertoire created a powerful combination, with each re-singing compounding layers of memory and communal bonds.[23]

> CONGREGANT #1: Their faith leading to our faith. I think it's a beautiful thing. God working through centuries . . . Sometimes my voice cracks when we're singing some of the songs. Just the history. Especially the saints that have gone, like my mother, my father, who have now passed on. It moves me to think about that.

> CONGREGANT #2: A lot of times, there'll be a really old school—and I can't name anything—like one of those old hymns, and it just, the sound of it, the, you know, I just really feel in a safe place. I just feel the presence of God around me . . . and it just feels really good.

108 / (White)Washing Our Sins Away

While these worshipers were singing from the Presbyterian hymnal in 2009, today's mainline Protestant ecumenicalism has resulted in Lutherans', Methodists', and other groups' hymnals having considerable overlap of many cross-denominationally appreciated "standards." The hymns in the latest Presbyterian hymnal do not target a historically tight Presbyterian ethnic heritage by sourcing mainly Scottish tunes and lyrics. In fact, "When you think of music, you don't think of Presbyterian churches. I don't think of them as having as strong an identity as Methodists or Baptists or even Lutherans . . . And even when you look in the hymnals, most Presbyterian hymnals are versions of other denominations," explains a Tennessee church music director.

The relative lack of historical *Presbyterian* hymnody demonstrates how Presbyterians, and some other mainline Protestant groups, have struggled to balance belief, heritage, and popular music. For Presbyterians, the problem dates to their Reformation-era foundation. The Scottish father of Presbyterianism, John Knox, followed Calvinist practices of psalm singing in local languages (as opposed to Latin) with localized repertoires of sacred music, often with heavy colloquial influences.[24] Singing vernacular psalmody was all the rage in sixteenth-century Europe, but the practice did not age well. Over the eighteenth and nineteenth centuries, psalm singing fell out of favor, especially with churches in the United States.[25] When US Presbyterian churches finally modernized to admit hymn singing, they usually just borrowed particular hymns they liked from neighboring Lutherans or other external sources.[26] As a result, though many tunes originally composed for Calvinist metrical psalms eventually migrated into hymnals, Presbyterian contribution to the common stock of hymnody—mainline and otherwise—has been modest.

Still, by the twenty-first century, as decreasing numbers of American Christians overall have been singing hymns, minor differences between Protestant denominations have faded in musical importance. Denominational boundaries have also become more porous due to more worshipers switching between subsets of Christianity, so congregants are increasingly bringing musical heritage from a wider variety of spiritual backgrounds into their current religious practice. Singing hymns is important, with familiarity, musical qualities, and theological content outranking concerns over their denominational sources. Two Presbyterian Traditional worshipers, who had been raised in the Church of Christ and Presbyterian Church, respectively, expressed an increasingly common postdenominational approach to incorporating old-fashioned evangelical hymnody.

WORSHIPER #1: It seems a shame. I mean, I think of the hymns of the church; it seems like we've lost something. Like when I go to a Baptist church, or think of my childhood in the Church of Christ, there is a set of songs that is closer to the earth. We joke about "When the Roll Is Called up Yonder," things like that, singing one of those a quarter would be a gas!

WORSHIPER #2: I had been out of town somewhere and they did "To God Be the Glory" and I thought, "Why aren't we singing that? I haven't sung that in ages!" And it is in the hymnal! The other one I asked for was "He Lives." Now that one isn't in the [Presbyterian] hymnal. Now I'd like to hear kids sing that because it's real basic. It's got the good bass part to it the men can sing. But that's not in the Presbyterian hymnal.

They both started singing, with enthusiastic echoes on the call-and-response chorus. I joined in.

In the simplified dichotomy of the Worship Wars, hymnody is hymnody and hymnody is Traditional. According to this calculus, explains church music historian Stephen Marini, hymnody provides an important mode of ritual expression in which hymns' specific origin details are less important than their "aura of factuality" that helps to "synthesize the doctrinal, communal, spiritual, and physiological dimensions of worship."[27] Just as with Traditional organs, a positive relationship with hymnody rests on interrelated dynamics of cultural heritage and personal history.

Hymnody is based in history, but consistent newly composed hymns try to keep the body of song from being ossified in the past. Yet, while worshipers liked the idea of a living tradition, newer hymns often received a less enthusiastic welcome. For example, a national survey of Presbyterian hymnal use showed that the newer hymns were the least frequently sung and most requested to be edited out of forthcoming editions: "Of the 100 hymns sung by the fewest congregations (sung in less than one in eight congregations), 76 percent had words or music—usually both—written after 1959. In sharp contrast, of the 100 most widely sung hymns, only five appeared after 1959."[28] Traditional congregants reported that the language and imagery of the newer hymns does not resonate with them. One long-time Tennessee Presbyterian explained, "There's not a spiritual experience for me in music written in the later part of the last century. Going back to the nineteenth century is very relaxing and that's where I keep Sunday

110 / (White)Washing Our Sins Away

morning." Another congregant voiced a popular complaint, asserting that more recently written hymns had distinct lyrical "differences" (by which he meant deficiencies). Making light of one hymn's title, he explained:

> We do things like "God of the Sparrow,"[29] God of the Aardvark, something along those lines, which is a wonderful sentiment, but the older stuff, the truly old hymns, don't sound like that. There's a phraseology to them. They talk about religion in a specifically theological way, and the more contemporary stuff, 1940 forward to where you get into praise music, seems to be trying hard not to have anything that could be taken wrong. So it's blander.

The syntax and "phraseology" of more recent language impacts congregants' perceptions of newer hymns.

> JUSTICE: You had said that if you were to sing a hymn, you want to sing an older hymn?

> CONGREGANT IN HER FORTIES: I think I would. I prefer the older hymns to the newer ones.

> JUSTICE: And "God of the Sparrow" is one of those?

> CONGREGANT IN HER FORTIES: Yes [citing one of the hymn's lines] "God of the creature." I think it's being called a creature. I don't want to be called a creature!

Although newer hymns have updated Traditional denominational hymnals, many mainline Protestants find the additions lacking. The older hymns still being sung are the relative few that have stood the test of time, but newer hymns often struggle to balance Traditional genre requirements, twenty-first-century aesthetics, and a mainline sense of theological authenticity. Still, as Hillsboro pastor David Kidd quipped, "Traditionalists consider classical church music 'contemporary'—they're still singing it, so it must still be current!"

Repertoire Sources: Praise and Worship Music

Contemporary congregational repertoire is far more fluid and dynamically emerging than most Traditional repertoire. Just as different hymnals have historically helped to draw denominational lines, physical hymnals in Traditional worship contrast an ephemeral, ever-evolving stream of praise choruses and songs in Contemporary worship. Contemporary repertoire exists as an unregulated, rapidly evolving body of music, gleaned from globally available media for use in local worship settings. An entire Contemporary worship industry has developed, with songwriters, worship leaders, tours, record labels, recording industry, and more.[30] Worship music scholars have been studying the development of Contemporary music in evangelical, charismatic, and Pentecostal communities since its origins in the 1960s.[31] Ethnomusicologist Monique Ingalls highlights how

> examining these several popular sub-genres of contemporary worship music affords an understanding of the different historical contexts out of which each style developed, along with which genre characteristics were adopted from mainstream popular music and their associated meanings that had to be negotiated as a result.[32]

Many mainline Protestant congregations were cautious in adopting Contemporary worship because of these "associated meanings." Secular associations aside, mainline Protestants often heard Contemporary music resonating with "the corporate mentality of the purpose-driven megachurch and McMansion evangelicalism."[33] Many mainline Protestants agreed with editorials like the following from *Christianity Today*:

> The evangelicalism in the '90s had a firmly established youth culture, built on the infrastructure of a lucrative Christian retail industry and commercial subculture. Huge Christian rock festivals, Lord's Gym T-shirts, WWJD [What Would Jesus Do] bracelets, Left Behind [a popular book series about the Rapture], and so forth. It was big business. It was corporate. It was schlocky kitsch.[34]

Much of the praise and worship music written during the 1990s, now "classics" within the genre, for example, "Lord, I Lift Your Name on High" and "As the Deer," seemed to be relics from that era, just like WWJD bracelets.

Although mainline congregants reported enjoying some of these earlier songs, the subgenre sounds of many older praise and worship songs also represented two issues. Traditionalists often associated them with simplistic, youth-oriented music and theology—better suited for Sunday

School programs or youth music nights than Sunday morning adult worship. The musical styles had not been updated, so while the music was Contemporary by comparison, it was no longer literally contemporary with current tastes. While this might sound like a problem with the church's praise band leader or musical director and not necessarily with the repertoire itself (because Contemporary songs are really just lyrics, melodies, and chord changes), such cultural lags were commonplace in mainline (and other) churches. Second, the rapid commercialism of Contemporary repertoire echoed suburbanized capitalism and "the privileges of Americanness, or those of whiteness, wealth, and cultural capital."[35] The Christian Copyright Licensing International (CCLI) charts that report the royalty-requiring use of worship music indexes a reporting pool of mostly White churches, so their preferences are projected. The rise and commercialization of Contemporary worship has remained predominantly White and middle class.[36] In 2008, a twenty-something Presbyterian praise band guitarist explained:

> GUITARIST: There's a whole lot of the popular Christian music which I don't like.
>
> JUSTICE: Why not?
>
> GUITARIST: I just think it's too sweet sounding, not really—like Michael W. Smith and all that stuff on WAY-FM. I was into it for like two or three months, and then you realize that it's like all the same selective group of songs. It all sounds the same. I just didn't like it. I liked it at first, but then it kinda started to grate on me.

Even though Mainline Protestants tended to gloss Traditional versus Contemporary repertoire as broad categories, they were hearing subtle value differences between styles and eras of worship music.

Understanding turn-of-the-millennium Contemporary music as "an amalgamation of nearly fifty years of songs"[37] helps explain the lack of a direct correlation between worship music genre and age. Having started gaining momentum in the 1960s and '70s,[38] Contemporary worship was firmly rooted in many American churches by the early 1980s. In other words, Contemporary worship music started nearly two generations before the Worship Wars reached their peak after the turn of the millennium.

Sonic Diversity / 113

"How is it that bifocaled Baby Boomers leading '70s praise choruses is Contemporary?" laughed Hillsboro pastor David Kidd. Worship teams that set the international standards of Contemporary performance are often comprised of musicians in their twenties, but, given the congregations they are drawing from, the average mainline Contemporary band skews a bit older. One singer in her late forties drew the analogy between the age of the repertoire and the age of the worship team at her church:

> SINGER: If it was more "Contemporary," they wouldn't let me sing!
>
> JUSTICE: Why not?
>
> SINGER: Because I'm too old! I mean, it seems like the mega-churches that are real Contemporary have all young people in their twenties singing!

At more than one mainline Protestant church, more than one Contemporary praise band member counts bifocals among their musical equipment.

Still, Worship Wars rhetoric often adopted seemingly logical assumptions that younger people prefer current popular musical styles, and thereby want to hear them in church.[39] Since mainline congregations have been aging much faster than the general US population, their churches often hoped that "younger" Contemporary music would bring in new, younger members. Many existing church members were less enthusiastic about worshiping with Contemporary music themselves, but they valued the perceived overall benefits of supporting it alongside Traditional.

> WOMAN IN HER FIFTIES: I haven't seen much downside at all. I feel like it appeals to more people . . . keeps the young people in.
>
> WOMAN IN HER SEVENTIES: Yes, I think it's been a good experience having a Contemporary service. It's brought in a lot of people, young adults. They're not old people like we are.

For Traditional congregants like these, even anecdotally supported assertions that Contemporary music sustains or builds the congregation as a whole makes its inclusion both pragmatically and ideologically appealing. Mainline Contemporary worshipers generally do not express a parallel belief

114 / (White)Washing Our Sins Away

that the Traditional service has more older members, likely because they see numerous elderly congregants every Sunday in their own services. As one older Tennessee man said, "I've been worshiping to the other stuff all my life, I might as well try something new while I'm still here."

Lyrics: Singing Theology

> Our praise band director, his stuff is [theologically] substantial. I've never heard anything he's done that hasn't been a lot better than an awful lot of crap you hear.
>
> —A Tennessee Presbyterian minister

When mainline Protestant churches decided to adopt Contemporary music, they were often concerned about lyrical content. Theologian John Frame highlights how Contemporary lyrical focus differs from Traditional music:

> (1) [Contemporary worship music] is far more contemporary and popular in its literary and musical idioms, rather than traditional or classical. (2) Most of it consists of one-stanza choruses as opposed to the multi-stanza poetry of traditional hymnody. (3) The texts . . . tend to be far simpler than those of traditional hymnody. (4) . . . there is far more emphasis on praise (as opposed to lament, confession of sin, teaching, personal testimony, or supplication) than in traditional hymnody, though other aspects of worship are also present.[40]

These content shifts posed substantial departures from mainline Protestant focus. If worship music came across as "too Contemporary" or "too evangelical," worshipers were hearing too much overlap of identities and denominational boundaries. Often, this judgment came together with "too simplistic," in regard to both musical and lyrical content, or more scathing critiques that Contemporary worship music only promoted "warm fuzzy feelings with a focus on self-fulfillment." [41] One Traditional choir director did not mince words: "A steady dose of that is, you know, (*pauses*) shallow. It's shallow music. It's not only shallow music, the text is shallow." Many mainline churches, like Hillsboro Presbyterian, actively worked to vet their Contemporary lyrical content:

PASTOR McCURLEY: We've worked with Stephen [Nix, the Contemporary worship leader] . . . It's not just the typical praise music . . . which is something that keeps that service from becoming too . . . [*pauses*]

PASTOR KIDD: Saccharine.

In terms of content, most of the lyrical controversies centered on two areas: agency and repetition. If these were only aesthetic questions, congregants could agree to disagree. Concerns over shallow text might be dismissed as perennial complaints that every new American generation is losing cultural literacy. Increasing national diversity has tempered previously unbending Eurocentric, elitist high-culture standards such that different types of literacy, rhetoric, and communication are valued. This evolution of language and culture worries many American mainline Protestants because—like many other people of all different spiritual systems the world over—they believe that worship lyrics "over time shape people, shape people's faith."[42] A Tennessee Presbyterian pastor explained, "I think that [singing] helps shape people's faith. You're talking about their choices and their decisions." Scholars like ethnomusicologist Jeffers Engelhardt and anthropologist Webb Keane have found that Christians from Estonia to Indonesia worry that singing the wrong way or the wrong materials creates "not only a theological error or an affront to God; it threatens to undermine the agency proper to humans."[43] As the old Sunday School song goes, "Be careful little ears, what you hear . . . be careful little tongue, what you say." What we sing can throw off divine-human relations.

Lyrics: Me and Jesus

Lyrics are especially pressing because, as a whole, the words of Contemporary and Traditional worship music take contrasting approaches to sorting out agency and negotiating relationships between human and divine. Historians Loveland and Wheeler observe that "rather than being written *about* God," Contemporary worship songs "were addressed *to* him, using second-person instead of third-person pronouns. They encouraged worshipers to seek a personal, intimate relationship with God."[44] Sometimes

116 / (White)Washing Our Sins Away

this relationship was seen as too close, with criticism of overly emotional "me and Jesus" sensibilities,[45] "Jesus is my boyfriend ditties" (songs ambiguously worded such that they could easily have been about either human romantic love or divine adoration, or (as one Presbyterian pastor put it) "sappy and individualistic." During my long-term fieldwork at Hillsboro Presbyterian, statistical analysis confirmed that the vast majority of its Contemporary songs[46] used the first person to emotionally call out to God. This focus pushes historical denominational boundaries; articulating emotional, personal relationships with Christ has characterized evangelicalism more so than mainline Protestantism.[47]

While many mainline Protestants would also identify as having such a personal relationship (keeping in mind that theological and sociopolitical identities such as evangelical are not always cut-and-dried), the music of mainline worship has historically focused on corporate, rather than individual, aspects of faith.[48] "All Creatures of Our God and King" and other favorite hymns call "we, your people" together as "partners in Christ's service." Hillsboro Presbyterian's associate pastor explains:

> McCURLEY: If you look at our hymnal, that is the case—"O, God, *Our* Help in Ages Past." "A Mighty Fortress Is *Our* God." There are very, very few hymns that talk about "*I* Walk in the Garden Alone" in the Reformed tradition . . . If you look at the hymnal, there oftentimes is "we." [*Pointing to the text*] "Bring *we*." It's not "I bring the frankincense of my love" no, it's "we." I mean, certainly there is the first-person singular used [*paging through*]. Here, "I'll Praise My Maker." But it's much more often out of a corporate sense.

For many mainline Protestants, the individual focus of much Contemporary worship resonates with the rise of evangelicalism, but also with related overall changes to the fabric of American society. Musically, affinity-based niche consumption has been rising. Musical stars and cultural icons used to have a more pervasive reach, but the idea of a dominant US musical culture has been receding as micromusic scenes have been replacing previous aesthetic superculture.[49] Sociologically, as scholars Robert Putnam[50] and Justin Wilford[51] chronicle, the nation has been shifting away from twentieth-century collective culture to increasingly individualistic modalities.

Sonic Diversity / 117

Lyrics: Repetition

How congregants heard repetition played a key role in how they valued Traditional and Contemporary musics. This section uses two songs—one Contemporary piece and one Traditional hymn—to provide a case study of how worshipers were hearing repetition differently across the Traditional-Contemporary divide.

In a "blended" worship service, Hillsboro Presbyterian's joint congregation sang the 1994 praise and worship hit "I Could Sing of Your Love Forever."[52] People who preferred the Traditional style reported a very different experience than did regular Contemporary worshipers. Their responses fell on a continuum between two main polarities, illustrated by the following representative comments:

> CONTEMPORARY WORSHIPER: Singing those words over and over again. It's like a mantra. I just love it. It helps me worship.

> TRADITIONAL WORSHIPER: Every time the praise band starts that song, I just shudder! [*Shakes shoulders and shudders*] Just because the lyrics say, "I could sing of your love forever," doesn't mean we have to sing that line forever, over and over and again!

The blended congregation also sang the Traditional nineteenth-century hymn "For the Beauty of the Earth":[53]

> TRADITIONAL WORSHIPER: I love the structure of the old hymns, with verse after verse building layers of theology and ideas.

> CONTEMPORARY WORSHIPER: When we sing one of those Traditional hymns, it's like it just keeps on going, verse after verse. It makes me tired! Can't we sit down already?

People were experiencing the lyrics in both types of music as repetitious. Yet, they assigned positive value to repetition in their preferred style and negative value to repetition in the "other" music. Contemporary worshipers positively compare singing praise choruses repeatedly to mantras. Traditional worshipers label the same music as "shallow," "boring," and "7-11s" (the same seven words sung eleven times over). Contemporary singers weary of the higher verse count of many Traditional hymns, whereas Traditional worshipers extol the lyrics' "rich theological content."

Congregants respond to word count and distribution over time when judging a song as excessively repetitive. "I Could Sing of Your Love Forever" and "For the Beauty of the Earth" illustrate these frames of perception (see figure 4.1). "I Could Sing" has thirty-nine different words and, in Hillsboro's

I Could Sing of Your Love Forever

- 39 words
- 2 minutes

For The Beauty of the Earth

- 76 words
- 3 minutes

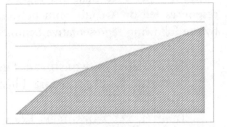

Over the mountains and the sea,
Your river runs with love for me,
and I will open up my heart
and let the Healer set me free.
I'm happy to be in the truth,
and I will daily lift my hands:
for I will always sing of when
Your love came down.

I could sing of Your love forever.

(repeat)

1. For the beauty of the earth,
For the glory of the skies,
For the love which from our birth
Over and around us lies;
Lord of all, to Thee we raise
This our hymn of grateful praise.
2. For the wonder of each hour
Of the day and of the night,
Hill and vale and tree and flower,
Sun and moon, and stars of light; Lord of all, to Thee we raise
This our hymn of grateful praise.
3. For the joy of ear and eye,
For the heart and mind's delight,
For the mystic harmony
Linking sense to sound and sight
Lord of all, to Thee we raise
This our hymn of grateful praise
4. For the joy of human love,
Brother, sister, parent, child;
Friends on earth and friends above;
For all gentle thoughts and mild;
Lord of all, to Thee we raise
This our hymn of grateful praise.
5. For Thy Church that evermore
Lifteth holy hands above,
Offering up on every shore
Her pure sacrifice of love;
Lord of all, to Thee we raise
this our hymn of grateful praise

Figure 4.1. Comparative lyrics. Chart by Deborah Justice.

rendition (which is typical of many mainline churches), usually lasts just over two minutes. "For the Beauty" has seventy-six different words and usually lasts just over three minutes. Only comparing words over time, the overall textual densities of these two songs are not remarkably different; "I Could Sing" moves at about twenty words per minute, which is similar to the twenty-five words per minute in "For the Beauty."

Larger differences in repetition emerge, however, when comparing the overall number of unique words and ideas in the songs. "I Could Sing" has roughly half the words of "For the Beauty." Like many older hymns, "For the Beauty" features multiple verses that deal with a variety of subjects relating to the work's central theme. "I Could Sing" does not continue to introduce new concepts over the course of the song. As a result, the distribution of words over time differs dramatically between the two songs. In "I Could Sing," the first thirty-seven out of thirty-nine nonrepeated words come within the first twenty seconds. The remaining minute and forty seconds are filled with the single phrase "I could sing of your love forever." The "over and over" repetition is easy to hear. In contrast, the words in "For the Beauty" are well distributed over the five verses. New verses, full of new words and ideas, just keep coming. Here, repetition comes through repeated introduction of novelty.

On the Contemporary side, band leader Stephen Nix explained the power of "simple," "redundant" music like "I Could Sing":

> You'll always have a chorus with a main thematic principle, sort of as a mantra that carries the weight of whatever you're saying. As simple as they are, that sort of redundancy helps people. Music is really not meant to inculcate you with massive theological concepts.

Although the term "mantra" comes from Sanskrit religious texts rather than being rooted in Christianity, its use in yoga has helped it become common in modern American society. Many Hillsboro congregants used this as a pan-religious word to describe positively valuing Contemporary repetition. One woman reflected a common theme: "[Repetition like 'I Could Sing'] is like having a mantra . . . I find that that is very soothing to me, and pulls me in to where I think I should be." For worshipers who prefer the Contemporary service, such meditative textual repetition enhances their experience of worship.

However, for Traditional congregants, the brief repeated choruses of "I Could Sing" and other Contemporary praise and worship music are repetitively excessive, both aesthetically and theologically. One typical congregant explains the effect, "You just repeat it over and over and over again until you'd killed it!" Even Hillsboro's pastors, David Kidd and Nancy McCurley, remained unconvinced about this type of repetition. Associate Pastor McCurley rubbed her temples as she unexpectedly volunteered, "You know the song that drives me absolutely bonkers? "I Could Sing of Your Love Forever." Four hundred times. Ugh. Every time we begin it, I go, 'Oh no! This is interminable!'" Traditional worshipers heard the same repetitive lyrical elements that Contemporary worshipers did, but they assigned negative values to the repeated lyrics.

Similar opposite value judgments occurred in Traditional music. The consistent introduction of new words and ideas stimulated Traditional worshipers. Proponents spoke of the "lyrical depth," "excellent theology," and "textual substance." Hillsboro's choir director, Sherry Kelly, emphasized the educational value of Traditional texts: "You probably learn more scripture through that music than most ways, other than preaching of the Word." Another congregant described the lyrical density of Traditional music as theologically sound because "it tells a coherent story, gives you a sense of God in more than one dimension." Traditional music's repetition came to be valued as the consistent, repeated introduction of new ideas.

Many Contemporary worshipers, however, perceived this repetition as negative. For them, the long strophic forms did not come across as helpful, but rather as erudite and pedantic. One Hillsboro Contemporary band singer summarized the repetitive nature of the experience, "I've been there, done that. I don't need the fourteenth verse." Another congregant voiced similar sentiments:

> If I am in that Traditional worship service and somebody says, "You have to sing five stanzas of a hymn," I'm like, "No, I really don't have to." It makes me tired; it doesn't energize me. It makes me feel like, "When are we going to be done with this and sit down?"

Both Traditional and Contemporary worshipers heard the same Traditional lyrical elements as repetitious, but they assigned different value to that repetition.

How to Sing: Screens, Hymnals, and Heritage

Contemporary and Traditional worship musics rely on different means of transmission, which are based upon different types of musical skill and literacy. Traditional music transmission relies on education-grounded Western music literacy; Contemporary relies more heavily on aural musical skills. The material culture of how the music is communicated impacts how congregants can embody worship. Yet, despite these differences, in the reality of a service, for most congregants, both styles of musical transmit similar information.

Contemporary musical transmission is based on learning by ear, on aural—instead of written—transfer of knowledge. Musicians receive lead sheets with chords and lyrics for the music (see figure 4.2), but most of the transmission happens off the written page. For congregational singing, lyrics are projected onto screens at the front of the worship space. No musical notation is provided. Worshipers listen directionally and try to follow the musical line by ear. For people familiar with basic Western pop and folk idioms, the repetitious nature and predictable structure of the music helps them anticipate melodic directions to sing along with new materials easily.

In contrast, for Traditional worship, musical literacy based on reading printed Western sheet music has been central to mainline Protestant worship. Organists and pianists follow detailed scores. Choirs read from four-part sheet music for rehearsals and Sunday morning services. Hymnals provide full soprano, alto, tenor, and bass (SATB) notation for all congregational songs (see figure 4.3). The printed scores allow formally trained or long-experienced participants to sing unfamiliar pieces.

These two styles of musical transmission assume different types of musical literacy: written and aural. For musicians participating in either service, experience and training in these types of musical transmission is key. Many Traditional musicians and congregants accustomed to written Western notation report difficulties coming to terms with the directional listening required in Contemporary worship. For example, a French horn player with a graduate degree in music explains, "Maybe that's my lack of musical talent, not to get it on the first time through, but it just, it makes me very ill at ease to be singing, and then singing the wrong note." A classical pianist agrees, "There's no notes! So, you're sitting there, and they've printed all these words, but what are you supposed to sing?!"

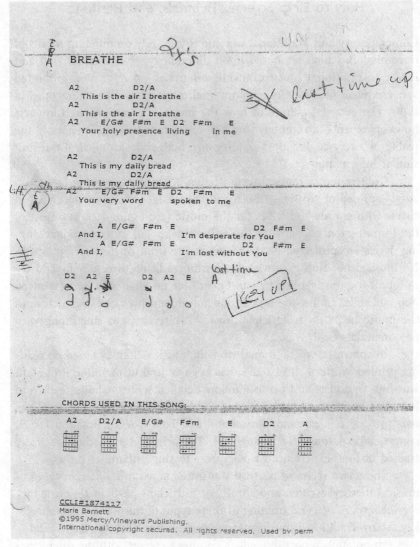

Figure 4.2. Contemporary song "Breathe," as transmitted to the Hillsboro praise band. Handwritten directions are my own with my own notes for playing. Photo by Deborah Justice.

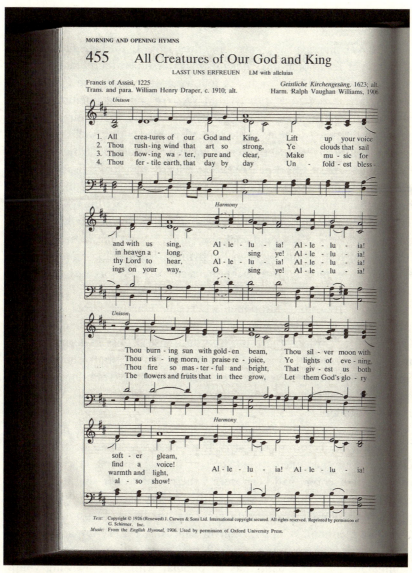

Figure 4.3. Traditional hymn "All Creatures of Our God and King," as transmitted to Hillsboro Presbyterian congregants and choir in the PC(USA) hymnal (1991). Photo by Deborah Justice

124 / (White)Washing Our Sins Away

Having had formal Western music education, these worshipers feel adrift without notation.

Many congregants, however, find themselves in the opposite position. A portion of Traditional and Contemporary worshipers reported directional singing as their primary means of following the music. Due to a lack of training and experience with written Western musical notation or lack of interest therein, many congregants, and even a few choir members, admitted that they were not able to read printed music well or at all. A former Hillsboro Presbyterian choir member explained: "Now, provided it's a churchy piece, most of those I can usually sight-read. Especially if it has traditional harmonies. It's where you got dissonance and minors, odd timing, that kind of stuff that really throws me." Another thirty-something Traditional worshiper says that the hymnal's notation actually hinders her rather than helps: "It would make no difference to me if they printed [the words] in the bulletin or in the hymnal, because I certainly am not looking at the music. It'd probably be easier, actually, because the words would be all together instead of having to skip all around."

Some Traditional proponents correlate congregational difficulties with reading musical notation with a perceived overall societal decrease in musical education. There is a specific sense of loss in terms of how many musical skills used to be taught in churches. Hillsboro choir director Sherry Kelly's perspective is representative of many Traditionalists who dig in their heels to staunchly defend the superiority of classical Western music education:

A few years ago, we did [Mendelssohn's] "Elijah" here and we dramatized it . . . Other directors would say, "That's neat, I want to do that in my church." And then they would look at the score. First of all, because of what their choirs had been doing, their choirs can't sing it. And the conductors can't conduct it because they're just used to doing this sim- plified music. Other Traditionalists, such as the liberal Mennonites of the Neffsville Mennonite Church choir in Lancaster, Pennsylvania, expressed more nostalgic introspection. Overall, they were happy that their church's Contemporary praise band was so popular with their growing youth demographic, but "our kids can't sing the four-part a cappella like we used to," noted an older congregant. "I guess the times are changing, but it seems like we failed somehow."

Not all older congregants preferred continuing with the material culture of Traditional worship, however. Many older congregants explained that singing from the screen made them feel younger because "I don't have to dig through the hymnal and put my glasses on to try to see." One woman said, "I don't know why, but it seems like it just sounds better, like how people are singing." Hillsboro Presbyterian's band director Stephen Nix highlighted how screens can help people sing:

> The reason why we do the lyrics, why I'm a believer in putting the lyrics up, is to get people's voices from singing to the floor to singing upwards is to create volume, and thus you get this greater sensation of music. It sort of builds the emotional, and spiritual, to me, it helps to build the volume, you know, to make the people feel more unified. That's the reason why I love to have the lyrics going up. Because most people don't read music, most people are elementary in their musical skills. They're really directionally hearing, that's all that they're doing, they're guessing.

This explanation helped congregants warm up to the new technology. "When that screen went up," remembers one woman in her fifties, "I said to the band leader, 'I don't like that screen. It just reminds me of a big church. It's too high tech, commercial!' And his words were, 'But when you guys sing, you're looking down. You're not lifting your voice' . . . When he explained that to me, the screen was a whole different experience" (see figures I.5 and I.11).

Contemporary worshipers of all ages also noted that the lack of hymnals freed them to raise their hands in the air to praise or to clap. (I have personally tried—and do *not* recommend—singing, holding a hymnal or choir folder, and clapping at the same time.) Nevertheless, given the more reserved worship behavior to which many mainline Protestant congregations are accustomed, there is relatively little clapping or hand-raising in mainline Contemporary services. As in other areas (see chapter 7), the possibility for participation is as important, if not more so, than actively participating.

Conclusion: Immanence and Transcendence

As mainline Protestants incorporated Contemporary worship music, they negotiated specific pragmatic questions: What instruments to use, what to sing, how to sing it? Contemporary worship brought in elements from beyond mainline Protestantism's historical limits. These sonic elements carried potential overtones of changing social and sacred identities. Looking at their own demographics, mainline Protestants knew that their institutions needed to make some changes, but how much change and diversity was too much? Would incorporating elements like guitars and Contemporary repertoire result in identity-compromising social and theological shifts? Could mainline Protestants retain core features and values while retaining (or perhaps reclaiming) relevance in America's shifting religious landscape?

The ways in which mainline Protestants answered the three sonic questions—What instruments to play? What music to play and sing? How to sing it?—depended on how they wanted worship services to relate to the rest of their lives. On both musical and theological levels, to what extent should "Sunday morning" exist apart from "the rest of the week"?

One group of congregants—comprised of both Contemporary and Traditional members—preferred continuity between music heard on Sunday morning and throughout the week. I refer to this as *musical immanence* because the sounds of worship encompass and manifest the everyday world "outside" of worship. This type of relationship to worship characterizes evangelicalism, which has been the main source of guitar-heavy Contemporary worship music. Most mainline Protestants who preferred musical immanence were Contemporary worshipers who regularly listen to Contemporary Christian Music and mainstream popular music outside of church. A praise band singer explained, "The music we do in the Contemporary service is music that I listen to. Not just because I'm rehearsing it or I'm singing it in preparation for something, but because I would *choose* to turn it on and listen to it." As another worshiper put it, for her, music in church was just like "what you'd sing in your car by yourself."

A small proportion of Traditional service attendees reported the same desire for and experience of musical immanence. They described listening to classical music and sacred music—both of which included some organ—during the week, but these people were used to searching out their desired music on particular radio stations or recordings outside of mainstream media channels.

Most Traditional worshipers reported finding little resonance between Sunday morning's music and the rest of their sonic week. They usually went on to explain that this was a good thing. These congregants wanted *musical transcendence*, with worship sounding different than the rest of the week. For them, the sounds of worship transcended mundane experience to demarcate a sacred time and place, a sanctuary (discussed further in chapter 6). Pipe organs provided a welcome counterbalance to the readily available commercial music these worshipers were usually exposed to during the week.

These two approaches of musical immanence and transcendence help explain why congregants found the two sides of the Worship Wars dichotomy to be so incompatible. When mainline churches supported both styles of music, they were supporting fundamentally different approaches to worship and relation with the divine. Churches could mitigate some lyrics, and, as the next chapter discusses, they often used hymnody as a stylistic bridge. But how were faith communities able to find enough common ground to support both styles and the resultant theological impacts?

Some churches, quite simply, could not. Part of the reason the Worship Wars simmered down after the first decade of the twentieth century was because Christians got tired of conflict. Having experimented with various configurations to accommodate worship styles that they perceived as fundamentally opposed, some churches eventually picked one or the other. Sustaining tension over long periods wears on resources.

When mainline churches did successfully incorporate and institutionalize Contemporary worship, both their Traditional and Contemporary congregants often expressed similar beliefs about the fundamental value of music in worship. At Hillsboro Presbyterian, congregants spoke about music as thoughtful prayer and praise:

> CONTEMPORARY CONGREGANT IN HER FIFTIES: To center and focus, to prepare a person to be open to God and to be an expression of praise to God, like a prayer.

> CONTEMPORARY CONGREGANT IN HER EIGHTIES: I asked for the lyrics to the song so I could post them here at home and look at them throughout the week. I like the chance to think about the words.

> TRADITIONAL CONGREGANT IN HER SIXTIES: I actually believe that it's to prepare the spirit and the heart in worship, in worshiping God, and getting you ready to receive the Word. And then the closing of the music is to prepare you to go out into the world.

128 / (White)Washing Our Sins Away

TRADITIONAL CONGREGANT IN HIS SIXTIES: I think it needs to speak to a person, make him feel like he's having a worship experience, or some kind of prayerful experience, and that's what I think it should do. That's what I think anyway. It's supposed to accompany, set the mood.

CONTEMPORARY CONGREGANT IN HER FORTIES: I don't want to go away with just this head-banging noise going on in my head. I want to have the words and the music together in my head and my heart to take with me. Because, to me, that would be the full blessing of all of it.

Similarly, although they work with different genres, both Hillsboro Presbyterian's Traditional choir director and Contemporary band leader also both emphasized the centrality of praise and emotion in worship music:

CONTEMPORARY BAND LEADER: Music is really not meant to inculcate you with massive theological concepts. It's meant to sort of emotionalize you to accept a spiritual truth, and to prepare you emotionally, whether it's to break down the walls because you're tired, or whether it's sort of to break down the barriers because you're jaded. Whatever they are. I think, by simplifying it, either people get lost in the rhythm, or the beauty of it, and they sing a lyric that's more simplified, and it makes them aware. It opens them up. It's sort of like caffeine for the soul [chuckles].

Even though she had often extolled the pedagogical value of Traditional worship music, she softened when I asked her to identify the basic purpose of music in worship:

TRADITIONAL CHOIR DIRECTOR: Music reaches the depth of the soul, and sometimes the spoken word does not. You can hear a piece of music, even if there are no words to it, and you can be moved to praise. If I had to put it in a capsule form, I would have to say that's what it is. It's praise and leading worshipers to praise, something that is going to move people to praise emotionally.

The reasoned, intellectual systematic theology of Presbyterianism remained important, but musical leaders and congregants alike spoke about music's fundamental power to awaken experiential spiritual parts of the soul.

Although Hillsboro musical leaders, congregants, and clergy were experiencing musics that they sonically judged as drastically different, they identified the same core values across those musics. Even if a Contemporary congregant could not personally hear that value in Traditional music, vice versa, they could agree on the principles and beliefs—and they trusted that their fellow worshipers shared those same values. Worshipers knew that they actually shared more core values than their alleged Worship Wars Traditional-Contemporary dichotomy suggests. Members of the same church might detest the sound of each other's worship services but knew that they were fundamentally united in sonic, social, and sacred values.

Still, the oppositional Traditional-Contemporary dichotomy nevertheless proved useful for mainline Protestants. Successfully supporting both Traditional and Contemporary worship helped the congregants at Hillsboro Presbyterian—and countless other mainline churches—genuinely feel that they were increasing their congregation's diversity. Individuals were participating in large organizations that devoted significant portions of their resources to worship styles that these individuals neither personally liked nor found spiritually effective: supporting guitars when they preferred organs or musical immanence when they preferred transcendence. The musical paradox was useful within the American religious and social landscape and Christianity is, after all, "a fundamentally paradoxical tradition,"[54] asserts anthropologist Fanella Cannell. As Episcopalian scholar and musician Scott Robinson observes, "Anyone who organizes life around the idea that God could appear in a form at once divine and human—shouldn't, theoretically, be in the business of setting up false dichotomies. At the very least, we ought to be comfortable with paradox."[55]

Chapter 5

"We're Only Medium Contemporary"
Creating Identity Boundaries

> They really have bastardized it. They popularized it. They put jazzy
> rhythms in it. But they use the same text. It loses all, I'm sorry, but
> it loses its profundity.
>
> —A Traditional worshiper

As mainline Protestants worked to incorporate Contemporary worship,
they were balancing creating difference while maintaining some degree
of overarching congregational unity. While every church with multiple
services (regardless of style) had to work to help individuals feel like they
are part of the greater whole, the contrasting values of Contemporary
and Traditional worship only exacerbated divisions of time and space
between services. The readings of Hillsboro Presbyterian throughout this
book serve to illustrate such broader trends in American Christianity. This
chapter explores three strategies—evangelical hymnody, retuning hymns,
and blending worship—that mainline churches often employed to bridge
Worship Wars tensions. All three strategies evidence increasing evangelical
influence on mainline Protestantism, a trend that holds implications both
for churches and American society as a whole.

Hymnody often provided a point of both connection and conten-
tion between Contemporary and Traditional worship. In many mainline
Protestant churches, rather than digging deeper into their own denominational roots, musical leaders were often drawing on outside repertoire:
older evangelical chestnuts. The repertoire resonated with a concurrent

132 / (White)Washing Our Sins Away

upswing in Americana in popular culture, with bands like Old Crow Medicine Show and Mumford and Sons cultivating massive followings for their banjo-heavy folksy sound. Using popular old evangelical hymns allowed mainline Protestants to tap into a useable, accessible heritage of Americana past—but often without engaging the specific racial, regional, or economic origins of the music.

Finally, this chapter explores the limits of congregational unity. While the Worship Wars rhetoric positioned Traditional and Contemporary as diametrically opposed styles, worshipers found they could choose to hear core commonalities between the genres. If congregations were finding enough common ground to stay together instead of splitting over musical differences, why could they not "blend" styles and combine the different musics in one service? Many churches did experiment with so-called "blended worship," but this compromise approach did not gain widespread popularity. Instead, most mainline congregations chose to double-down on the differences between Traditional and Contemporary worship. Why did mainline Protestants decide that emphasizing stylistic diversity was the more effective strategy? Most congregants were willing to support the "Other" style for the perceived good of their congregation, but they were generally not willing to worship with it themselves. What broader implications does institutionalizing a "separate but equal" stye of musical diversity hold for White mainline Protestants in twenty-first-century America?

Evangelical Hymnody

By the turn of the millennium, mainline congregations—from both the Traditional and Contemporary sides of the Worship Wars—had a growing interest in the sounds of evangelical heritage. Most mainline churches had used evangelical chestnuts peripherally, often incorporating them outside of Sunday morning worship: "We had a hymn-fest that was all of the old evangelical 'Jesus died for my sins and the blood of the cross,' all of that. That was on a Wednesday night," explained Hillsboro Presbyterian's associate pastor Nancy McCurley. In the early 2000s, many mainline churches had begun adopting old evangelical hymns, often infusing them with the sounds of Americana through bluegrass, old-time music, and folk rock to reimagine a shared sonic and sacred heritage. This new musical renegotiation was repositioning the sounds and symbols of evangelical Americana as "authentic" and "useable" in worship.

"We're Only Medium Contemporary" / 133

Mainline Protestants were not simply expanding their hymn selections. Rather, they were reimagining their relationships with neighboring evangelical traditions. While not generally a consciously deployed strategy, Presbyterians and other mainline Protestants were using evangelical hymns to access a useable history that contrasted their own heritage. As sociologist R. Stephen Warner notes,

> The past that evangelicals invoke is not that of the historian. . . . In many ways, today's evangelicals are heterodox, expecially [*sic*] in the formerly Calvinistic Presbyterian church. . . . But they can better, with alacrity, embrace the very language and imagery of the mainline's theological symbolism— in hymnbooks, ritual confessions, and scriptures—than can the mainline itself, whose leaders may be more rigorous historians.[1]

In fighting the Worship Wars, many mainline Protestants had indeed staked out defensive positions protecting their histories. Yet, they could see that in honoring Tradition and heritage so specifically, they risked erecting barriers and hurdles for new participants. Selectively embracing time-tested evangelical repertoire offered a compromise.

In the mainline magazine *Christian Century*, Minnesota pastor Russell Rathbun described how his mainline Lutheran congregation was using the foreignness of the "old-time-gospel angle" to subvert the terms of the Worship Wars altogether: "It's a tradition of sacred music that's outside the experience of most of the people. . . . So there are not these battles over whether we play 'our music' or 'their music.' "[2] The origins, rural settings, and sense of "crossing over" in these songs drew far more strongly upon tropes of American religious heritage (read: a mix of Baptists, Methodist camp meetings, African American worship, and more traditions) than European-based denominational histories.[3] Specific ethnic and theological histories faded into a usable past.

The repertoire easily lent itself to an increasingly popular Americana twang. "I sometimes feel rootless," explained a thirty-something Presbyterian. Traditional mainline hymnody fell flat for her, but Contemporary worship also lacked something. What did resonate for her? "Older folksy hymns," Mumford and Sons, and the banjo-driven folk-rock sound that was increasingly dominating popular Christian worship music.[4] The acoustic guitarist with Hillsboro Presbyterian's Contemporary praise band equated songs of this sort with a musical sense of Americana: "Like 'Just a Closer

Walk with Thee'—[that would be] some old-timey song that would lend itself to a western swing feel, or let's do it in bluegrass style, because I can play mandolin on it or something."

In creating a usable past through music, mainline Protestantism often overlooks or revises specific or unpleasant details in an attempt to use the past to secure the future. Repertoire origin is one such example. Rather than coming from "timeless" aural traditions in rural areas, much of this "old-time religion" repertoire comes from well-connected turn-of-the-century songwriters. At the time, their musical genres and lyrical settings would have sounded quite new. Old-timey, folksy instruments like guitars, banjos, and mandolins also emerged into mass popularity around that same time.[5]

A century later, the "old-timey" sound was remerging to cultural prominence. In 2000, the popular movie *O Brother, Where Art Thou?* put fairy-tale glow onto old-timey music. The film became a cultural phenomenon and sparked the Down from the Mountain concert tour, featuring musicians like Ralph Stanley, John Hartford, Alison Krauss, and Emmylou Harris. Instrumentation is often used in conjunction with older evangelical hymns to establish Americana by evoking the "timeless" rural culture of Appalachia. By 2007, international folk band sensation Mumford and Sons was dominating music charts with slick banjo riffs and spiritual-sounding vocals. In 2010, the Coen Brothers' movie *True Grit* used "Leaning on the Everlasting Arms" centrally in the soundtrack. In a corrective to the synthesized sounds and slick production of 1980s and early '90s country music, many big-name country stars were returning to simpler, folksy roots. Soon Christian musicians like David Crowder were gaining large followings by bringing bluegrass to contemporary Christian music.[6]

The undefined "old-timey" and older "folksy" sound references nostalgia for a generalized American past—but given the nation's history of colonialism, slavery, racism, gender bias, and other forms of discrimination, only certain demographics will understand the American past as an overwhelmingly positive place. Mainline denominations like the PC(USA) aim to "engage the Church in its mission to become more diverse and inclusive of racial, ethnic, cultural and language groups,"[7] but as discussed in the preceding chapters, the mainline demographics themselves are over 90 percent White. Unlike other Americans who have a strong sense of their specific cultural roots, many White Americans describe themselves as "simply American."

Ethnomusicologist Mirjana Lausevic has written about how some White people develop specific musical affinities as compensation for their own perceived lack of self-identity within America's increasingly multiethnic milieu.[8] This lack of distinct worship music identity resonates with many Mainline Protestants. For example, when the PC(USA) did issue their new *Glory to God* hymnal in 2013, revisions reflected new openness to evangelical repertoire and a grassroots desire to move away from many of the historical backbones of the denomination's music. National survey results by the hymnal committee showed that postmillennial congregants wanted less psalmody (historically the hallmark of Presbyterian worship) and more diversity. In addition to "music from six different continents. . . . music covering all major historical and contemporary sacred genres, including approximately thirty-five African American/Gospel hymns,"[9] the editors included "some gospel, tent-revival hymns rarely seen in recent books."[10] Nearly all these additions to the Presbyterian hymnal were from different key points in the history of evangelical hymnody.[11] The Presbyterian Church's use of these songs demonstrated a new openness toward evangelical orientation and decreasing denominationalism, but this new music also referenced a heritage of American revivalism and populist Protestantism from which twentieth-century mainline Protestants had often distanced themselves.

In America's current demographic landscape, "just being 'White'" confers socioeconomic advantages, but socially and theologically progressive mainline Protestants find these dynamics of identity and privilege to be ethically problematic. As a result, mainline Protestants find themselves in a conundrum over how their religious identity and racial background is reflected in their congregational music. In keeping with broader American cultural dynamics, many musicians, clergy, and laity came to hear Americana roots music as communicating nonspecific Whiteness that could symbolize an imagined cultural past. Drawing a lineage with modern mainline believers as metaphorical descendants of *O Brother, Where Art Thou*–style rural White folksy Christians glosses over heritage that includes racial violence and class tensions to present a romantic, yet highly usable version of Americana past.

The older evangelical hymns that were incorporated into Contemporary worship often displayed evangelical roots that shared common musical and lyrical traits with newer Contemporary repertoire (see chapter 4). Editor of *United Methodist Book of Worship* Andy Langford notes a

136 / (White)Washing Our Sins Away

correlation between Contemporary worship music and "African American spirituals, camp meeting choruses, nineteenth-century gospel hymnody, the venerable *Cokesbury Hymnal* (published fifty years ago for 'young Christians'), youth retreats, campfire songs, and Hispanic corridos."[12] For example, the most frequently sung evangelical hymns in Hillsboro Presbyterian's Contemporary service included "I'll Fly Away," "Leaning on the Everlasting Arms," "I Surrender All," "Standing on the Promises," and "In the Garden." These hymns all emphasize the first-person individual and emotion, often speaking of an intimate personal relationship with a loving Savior. Additionally, similar to modern Contemporary music, the lyrics feature frequent repetition: "Leaning, leaning/ safe and secure from all alarms/ Leaning, leaning/ leaning on the everlasting arms" or "Standing, standing/ Standing on the promises of God my Savior/ Standing, standing/ I'm standing on the promises of God." Just as Contemporary worship often features raised arms and swaying, many of these songs encourage physical movements, such as singers rising to one's feet to "Stand Up, Stand Up for Jesus" or to be "Standing on the Promises."

Hillsboro Presbyterian often played "I Come to the Garden"[13] in their Contemporary service, and the lyrics provide a representative example of these features: "And He walks with me, and He talks with me/ And He tells me I am His own;/ And the joy we share as we tarry there,/ None other has ever known." Often, in evangelical services, such emotional songs are used to call worshipers to the altar to be saved (a simultaneously emotional, public, and personal liturgical element not present in Presbyterian worship). When interviewing Hillsboro's associate pastor Nancy McCurley, I mentioned that I had noticed this similarity to gauge her reaction:

> JUSTICE: This Sunday, Stephen played "He Leadeth Me" for the offertory and then the praise band sang "In the Garden." I was like, I'm ready for the altar call now!
>
> McCURLEY: (*Laughing*) I know, right!? I know, I know!

While Presbyterian Hillsboro would not be implementing evangelical altar calls, McCurley had felt how the church's new musical practices referenced other traditions of Christianity.

While mainline Protestants want to absorb the musical energy, they have not been willing to blanketly incorporate historical evangelical hymnody without considering the repertoire's content in light of current theological and social dynamics. For example, while mainline Protestants believe that Christ physically died on the cross, they tend to avoid hymns that dwell on gorier aspects of the crucifixion like "There Is a Fountain Filled with Blood" or "The Cross, the Cross, the Bloodstained Cross." As one Hillsboro Presbyterian congregant observed: "There's certainly no 'Onward Christian Soldiers.' Or having grown up in the mountains of eastern Kentucky, there's no 'Old Rugged Cross' or anything like that. Those songs are gone forever in the Presbyterian Church." While Presbyterians do not tend to be pacifists, another congregant found that while "it's a nice tune," the words to "Onward Christian Soldiers" were distasteful in light of then-current political events: "I mean, invading Iraq was not part of our theology! That was something else!" Mainline congregations have been selectively filtering repertoire based on lyrical content, rather than blindly embracing older evangelical hymnody as a whole.

As they renegotiate their place with an increasingly diverse America, Presbyterian churches and other predominantly White mainline Protestants have selectively been embracing evangelical hymnody across both sides of the Traditional-Contemporary divide. This move is not purely ecumenical; rather, it grants mainline Protestants access to other American Protestant musical heritages. Through a mix of banjos and hymns, Presbyterians can feel a sense of diverse American belonging through musics developed by and for worship by lower-class Whites and African Americans—rather than feeling ossified in the musical history of White Protestant privileged classes.[14] The mainline's new usable past is both authentic and imagined, anchored in historical values and modern sensitivities, hoping to ground present identities and future possibilities on a powerful heritage.

Retuning Hymns as a Bridge

The general idea of mixing and matching lyrics with musical settings is nothing new. Musicologists even have a term for it: contrafactum. From Weird Al Yankovic's parodies to updated versions to remixes, people like to experiment with the old and new. Creating a Contemporary version of a Traditional hymn requires a balance of musical changes and continuities. The new version has to be just that—new—while also retaining enough melodic or lyrical anchors from the original version that the song is still recognizable. Retaining the old element gives a sense of familiarity (whether that is positive or negative) that highlights how different the new part is.

138 / (White)Washing Our Sins Away

As churches adopted Contemporary music, using old hymn lyrics with new musical settings was often a central strategy. It became such a common practice that a "Retuned Hymns" movement emerged, generating discourse and materials for congregational use.[15] Bruce Benedict, chaplain of worship and arts at Hope College, describes the retuned hymns movement as responding to "a pressing need for grassroots sacred song"[16] across the evangelical to mainline spectrum. Individual congregations sometimes used external materials, but local musicians often took inspiration and applied their own skills to update tradition.

Hillsboro Presbyterian's Contemporary worship provides a case study of how mainline churches were retuning hymns. Senior Pastor David Kidd explained, "I have asked Stephen [the praise band director] to have one hymn most Sundays, and he does. He does them the way he wants to do them, but they're there." Leadership and worshipers felt that at least one hymn per week anchored Hillsboro's Contemporary service to the Traditional service's musical heritage. This section analyzes musical changes that transform a Traditional hymn for Contemporary worship in order to demonstrate what exactly people were hearing as different between the genres.

Penned by master hymn-writer John Wesley in 1747 and usually set to John Zundal's 1870 tune "Beecher," the popular hymn "Love Divine, All Loves Excelling" appears in over two thousand hymnals. "Love Divine" was a favorite in Hillsboro's Traditional service and became one in the Contemporary service, as well. Contemporary band leader Stephen Nix talked about his process in transforming the hymn:

> NIX: How do I change a hymn? I first take, in context, the lyrics. I say the lyric as I would normally speak it. That kind of denotes where the rhythmical lines should fall. And that's how I change it, based off of what is natural. Because a lot of the hymns that we have inherited over the years, they took tunes that were previously written and maybe the [first] lyric for that tune was correct for that tune, but they sort of force-fed their lyric to a tune that really didn't fit. And song writers still do it to this day, but they wait tables! [*Laughs*] So, you get a lot of hymns that just feel awkward. They feel awkward, they feel weird, they feel left-footed.

> JUSTICE: What about the example of how you changed "Love Divine, All Loves Excelling" from last Sunday? The chords are different, and it seems like you make changes to lots of hymns

"We're Only Medium Contemporary" / 139

in similar ways. Would you describe it as changing them to a particular genre?

NIX: When you distinctly go with more a speaking tone, you can move genre into jazz. You can move into a lot of R&B—you can move into a lot of genres—country, rock. You can change a lot of things. And then it becomes a matter of personal taste. What do we want to do? [*Looking at the chords from the band's lead sheet for "Love Divine"*] Yeah, that, the F is really an F6 going to a Gm7, and that's like a B-flat major 7 and there are a lot more altered chords in there that lend themselves more to a jazz thing.

JUSTICE: So, if you had to put a label on it, what genre would you call it?

NIX: I would say "Love Divine" is a light jazz. A *very* light jazz. Easy listening, not too far out there. It's just light jazz. It's not hard-core jazz and Herbie Hancock and everything with flourishes, just very light.

JUSTICE: Is that how you would describe your changes in general?

NIX: As light jazz? No. I try to run the gamut of styles—county, bluegrass, Traditional, etc. It's like ice cream in that you don't want too much of one thing. You need variety. What may reach one person might not help another. I will sometimes pull a hymn and take it to more of an Appalachian style where it's real pure and less altered. And sometimes, last week, I wanted to do a song, I wanted to do like "Blessed Assurance," and I wanted to do a rock thing with the melody [*sings example*]. Some songs lend themselves to certain styles more than others. It's just certain lyrics also. I think "Love Divine" lends itself to that jazz standard type of thing.

Figure 5.1 illustrates the changes made to "Love Divine, All Loves Excelling." The rhythmic swing of the song has been shifted, but that change would be communicated aurally. A four-measure turnaround has been added as an introduction, between the hymn's first two lines, and after

140 / (White)Washing Our Sins Away

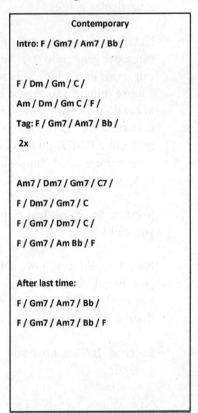

Figure 5.1. Comparison of form and chord structure for "Love Divine, All Loves Excelling" in Hillsboro's Contemporary and Traditional services. Source: Deborah Justice.

the chorus. The melody line remains basically unchanged, but the band singers' harmonies reflect the new chords.

Creating a Contemporary sound for musical leadership requires more than just changing the melody line, harmony, and swing. Vocals styles play an important role in defining Contemporary and Traditional sound. Nix further explained the key role that vocals play:

I break it down and say, "OK, let's do this, let's change this." We're not dealing with a choral situation, but more of a "praise and worship team." I like to make the hymn a reflection of the vocal power of that group, so I'll make the arrangement customized to fit their needs. And that's in voicing.

For instance, in some hymns, I'm not a traditionalist who believes that the soprano gets the melody and the alto gets the harmony, and right now we don't even utilize the bass line because I don't want the group to sound like a quartet.

A professional vocal coach, Nix worked with his singers to create tone quality that contrasts classical Western vocal production: "They've sort of broken out of the box in regard to their training and realized, 'Oh, my voice can do a whole lot of things and I'm not injuring it.'" Members of the praise band who used to sing with the Traditional choir explained:

> SINGER: Vocally, technique-wise, it has been an unbelievable journey. And I could talk about that for an hour! It's been real difficult for me because I sang classically for so long . . . It's a different placement, a different way of singing. It's been a fun challenge.

> JUSTICE: What's different about it, placement-wise? If I was a classical singer, what would you tell me to do?

> SINGER: Throw away everything you know! Everything. Completely. Throw away the vibrato. Throw away all the training. Throw away everything you know about where you place your voice, what you do with your voice. It's about adding a commercial edge to your voice.
>
> It's hard. In classical singing, I never had a break in my voice. It was all smooth from top to bottom. I never really sang in a chest voice . . . In classical singing you don't use a microphone. With other groups I've worked with, done solo work over an orchestra, in a huge auditorium with no microphones, and you know, you gotta lay that sound out there and it better go across the street! But not in commercial singing, not in the type of singing in praise band. If we scream like that—good grief. Well [*laughing, checking herself*], not scream, but you know what I mean. It's all different placement. You make it smaller rather than big. It's hard to explain.

142 / (White)Washing Our Sins Away

JUSTICE: So, it's more nasal?

SINGER: It's more [*rubs face*] mask. Not nasal. It's mask. Very up front, out this way.

I later asked Nix to demonstrate the physical techniques behind the change in tone. After singing a few words with an O-shaped mouth in classical Western/Traditional style, he suddenly changed the sound dramatically by smiling and pulling the corners of his mouth back toward his ears. This physical change altered his mouth's resonating space and made a smaller, thinner-sounding tone.

Understanding what is happening in terms of tone production is not the same as appreciating the results. One Traditional service musician pulled no punches in her unfiltered reaction to Contemporary singing: "They're up there with the microphone . . . And the singing is bad. They're trying to imitate what they hear on television. And consequently the music's not very good."

Another Traditional choir member expressed a racially charged response to Contemporary vocals. Hillsboro's Contemporary praise band director Stephen Nix had accompanied himself on piano singing an arrangement of Thomas Dorsey's gospel classic "Previous Lord, Take My Hand" for an offertory.

CONGREGANT: It's just—just talking about musical tastes here, I guess. The piano works appropriately for the song. And if he was really Black, it would—and if he was a little Blacker. Just, it's a White guy trying to sound Black.

JUSTICE: So it's getting there, but not exactly for you . . . ?

CONGREGANT: It's just, you know, that's just blunt prejudice, I'd say. But overall, I think, there's a reason for that song. If you're honoring the Black spirituals, and the Black man's place in America, and how he got where he was spiritually, and how he—helped, helped us have the music, you know, to know where that came from, that's wonderful.

The congregant's perception of the entire song was strongly impacted by his perception of the vocal style. While value is in the ear of the beholder, the contrasting techniques used to produce these classical and commercial sounds result in different expressive behaviors, postures, and facial expressions during singing.

Retuned hymns gained popularity, but never became the face of Contemporary worship. Some retuned hymns added choruses and bridges, like superstar worship leader Chris Tomlin's "Amazing Grace (My Chains Are Gone)," and became part of the Contemporary canon. However, most of the Contemporary worship songs coming out of flagship megachurches like Hillsong and Willow Creek were new material.

For local mainline Protestant congregations, Contemporary repertoire was more of a balance. These congregations were generally not writing new Contemporary material, but skilled worship leaders like Hillsboro's Stephen Nix could easily retune hymns. This in-house practice created local meanings that anchored congregations' participation in the broader Worship Wars and Traditional-Contemporary dynamics.

Mainline Protestant Contemporary musicians often explained that the purposeful inclusion of hymnody gave their Contemporary worship a unique character in comparison to other Contemporary worship. "I think it makes us unique from other praise bands," says one Hillsboro Presbyterian singer. "Most praise bands stick to Christian rock stuff," and the bass player added, "I like that we take old hymns and adapt them for Contemporary styles." The praise band electric guitarist in his twenties agreed:

> I like this [music that we play] because it's kinda an alternative sound, I guess. And we get to play all kinds. We do play some of that [Christian radio] WAY-FM type stuff, and we do play a lot of the hymns, changed up. And some of the slower actual hymn-singing hymns. It's good variety. It keeps it interesting, I think.

This guitarist described the incorporation of hymnody as significant; hymnody contributed to a Contemporary sound that differentiated the congregation's identity from local religious neighbors and global flows of Christian media.

Hearing Difference

Trained musicians in either Traditional or Contemporary worship are bound to have strong opinions, but what do average congregants think? Do they notice these changes? If they do, where are they hearing value and why?

144 / (White)Washing Our Sins Away

Gathering data from people about their experiences during a worship service presents challenges. Ideally, a researcher would defy space and time to hit "pause" to ask a participant what they are experiencing. Instead, I used an anthropological technique called feedback interviewing to hear from congregants. One Sunday, Hillsboro Presbyterian used the well-known hymn "Be Thou My Vision" in both its Contemporary and Traditional services. I recorded both versions of the hymn. In individual interviews, I played the recordings of both versions and then asked the worshipers to comment on the two different musical renditions. This technique allows the congregant to reexperience the music and to hit "pause" or "replay" to talk about their perceptions. The following comments provide an overview of worshiper responses:

Traditional Version

CONTEMPORARY CONGREGANT IN HIS SIXTIES: That organ stuff doesn't do it for me. I can't relate to it.

TRADITIONAL CONGREGANT IN HIS THIRTIES: It just seems like a better fit to me with the choir singing it and an organ leading it.

TRADITIONAL CONGREGANT IN HER THIRTIES: I'd say it sounds more ancient. It's a little less personal and a lot more formal.

CONTEMPORARY CONGREGANT IN HER FIFTIES: Oh, I can't believe it—this is what came to me. And it's [the music] beautiful. [*Shaking her head and laughing.*] "Addams Family." I think "old." I think "somber."

CONTEMPORARY CONGREGANT IN HER THIRTIES: Is that the same song? [*Listens*] You know, this is just more formal and stuffy! [*Laughs*] It's not my style.

CONTEMPORARY CONGREGANT IN HIS FORTIES: The arrangements are very lush. Those are just gorgeous and the messages are all there. It's just, it got stale to me. I just didn't get the emotion out of it.

Contemporary Version

CONTEMPORARY CONGREGANT IN HIS SIXTIES: That would certainly make me focus on a prayerful attitude, that piece of music anyway.

TRADITIONAL CONGREGANT IN HIS THIRTIES: It seems like an older song. It doesn't seem contemporary.

TRADITIONAL CONGREGANT IN HER THIRTIES: It sounds very communal.

CONTEMPORARY CONGREGANT IN HER FIFTIES: The two words that come to mind would be "community," "prepare." It's kind of like preparing, when I hear that. It's like I'm preparing to be a part of a worship group.

CONTEMPORARY CONGREGANT IN HER THIRTIES: Calming. Calming and inspiring.

TRADITIONAL CONGREGANT IN HIS FORTIES: "Don't jazz it up! I just can't take it, I have to leave. It's in rigid meter, it's locked in. I mean, is your relationship with God locked in, or are we just making it up as we go? That's it. I would almost rather the 8:30 do new things than massacre the old things. Massacre, wait. That's a pejorative word. Rather than "embellish" the old things.

Every respondent found a significant difference between the two versions. Overall, the musical style proved so powerful that it overrode the text in coloring congregants' reactions to the hymn. One Contemporary congregant explained how the transformation was both jarring and helpful:

I don't know the musical word for it, the rhythm, you know, the time. It's not the same beat or whatever you call it, and that was kind of weird. But then after you do it a few times, it's kind of like, "Oh, I like it better." Then, when I go to the Traditional service, it's like [*rolls eyes and looks distressed, tired*], "Ugh." [*Groans*] And, I mean, I really do kind of like doing the old Traditional songs.

146 / (White)Washing Our Sins Away

For this man and other worshipers, keeping the lyrics but resetting the music and changing the instrumentation redefined congregants' perception of the entire piece of music.

Retuning hymns to bridge Traditional and Contemporary repertoire met with varying reception in different faith communities. From a mainline theological perspective, incorporating some hymnody into Contemporary worship safeguarded against excessive evangelical shift. Yet, while the lyrics might offer a common ground, congregants still tended to react to the music on the basis of style. Very few congregants were willing to worship through both styles, usually having a strong preference for one or the other.

The Limits of Congregational Unity: Blended Worship

As Hillsboro choir director Sherry Kelly explained, "Any time there's an early service and a late service, it divides the church. There are many people in the early service that never come to the other, and vice versa." However, having dichotomized Traditional versus Contemporary musical choices made things more disconnected. Band director Stephen Nix emphasized how stylistic differences build upon time differences: "When you create two *different* worship services, you basically start being two different congregations. Some people prefer this style, and it may not even be style, it may be the time of worship services, but a lot of it's style."

Although most worshipers expressed clear stylistic preferences, as congregations worked to incorporate Contemporary music with Traditional worship, some faith communities tried putting the two genres within the same service. So-called "blended worship"[17] became a controversial technique. Overall, it did tend to result in Traditional and Contemporary congregants agreeing with each other; both Traditional and Contemporary participants generally felt that blending worship was unpleasant.

And the congregants let church leadership know. An usher from Hillsboro Presbyterian explained:

> I was really surprised [at] all of the complaints we got by mixing the two . . . They said that they just didn't like *that* kind of music, and *that* refers to the Traditional or the Contemporary. They just didn't like it. And from an operational point of view, from ushering, I hear all that.

"We're Only Medium Contemporary" / 147

Pastoral leadership also felt that blending the two services was undesirable. Associate Pastor Nancy McCurley shook her head in agreement as Senior Pastor David Kidd explained:

> [Blending] works at cross-purposes with the intentions of the different services . . . People make those choices, "I want a Traditional service, I want a Contemporary service." And that's what they want. There are an awful lot of churches that offer blended services, and we do, as I say, occasionally they'll be different ways in which something will be played in between the two services, but I don't feel pressure to do that [all of the time] because I really think there's a legitimacy in those two different styles. They don't need to be blended.

Attitudes from Hillsboro's musical leadership agree that blending unmitigated versions of Traditional and Contemporary worship was unlikely to yield positive outcomes. Choir director Sherry Kelly had strong opinions:

JUSTICE: Did you ever try making it a blended unity service?

KELLY: [*Quietly and firmly*] It doesn't work. It doesn't work.

JUSTICE: Did you try it here at Hillsboro?

KELLY: I don't know, maybe at the very beginning. It doesn't work. It's oil and water.

JUSTICE: Why doesn't it work?

KELLY: It's two different styles, and really you want to do one or the other. You just don't want to mix them! It's disjointed. A service needs to have a rhythm to it. It needs to have a cohesiveness to it. And you get up there with the instruments and individual singers, versus choral—it's just not cohesive.

JUSTICE: Not cohesive musically? Or theologically?

KELLY: In any way. There's not flow to the service.

148 / (White)Washing Our Sins Away

For Kelly, blending led to multiple levels of disjuncture. During our interview in 2008, band director Stephen Nix emphasized that logistical difficulties prevent blending, although he also emphasized how providing a slightly modified version of Contemporary worship to Traditional congregants helps bridge differences:

> NIX: Initially, we were utilizing both styles, both formats of music, but we found because of the band having so much equipment . . . when we get band equipment up there, combined with the choir, and all that stuff going on, it's just not designed for that. So, we had to back out of that and so they do a Traditional style, and then we'll do a Contemporary style.
>
> Although when we do a Contemporary style, I have a lot of people from the Traditional service say, "That was wonderful," you know, because I tend to not lean toward labels . . . I will sing a hymn and keep it more straight and just to the traditions of the years past. But I might sing the next hymn and totally blow them out of the water, do it totally different, or do a different song that makes them enjoy it, jump up and down [clarifying what he means], or kind of move. So, that's my version of the Contemporary service is to unify the groups.

Given that Hillsboro's version of Contemporary has been described by congregants as "medium Contemporary" (see chapter 4), the service could arguably be called "blended." As one Traditional usher at Hillsboro Presbyterian put it, "Blending just annoys everyone."

With blended worship off the table as an option, Hillsboro tried to implement a unique strategy for bridging the Traditional-Contemporary divide. Once a quarter, the church began holding "unity services." Held on Sundays that would typically have low attendance,[18] a single unity service, at the compromise time of 10 a.m., replaced both 8:30 Contemporary and 11:00 Traditional services. Attendance was slightly lower than the two services' usual combined average, but still generally exceeded that of either single Sunday morning service. The entire congregation was invited to unify together, first by worshiping in the sanctuary and then by sharing a meal in the fellowship hall.

Despite many of the congregants coming together for unity services, musical styles remain dichotomously separate. A single unity service has *either* Contemporary or Traditional, but not both. Even in uniting

Traditional and Contemporary congregants, so-called "blended worship" did not prove to be a viable option. "It turned out that there were people who didn't want to come to a unity service that mixed the two," said an usher. He continued:

> When I usher a unity service that's going to be Contemporary, then there will be fewer people who would normally attend the Traditional. And it works the same way in the Contemporary service. And always some really vociferous comments about not liking that *other* music.

Worshipers and musicians with strong stylistic preferences often describe the unity services as "just not fun to go to, that's a good one to skip because it doesn't feel like it's really a unity service! It feels like it's the late service early and sometimes they stick the band in there, like every other time." Despite being intended as a time of compromise, for many worshipers the unity services also highlight the importance of sticking to convictions about worship preferences. Many congregants express stubborn musical sectarianism,[19] reluctant to even temporarily sacrifice their worship musical preferences in exchange for celebrating congregational unity.

Particularly for musicians and congregants who strongly identify or disidentify with a musical style, unity services become what ethnomusicologist Timothy Rommen describes as a moment of "ethical conviction."[20] Ironically, a number of Hillsboro musicians find solidarity in their shared dislike of attending the unity services when their own ensemble is not providing the music. Two singers, one from the praise band and one from the choir, admitted:

> PRAISE BAND SINGER: To be truthful, if it's a unity service that we don't sing at, I would probably pick that week to take a week off.

> CHOIR MEMBER: For a lot of people, we think, "Well, this would be a good time to go visit [neighboring] Covenant [Presbyterian Church]," or "Why don't we go early to the football game today?"

They still disliked each other's music but could agree that acting upon one's artistic integrity formed a shared conviction.

150 / (White)Washing Our Sins Away

During interviews, most congregants expressed positive opinions about the opportunity for unity through shared worship that these services offer. But Presbyterian worship does not allow a lot of opportunity for personal interaction (see chapter 6). The interaction might be fairly subtle, as Pastor McCurley explained:

> It connects them in the same worship service. They're sitting by people they don't normally get to sit by . . . A church is a social place and people kind of get caught in with "OK, I sit on the third row, second pew." All of a sudden, there are people sitting on *your* pew that are not normally there during the time, and you sort of connect with them.

How exactly, then, were congregants finding the opportunity to attend a unity service to be helpful? During interviews with Hillsboro congregants and musicians who were particularly enthusiastic about the unity created during these services, I tried to understand how they perceived this transformative interaction. One Contemporary worshiper provided a succinct response typical of most congregants: "Yes, they do [create unity], because I am able to see some of the people that attend the Traditional service. So, yes." Quickly, he self-reflectively qualified, "Well, for me they do." I asked more follow-up questions. Beyond seeing people across the room, specifically *how* did the service create the experience of unity for them? Responses tended to begin with phrases like "I don't know," "I never thought about it before," "Good question," and to end with affirming smiles, laughter, and "But it does!" "Although there are some people who won't come if it's the band or there are some people that won't come if it's the choir," explained one Traditional singer, "in general people are kind enough to do the same thing that someone else is doing." While these congregants could not articulate any specific element of the service as unifying, they perceive the overall experience as generating an ideal sense of faith and community, described by theologian Lawrence Hoffman's phrase: the liturgical whole.[21]

One Hillsboro elder explained unity services as supporting the congregation's vision of itself as diverse but unified:

> JUSTICE: Now the unity services, when they're doing the other style of music from the other services, do you go?

ELDER: Oh yes. And I enjoy the choir, um, just on a regular basis, given the choice of the two, I prefer the Contemporary. I like the unity services. I think one of the negatives about being in two services is that you don't get to be with the other people and get to know the other people.

JUSTICE: Do you feel like the unity service helps in creating unity?

ELDER: [*Pause*] Um, I guess so, but I don't think so. I don't think you can do that just in the unity service. I think the unity is created more in the Wednesday night services, or with different functions that we might have after both services, Sunday school for example, or different special services that we have, more so than just the unity service. The unity services are good, but that can't be the only thing.

While the unity services enjoyed limited success, for Hillsboro, blended worship was even less effective. The expressed desire for congregational diversity did not necessarily translate to willingness to undergo the lived experience of the Other. Levels of diversity were realized, but also mitigated.

Conclusion

Mainline Protestants tailored the broader Worship Wars Traditional-Contemporary dichotomy to fit their turn-of-the-millennium social needs. In creating a musical strategy for diversity, they used a combination of older evangelical hymns, retuned hymnody, learned to hear differences, and found that blended worship pushed limits of congregational diversity.

In implementing Contemporary worship, mainline Protestants had to renegotiate their relationships with some of their oldest, closest American Christian neighbors: the evangelical communities producing most of the Contemporary worship materials. Historically, mainline Protestants had spent a great deal of time and effort disidentifying themselves from evangelical denominations, and music had been one of the ways that they had achieved a sense of difference.

152 / (White)Washing Our Sins Away

Within the Traditional-Contemporary binary, however, mainline Protestants turned to old evangelical hymnody chestnuts to create a sense of useable Americana past. The predominantly White, affluent, educated mainline could more easily look backward with nostalgia than some of the diverse demographics now displacing them from social dominance could. Many of the hymns had to be theologically and culturally vetted for mainline use, but the ecumenically popular body of song shared basic congregation-friendly musical and lyrical structures with Contemporary music. The old repertoire provided a bridge to the new, and between mainline and evangelical groups.

While the older evangelical hymns were often adapted for Contemporary use through instrumental shifts drawing on the banjos and guitars of American string band tradition, Contemporary services also altered broader bodies of hymnody for worship. Between altering chord progressions and adding new bridges or choruses, changing the musical settings of Traditional hymns for Contemporary use "retuned" the older repertoire.

Congregants learned to hear clear differences between Traditional and Contemporary musics. When hymns were retuned, worshipers had strong reactions to the different musical settings. They heard the sonic elements, with related social and sacred dimensions, as more powerful than the lyrical content of the songs.

Musical leaders, congregants, and clergy heard these differences so strongly that combining Traditional and Contemporary worship in the same services proved extremely challenging. Out of space concerns or a desire for congregational unity, many churches tried "blending" worship. As discussed in chapter 4, Traditional and Contemporary musics communicate contrasting senses of musical immanence and musical transcendence to most congregants. Most mainline participants reported that trying mix those two approaches in a single worship service created unsatisfying, incongruous worship experiences. Some churches, like Hillsboro Presbyterian, would occasionally try to promote cross-genre unity in order to preserve and nurture a sense of congregational oneness. While some congregants chose not to participate, those who did generally felt that they were performing a service of tolerance and diversity. They would attend in spite of the "other" music in order to show support for the church as a whole.

For turn-of-the-millennium mainline Protestants, drawing a distinct line between Traditional and Contemporary worship styles served their broader purposes. Having a few elements that provided bridges between the worship genres—like hymnody—prevented a sense of total disconnection. Yet congregants were generally choosing to hear more differences than similarities between the styles. Learning to perceive sonic, social, and sacred differences allowed mainline Protestants to celebrate overcoming them.

Chapter 6

Spatial Diversity

Making Places for Traditional and Contemporary Worship

Stage lights from behind the praise band cast a soft glow over the congregation in a former-car-dealership-turned-worship-space in York, Pennsylvania. Rather than build traditional church buildings for its branch campuses, evangelical megachurch Lives Changed by Christ had decided to refurbish old retail and warehouse locations like this one for its branch locations. The look and feel of the entire organization purposefully contrasted with neighboring historically established churches. And so, in this former auto showroom, worshipers closed their eyes and raised their hands as they repeated the chorus of a slow praise ballad:

> Lord, prepare me to be a sanctuary
> Pure and holy, tried and true
> With thanksgiving, I'll be a living
> Sanctuary for You[1]

Ironically, the hit Contemporary worship song "Sanctuary" was often sung in spaces like this one: spaces designed *not* to resemble traditional church buildings with sanctuaries, steeples, and stained glass. Since its beginnings in the 1960s and '70s Jesus People counterculture,[2] Contemporary worship has attempted to redefine people's relationship with the church, both figuratively and literally.

155

156 / (White)Washing Our Sins Away

America once had "church steeples as the most common defining characteristics of civic space . . . church spires once stirred citizens to look upward to the heavens."[3] Most of these churches were built—in terms of architectural style and function—to accommodate worship that is now classed as Traditional in the pervasive Traditional-Contemporary Worship Wars binary. At its highest implementation, Traditional worship fills a sanctuary with features like pipe organs, large choir lofts full of professionally directed singers in matching robes, sets of glimmering handbells, a pastor behind an impressive pulpit, and solid wooden pews with hymnals for the congregation. Careful architectural planning ensures that Traditional sanctuary design projects unamplified acoustic sounds to maximum effect. Sightlines pull eyes heavenward, sacred symbols like crosses and Trinitarian groupings (reflecting God the Father, Son, and Holy Spirit) add meaning, and stained glass tells biblical stories. Everything about the physical setting and material culture has been designed to enhance the acoustic and aesthetics of Traditional worship.

As Contemporary worship rose in popularity, however, some churches discovered that ideal Contemporary gathering spaces require different features than Traditional spaces. Contemporary worship arose to counter perceptions of ossified, formal churches disconnected from modern society. For the early pioneers of Contemporary worship, "changes in churches mirrored the general tone of the times: there was a distrust of inherited institutions, a desire to create forms authentic to the people, and a reveling in the creative process itself."[4] During the 1960s and '70s, many early Contemporary services started meeting in nonchurch locations: coffee shops, people's living rooms, outdoors, and other typical venues of hippie counterculture social life. California evangelist Robert Schuller even began holding wildly popular worship services at drive-in movie theaters. While these communities claimed inspiration from the first-century informal gatherings of Jesus and his disciples, the underlying theology of Contemporary worship spaces also echoed colonial-era American Puritan congregations that "repudiated the notion of a consecrated place of worship and the idea of a church building as a sacred space, instead defining 'church' as a body of people who had entered into a covenant for the purpose of worshiping God."[5]

Twentieth-century Contemporary worship communities soon outgrew their initial spaces. As they moved to larger, institutional-level gathering places, they took two main approaches to space. Some congregations continued to hold worship in larger secular venues like nightclubs, movie theaters, shopping malls, or bowling alleys.[6] Others developed fixed worship spaces—generally neutral, modern venues purposefully designed without the architecture and sacred symbolism that typified mainstream, Traditional American Christianity.

Worship music played a central role in growing Contemporary faith communities, often spreading faster than the congregations themselves. As Contemporary worship expanded from its simple roots to the Christian recording industry and to churches nationwide,[7] new technological needs took center stage. By the turn of the millennium, Contemporary worship at flagship megachurches involved expensive professional audio, visual, and lighting systems to create state-of-the-art experiences for worshipers. Detailed videography allowed congregants to see close-ups of musicians and pastors, both on large screens during a live service or virtually as churches grew their web presence.[8] The musical instruments were the same high-end gear—keyboards, guitars, basses, drums, and more—that secular stars used. To support Contemporary music at that level, churches had to design their spaces with audiovisual priorities in mind.

This chapter explores how mainline Protestant congregations transformed their relationships with sacred space in order to support both Traditional and Contemporary worship. It examines historical approaches to physical worship spaces, as well as specific dynamics of race, class, economics, and theology as America's mainline Protestants incorporated Contemporary worship. Because they saw accommodating—if not personally experiencing—both Traditional and Contemporary worship as important for their institutional survival, mainline Protestants were willing to alter both physical and ideological spaces.

Creating Spaces for Sonic and Sacred Success

Different theological beliefs propelling faith communities to build specifically designed spaces for worship is nothing new in the sonic landscape of American Christianity.[9] American Christianity loves a good schism, and over the centuries, disgruntled parishioners have tended to vote with their feet and create new religious groups whenever major stylistic conflicts arise. Such conflicts have long histories in the United States. For example, in his 1702 *Magnalia Christi Americana*, colonial minister Cotton Mather had already been railing against neighboring groups' worship spaces: "To prepare and repair places for the public worship is but an act

158 / (White)Washing Our Sins Away

of obedience to him who requires worship from us . . . but the setting of these places off with a theatrical gaudiness does not savor of the spirit of a true Christian society."[10]

Churches have generally not tried to contain too much tension under a single steeple. Eighteenth-century Presbyterians were a case in point (see chapter 3): they were so upset about musical reflections of theological differences that congregations, presbyteries, and even synods split. A reflection of these schisms is that historically White churches have long used the contrast between worship venues as points of identification.

In addition to limiting *what* was happening in worship, some of the longest-standing Christian spatial distinctions in America have been based on *who* was worshiping. While White colonists' buildings echoed distinctive European worship spaces, their laws and customs often erected hurdles for worshipers of color to gather, form congregations, and erect worship spaces.[11] As Christianity expanded in the Americas and non-White congregations finally grew, systemic racism generally kept Black, Native American, and White churches separate for centuries. By 1963, Reverend Dr. Martin Luther King Jr. was still able to declare, "It is appalling that the most segregated hour of Christian America is 11 o'clock on Sunday morning." That de facto segregation remains true into the twenty-first century: by 2012, eight out of ten American congregants were still attending worship at a place where a single racial or ethnic group comprised at least 80 percent of the congregation.[12]

By the turn of the millennium, however, American culture was shifting toward diversity. Increasingly "musically omnivorous" people packed their iPods and playlists with multiple genres.[13] Having narrow preferences flipped from being a sign of high class to an indicator of outdated, elitist snobbery. Many Christian institutions were eager to take advantage of these trends, thinking that diversifying their music would make them seem accessible and organically bring in new congregants, while keeping older musical forms in place would retain existing members. Mainline Protestant congregations experiencing consistent membership loss were especially interested in the idea of "singing in new members." The Worship Wars had positioned Traditional and Contemporary worship in opposition to each other; but, perhaps, if so many people thought Traditional music was good—and so many other people thought Contemporary music was good—then one church having both of them might be even better. Maybe Contemporary music would bring a diverse range of new congregants. Thus, many White American churches optimistically decided

Spatial Diversity / 159

to buck historical precedent and try to accommodate *both* Traditional and Contemporary worship.

If concerns over *what* to sing had ignited the Worship Wars (see chapters 4 and 5), concerns about *where* to sing fanned the flames. Worship space, according to sociologists Jim and Sarah Lewis, became a "flashpoint leading to an eruption of latent hostilities."[14] Battle lines of class and heritage came into play as congregations began to fight over spatial aesthetics, theologies, and allocation of human and financial resources. The new challenge of creating spaces for both Contemporary and Traditional worship pushed mainline Protestants to reconsider how they related to things, people, and the divine.

Where to Worship

Human and financial capital played a central role in deciding how mainline churches could implement the Traditional-Contemporary binary. On one hand, worshipers were looking to large flagship congregations to see well-articulated, well-funded "ideal" iterations of both styles. On the other hand, most mainline congregations were relatively small with modest financial resources. Since mainline churches had largely been worshiping in ways now understood as Traditional, Contemporary worship was either a stylistic addition or substitution. As a result, implementing Contemporary worship required new spatial considerations; idealistic visions for musically diverse futures had to be balanced with congregational realities.

Before considering Contemporary spaces, most mainline congregations held worship in their church sanctuaries. Coming from *sanctus*, the Latin word for "holy," the word "sanctuary" suggests a separation from secular space and denotes various kinds of protection. Following Greek and Roman custom, early Christian churches often provided sanctuary, or protection, for those fleeing from punishment or retribution. Today, the United Nations High Commission for Refugees notes that a role of twenty-first-century religious communities around the globe still is to provide sanctuary. When violence happens within sanctuaries, the horrific actions take on extra dimensions of transgression. This elevated transgression can be seen in countless church burnings since the Civil War: the 1963 bombing at 16th Street Baptist Church in Birmingham, Alabama, that killed four school girls; the 2015 shooting of nine Black parishioners during Bible study at Emanuel African Methodist Episcopal

Church in Charleston, South Carolina; and more. Such actions especially stand out as evil because sanctuary space calls for a different, higher level of behavior than secular space.

Architecturally, within church buildings themselves, the term sanctuary denotes a type of protected space, separate from the chaos of the outside world. Just as with their beliefs about musical instruments (discussed in chapter 4), most mainline Protestants would not decree that altar tables, stained glass windows, hymnals, pews, or even the room of the sanctuary itself are inherently sacred. Instead, they believe that since people use these inanimate objects and space in ritual ways that produce sacred experiences, those experiences impact the people's expectation of future experiences. From this perspective, the sanctuary becomes a space where events beyond the mundane world have happened, are happening, and will continue to happen. The sanctuary's ritual items similarly have added layers of significance because, like the sound of the pipe organ, these tangible "sacred" things are unusual to encounter in everyday life. As historians Loveland and Wheeler summarize, a major uniting feature of sanctuaries over the ages is how congregants understand the space and its decorum as removed from the everyday. One Hillsboro congregant explained, "It's the sanctuary and I have these *feelings* about how you behave in the sanctuary as opposed to the gym, or fellowship hall." What takes place in a sanctuary has a special relation to occurrences outside its doors.

In contrast to Traditional worship's development in sanctuaries, Contemporary worship spaces have sought to blur boundaries between the sacred and the secular, between the church and the world. When adopting Contemporary worship, many mainline churches articulated goals of reaching potential new members who were unfamiliar with Christian traditions and churches. Since so many aspects of Traditional worship have deep histories and ties to liturgical practices, mainline Protestants reasoned that many people might be experiencing barriers to participating in them due to lack of familiarity. Encountering liturgical rituals and symbols that others had learned since childhood could be confusing to new adult seekers. Other potential new worshipers were people experiencing barriers to participation because their previous experiences with Traditional Christianity had been overwhelmingly negative. As a result, through informality and invitations to people to "come as you are," Contemporary worship and spaces emphasize access to the sacred in everyday life outside of Traditional institutional and liturgical structures.

Contemporary worship offered a counter to the overall mental and physical space of Traditional mainline Protestant worship. Instead of continuing high-context liturgical approaches that assume people have understandings of or positive experiences with historical Protestantism, Contemporary worship prioritized the everyday: "I drink coffee with God in my jeans every morning. Why should Sunday be different? Why should I act fake?" In positioning the *everyday* as more authentic, the Contemporary worship movement found identity through defining itself in contradistinction to the historical practices, structures, and spaces of mainline Protestants and other liturgical churches.[15] The idea fell on fertile ground: in contrast to flagging mainline numbers, Contemporary faith communities grew rapidly in neutral spaces outside of established Traditional churches, often in spaces free from overtly Christian symbolism.

Affording Spatial Diversity

Mainline Protestant churches knew that incorporating Contemporary worship posed a spatial challenge. Traditional and Contemporary worship flourished best in two different physical environments, the former of which was familiar for mainline churches and the latter of which was new. Creating new Contemporary spaces would require reallocating human and financial resources. Subsets of congregations would need to support worship styles that they did not personally like. Traditional congregants would have to approve funding for Contemporary worship, and Contemporary congregants would have to continue their church's support of Traditional worship.

In the United States' turn-of-the-millennium religious marketplace, being able to support genre-ideal forms of *both* Traditional and Contemporary worship signaled financial, spiritual, and social vitality. Churches capable of supporting both Traditional and Contemporary worship without schism-level tensions rightfully congratulated themselves on their resource allocation, tolerance, and diversity. Reaching difficult compromises and understandings of opposing positions produced a sense of united cultural vigor through triumph over discord.

The playing field was not equal, however. The more resources churches had, the more flexible and accommodating they could be. While the largest, most affluent mainline congregations were able to emulate

162 / (White)Washing Our Sins Away

Contemporary worship at evangelical megachurch scale, "churches that [were] too small to sustain separate congregations with separate worship styles," notes historian Michael S. Hamilton, "[were] either trying to mix musical styles. . . . or they [were] fighting and dividing over which music to use."[16] If a congregation did not have the resources to support both types of worship, then hard choices had to be made.

An important distinction is that most turn-of-the-millennium mainline churches *were* small congregations (see chapter 3). In 2007, for example, over two-thirds of PC(USA) congregations reported having 150 members or fewer.[17] Splitting a congregation of 150 people evenly along Traditional-Contemporary lines would theoretically produce two services with seventy-five worshipers. Since only about one-half of a church's members generally attend worship on any given Sunday, however, the reality of each service would only be about thirty-five worshipers. Whatever their enthusiasm, there are spiritual and financial limits to participation for groups this small. Executive Presbyter Phil Leftwich's voice belied his frustration as he described seeing these dynamics in his churches: "We have limited options here around money and around levels of tolerance of how much change people can absorb and you've got to understand that." When people have modest resources—and if they perceive those as threatened—they are less inclined to support options they do not personally enjoy or find effective.

Regardless of their resources, mainline churches felt pressure to incorporate high-production-value Contemporary worship. When congregations did not implement Contemporary worship to the highest standards, they heard their efforts being compared to flagship Contemporary congregations. In interviews, people often compared their own mainline congregations' Contemporary services and facilities to "my daughter's big megachurch," "that new worship center across town," or "more professional multisite congregations, like Willow Creek or Saddleback or Hillsong." When I asked one longtime member to describe her Presbyterian church's Contemporary worship space, she laughed and said, "They ran out of money! It's functional. It's fine for fellowship hall, but I would like to see something a little more updated and pleasing in terms of a family life center." Being forced to follow, rather than set, these cultural precedents of worship style and space subtly reminded average mainline congregations of their shifting cultural position within the American religious landscape.

Some mainline churches, like First Presbyterian in Bloomington, Indiana, decided to incorporate Contemporary worship to accommodate

Spatial Diversity / 163

their growing numbers. Located in a booming university town, by 2010, First Presbyterian's Traditional service was overflowing the sanctuary. Instead of simply duplicating their existing successful worship formula in a different slot to accommodate more worshipers, the church felt social pressure to offer Contemporary worship. Locals were talking about how a nondenominational evangelical group had just started holding Contemporary services in a vintage movie theater near the Presbyterian church. Studying national Presbyterian trends and now suddenly worried by their "competition," the church formed a committee to study their own non-Traditional, nonsanctuary options.

Many larger churches that built or remodeled during the twentieth century often featured a multipurpose fellowship hall. Frequently designed as gyms with kitchen service windows and public-school-style stages, fellowship halls supplemented worship space by serving the social life of many congregations. Generally slightly smaller than the sanctuary, these utilitarian rooms often accommodated AA meetings, soup kitchens, scout meetings, yoga classes, and the like. While fellowship halls fit the Contemporary aesthetic of neutrally decorated multipurpose spaces better than sanctuaries, many mainline churches tried implementing Contemporary worship in their sanctuaries out of both practical necessity and habit. First Presbyterian Bloomington did just that, as did Hillsboro Presbyterian in Nashville, Tennessee. What happened when Hillsboro initially tried to hold Contemporary worship in the sanctuary provides an example of the difficulties that many congregations faced in these attempts.

Prepare Me to Be a Modern Sanctuary?

Hillsboro's new Contemporary service initially began with folding chairs, a keyboard, and an overhead projector; within three years the service had outgrown its temporary chapel space. Worshipers packed into the room, pushing fire code capacities, spilling out into the hallway and around a corner. A practical solution was necessary. As in so many American churches built around the mid-twentieth century, only two rooms within the building could accommodate so many worshipers: the sanctuary or the gym.

The sanctuary seemed like the easiest choice—after all, it was already a gathering space for worship. While in this new Traditional-Contemporary binary, sanctuaries writ large were being classified as Traditional spaces,

164 / (White)Washing Our Sins Away

Hillsboro congregants thought that Contemporary worship might fit in *their* sanctuary. Many commented that their church's architecture barely counted as Traditional. One Hillsboro Traditional congregant laughed and said, "Ours is the most really unappealing sanctuary I've ever been in . . . So, that obviously was not the reason we picked this church!" Maybe the sanctuary—that had been built years ago to be trendy and "contemporary" but now culturally coded as Traditional—could be a good pragmatic compromise for Contemporary worship space?

For Hillsboro, as in so many similar churches, after a short trial run the answer was a resounding "No." For the vast majority of congregants, the experiment only confirmed the practical and ideological incompatibility of Contemporary worship in Traditional space. Musicians from both services were dissatisfied. Sonically, plugging in all the praise band instruments and equipment resulted in a continual low-pitched feedback buzz. After a few short circuits, the band was seriously concerned about the old sanctuary wiring handling all of their electricity requirements. The Contemporary musicians also quickly tired of having to set up and break down their gear hurriedly each Sunday service so the Traditional choir could also use the space. The mostly elderly choir had (quite reasonably) insisted that leaving so many cords plugged in throughout a high-traffic area posed a safety hazard, especially with choir members' long robes and stoles.

Congregants also complained. Blocking the central cross and communion table with a large projection screen "did not seem quite right," even if Contemporary worshipers needed to be able to see their praise song lyrics. A possible solution of putting the screen off to one side resulted in some people then countering that they could not read the words at such an angle. It seemed sacrilegious to have the pastors wearing robes for one service and casual clothing for the other. The Traditional sanctuary architecture of solid wooden pews, raised pulpit and lectern, and communion railing now "separated the pastors and musicians from the people" and was too "formal," "stiff," and "boxed in" for Contemporary worship.

After a few weeks, both Traditional and Contemporary worshipers were fed up. "People are more interested in Contemporary music, a more laid-back style, something that isn't in the sanctuary. That whole subculture that you think of when you think of Contemporary service these days," explained the senior pastor. Revisiting the budget, the congregation voted to refurbish the fellowship hall.

Hillsboro's turn-of-the-millennium facilities woes demonstrated another arena in which White mainline Protestants felt themselves struggling to project continued cultural relevance in the United States. They had hoped their sanctuary might be a reasonable Contemporary fit because it had initially been designed to "keep pace with the times"—but the times had changed. Midcentury modern churches like Hillsboro in Tennessee (figure I.1), First Presbyterian of New Haven, Connecticut (figures 6.1, 6.2), and First Presbyterian of Tucumcari, New Mexico (figures 6.3, 6.4) were built as part of America's post–World War II church building boom, with modern minimalist aesthetics.

The era had seen a dynamic pushback against "ossified beliefs and practices" of the past and "puerile American copies of Gothic Cathedrals." Instead, new church buildings triumphantly promoted "'the gathered church' . . . [with] intimate spiritual fellowship and full congregational participation" harkening back to ideals of the earliest followers of Christ.[18] During the postwar building boom, up to 50 percent of churches were built in styles that fell under this modern approach. The relative economy of building in the modern style (as compared with the exorbitant cost of constructing traditional, especially neo-Gothic, edifices) combined with the function of witnessing to those outside the church through a "modern

Figure 6.1. First Presbyterian of New Haven, Connecticut, exterior. Photo by Martha Smith.

Figure 6.2. First Presbyterian of New Haven, Connecticut, interior. Photo by Marth Smith.

Figure 6.3. First Presbyterian of Tucumcari, New Mexico, exterior. Photo by Reverend Amy Pospichal.

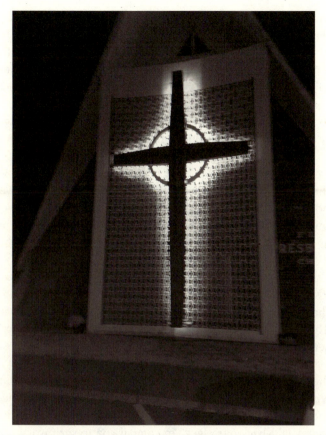

Figure 6.4. First Presbyterian of Tucumcari, New Mexico, cross. Photo by Reverend Amy Pospichal.

idiom [that] proclaimed the relevance and significance of the church's message in men's and women's lives and for the modern world."[19] The vast majority of these churches were built by progressive White mainline Protestant congregations moving to the suburbs.

Although their midcentury architectural choices had once projected progressive beliefs, by the early 2000s, as the Traditional-Contemporary Worship Wars moved across the United States, most White churches that had built or renovated facilities when they moved to the suburbs had a problem. Their building styles had aged out of seeming chronologically contemporary but were definitely not "traditional." In contrast, now many neighboring faith communities that had retained older buildings or built

168 / (White)Washing Our Sins Away

new designs inspired by their European cultural heritage seemed to provide perfect settings for Traditional worship. For example, in Nashville, Westminster Presbyterian featured a classically Calvinist look with colonial design, neutral tones, rows of impressive organ pipes, and glistening pewter chandeliers. Another newly built Presbyterian Church in America (PCA) congregation just up the road provided a stunning, textbook example of neo-Gothic architecture inside and out. Congregants worshiping in mid-century modern Hillsboro noticed the differences:

> CONGREGANT #1: We're kind of a second-rate church if you think of size and style within the Presbyterian church. We're no big First Pres[byterian], we're not the socially correct Westminster Pres[byterian]. You know, we're liberal but we're not as liberal as a couple of them in town.

> CONGREGANT #2: Hillsboro is pretty loosey-goosey! Let's face it. It's not uptight at all! Like, but if you went to Westminster Pres, that's a very strict service. And down on the corner, Covenant? That Gothic cathedral that they're building? It's PCA [the conservative Presbyterian branch], but they do *wonderful* music.

Even the senior pastor weighed in, chuckling at the idea of Hillsboro as an archetypal Traditional church: "We're not high liturgy at all! I mean, even our Traditional service is *nothing* like a lot of Presbyterian churches do. We're pretty laid-back ourselves." In comparison to such worship settings, both locally and globally, formerly trendsetting churches like Hillsboro now saw themselves as occupying a middle ground of quality.

The Sisyphean task of offering worship with timeless truths to ever-changing contemporary society has posed consistent challenges to mainline Protestants. Many of these congregations had made bold progressive moves in updating their style within the last fifty years, only to find themselves *again* being dismissed as old-fashioned. Still, those who do pick Hillsboro and churches like it often rationalize their decision, stating that the now sub-ideal architecture reflects ideal ethical priorities. Many congregants explained that they chose to bypass neighboring "high class," "snooty" churches "with their perfect liturgy, choirs, and ladies in fur coats" and "flashy music" that "just focus on a performance." Another woman interpreted her church's "beautiful imperfections" as following biblical principles. "Go reread about Mary and Martha," she smiled.

As Jesus and his disciples were on their way, he came to a village where a woman named Martha opened her home to him. She had a sister called Mary, who sat at the Lord's feet listening to what he said. But Martha was distracted by all the preparations that had to be made. She came to him and asked, "Lord, don't you care that my sister has left me to do the work by myself? Tell her to help me!"

"Martha, Martha," the Lord answered, "you are worried and upset about many things, but few things are needed—or indeed only one. Mary has chosen what is better, and it will not be taken away from her."[20]

The parable from the gospel of Luke tells a story of prioritizing learning and relationship over a perfect physical setting. Congregations like Hillsboro felt more validated in spending money on outreach—often including Contemporary musical diversification—instead of spending it refurbishing their now-outdated architecture. For these congregations, working within their existing spaces could be rationalized as demonstrating proper priorities.

Prepare Me to Be a Fellowship Hall?

While the old-fashioned sanctuary was deemed incompatible with Contemporary worship, the aesthetics of mainline Protestantism still ran strong. Both congregants and clergy agreed that they did not want the fellowship hall to seem like an entirely secular space. When congregations like Hillsboro dedicated resources to remodeling existing spaces, or building new ones, to accommodate Contemporary worship alongside their existing Traditional services, they felt that they were giving physical form to their beliefs of tolerance and diversity.

Even though the Contemporary service took place only once a week, certain material changes were still deemed necessary for the room to serve as a worship space:

When we had to move into fellowship hall, the feeling was, it's been so nice to have the symbols of faith [in the sanctuary] that made it seem like sacred space, let's do the same with fellowship hall. But it was a little more difficult because it was

170 / (White)Washing Our Sins Away

referred to as fellowship hall, or even "the gym." You know, there's a basketball court [*laughs*].

At the time of the move, the fellowship hall hosted sports and games, had an attached kitchen for facilitating covered dish dinners, and had a raised stage for performances. To transform the space for worship, a number of physical changes were made. The stage was lowered to a platform. The basketball hoop was moved across the room so the grand piano, drum set, and sound gear could safely remain on the platform throughout the week. Artificial plants were brought in to hide amplifiers, monitors, and "give the space a more friendly feel." Overall, congregants agreed that they had created "a more worshipful space."

Performance Space or Worship Space

I felt entertained by that. I didn't feel like that experience was spiritual, even with the drums and the guitar, and many of the same instruments that we have, and the vocalists and the soloists. It's not the instruments. It's not the composition. It's how it's presented, in the sense that, do you really allow the Spirit to shine through you, or do you give a good performance?

—A former-Catholic-turned-Contemporary-Presbyterian's
critique following a visit to a neighboring
Contemporary megachurch

One of the main tensions between Traditional and Contemporary worship spaces deals with worship versus performance. Since Contemporary worship often has spatial features—staging, lighting, and audio technology—similar to secular popular music, many Traditional congregants have trouble perceiving Contemporary settings as appropriate or effective for their worship. Hillsboro was typical of mainline congregations in identifying staging and lighting design as problematic. While these points seemed to be hurdles, the congregation wanted to understand their new Contemporary space as worshipful. In order to achieve that goal, many worshipers became willing to accept relatively small physical changes as creating substantial transformations.

For example, many Hillsboro congregants only felt that the secular performance space of the fellowship hall was transformed into a worship space when the "stage" was remodeled into a "worship platform." The physical work was fairly simple: a three-foot-high raised stage with curtains (similar to the style found in public school auditoriums or gyms) was lowered to a half-foot-tall open platform (see figure 6.5).

The linguistic and philosophical transformation was more complex than the physical one. As congregants told me, it was important that the main action of the Contemporary service would happen on this "platform" rather than a "stage." The praise band bassist explained:

> BASSIST: At that time there was a stage in there, and it was a *stage*. Not an altar like we have in there, but it was a stage.
>
> JUSTICE: What's the difference between an altar and a stage?
>
> BASSIST: There was no lectern, no proper place for the sermon to be delivered. The stage looked like a high school gym stage, if that makes sense. And ultimately all that was torn out.

The physicality of the altar platform was minimal. In contrast to the large wooden pulpit in the sanctuary, the "proper place" for sermon delivery

Figure 6.5. Hillsboro's fellowship hall platform during the Contemporary service. Photo by Deborah Justice.

was a simple black music stand, identical to those used by the praise band (see figure 6.6). If anything, the configuration was less formal than the preceding "stage." For the Hillsboro Contemporary congregation, however, these physical and semantic alterations were important—and enough to transform the hall into a worship space.

How congregants understood the platform and the music-stand-turned-pulpit feeds into one of the most central questions of the Worship Wars: What is performance and what is worship? Traditional church architecture and layout frequently addressed this question by deemphasizing the visual presence of musicians. Organ pipes might be on display, but organists themselves were generally hidden by large keyboard consoles or placed in rear-facing elevated lofts, where they had to use well-placed mirrors to see the pastor and congregation behind them. Choirs, generally wearing uniform robes, sat in elevated lofts behind the congregation with the organ or in special sections of the chancel area. The musicians' lack of visibility or presence within a homogenized group supported a sense of disembodied, impersonal sacred sound. As a result, the music elevated worship but did not emphasize the individuals as performers.

Figure 6.6. Pastor Kidd preaching from a music stand in the Contemporary service. Photo by Pam Kidd.

This distinction is important to Traditional proponents who appreciate the transcendence and reserved decorum, but at the same time many Contemporary worshipers feel: "It's like a big wall between us and them. Like trying to make them seem more holy or something."

In Contemporary worship, the architecture and layout of the space usually put musicians front and center. Lighting and video close-ups often further emphasize individuals. Generally, the band is not separated from the congregation by a substantial height difference or railings. Rather than communicating through mirror signals or aural cues alone, praise band arrangement allows all musicians eye contact with each other and to "create a feeling of inclusion." The band leader, too, faces the congregation, fully visible and visually interacting with them rather than tucked behind the piano or organ. Musicians look at each other to coordinate entrances, emphases, and endings, and congregants notice how the open sightlines promote high levels of communication.

Worshipers who appreciate this individualism describe it as creating an overall perception of the church as a living community. Worshipers who dislike it emphasize how too much focus on individuals highlights their role as performers, detracting from worship as praising God. One older Presbyterian was direct: "I look at those praise singers, all done up and grabbing the microphones with lights on them and I think, 'Honey, you're trying to make this about you. You're trying to outshine Jesus.'"

Lighting became a major point of Contemporary controversy at Hillsboro. While lighting was part of the sanctuary's architectural plans, introducing professional-entertainment-venue-style lighting into the fellowship hall for the Contemporary service was heavily debated (see figure 6.7). Band leader Stephen Nix remembers:

> NIX: When I determined that lighting should be helpful in the worship service, you would have thought I'd said, "Let's start having a rock and roll band and sing punk music." I mean, it was like, "WHAT?!"
>
> JUSTICE: The lighting?
>
> NIX: Yeah, like lighting the stage with different cans and having lighting that can move, what they call intelligent lighting. . . . But you'd think I had just murdered Jesus again, you know! But it's people holding to stuff that, really, the only

Figure 6.7. Contemporary service lighting, Hillsboro Presbyterian Church. Photo by Deborah Justice.

sacredness you have is in your mind. They really have no validation in regard to God.

JUSTICE: Did people have any solid reasons?

NIX: No, that's the problem. They didn't. And then they started commenting, "Well, it might be an eyesore," and it might do this and it might do this, and I kept going, "Well, when you go here and you see this show, when you go see the symphony, there's lighting all over them. Do you think of that as an eyesore?" "No." "OK, well that's not valid anymore. Let's think of another excuse." And they kept trying to think of excuses that were logical, but they didn't. That stuff. You know, again, it is when you're moving from, and I use the Traditional term, it's when you're moving from a Traditional frame of worship style.

Nix tried to use Traditional congregants' positively associated points of reference—like the symphony—to help them understand lighting as a neutral technology rather than a negative symbol of secular popular music performance. While this worked for many congregants, for some Traditionalists—like those who objected to electric instruments and amplification in church—the similarity to secular performance remained too much. Just as easily as a small transformation or argument can convince someone who wants to be convinced, another person can use the same level of detail to hold fast to their position.

Conclusion

> CONTEMPORARY WORSHIPER: It took me a really long time to feel like I was really worshiping [sitting] on folding chairs in a gym . . . worshiping in that area is a little hard for me because I get distracted by the things that are messy, dirty, out of place, not seeming to be [*making air quotes*] "holy" or "sacred."

> JUSTICE: So, would you rather worship in the sanctuary?

> CONTEMPORARY WORSHIPER: No! Because the band would be separated from you, for one thing . . . I kind of am used to the fact that I'm not in a cubicle. You know, the pews are kind of like cubicles actually, and I've kind of gotten used to that where it feels more open and inviting, not being in a pew.
> So, it's kind of funny, I don't like this and I don't like that, I don't like any of it! [*Laughs*] But really I manage OK either place.

As figures 6.8 and 6.9 illustrate by way of example, in both Contemporary and Traditional services at most mainline churches, congregants assemble in rows of seating to worship. Some Contemporary congregants describe Traditional pews as restrictive, as "boxing us in," but Contemporary worshipers also sit in lines. The folding chairs are generally put away by building staff after worship so the space can be used for other activities throughout the week, but during worship, the chairs stay in place. People move around to the same extent that they do in the pews. Yet, the chairs are not pews; they *could* be moved.

The aforementioned worshiper's summation illustrates how mainline Protestants are aware of the mental constructs separating Traditional and Contemporary worship. The following three stories illustrate how people can change their definitions of worship space.

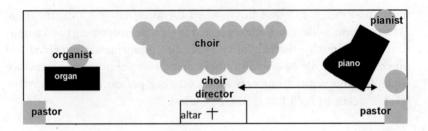

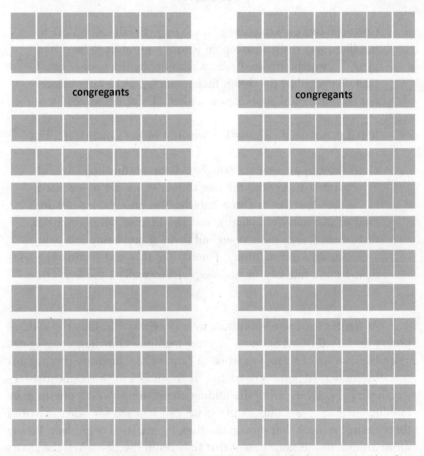

Figure 6.8. Layout of Hillsboro Presbyterian's Traditional service. Note: The choir director remains on the right, coming center to direct the anthem. Chart by Deborah Justice.

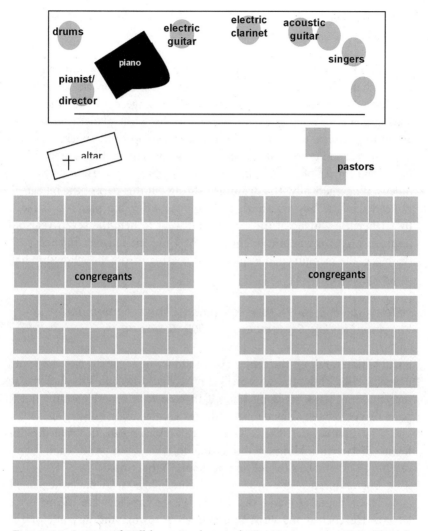

Figure 6.9. Layout of Hillsboro Presbyterian's Contemporary service. Chart by Deborah Justice.

178 / (White)Washing Our Sins Away

Fellowship Hall, Hillsboro Presbyterian Church Band Practice,
Thursday, September 18, 2009, 5:30 p.m.

A small boy was playing with a paper airplane in the fellowship hall while his mother rehearsed with the praise band. The folding chairs used for Sunday services had been packed into the storage closet for the week, leaving plenty of open space for the boy to throw the plane. He chased it around the room, underneath the basketball hoop in the back, and past the large rugged cross and stained glass panels. His mother watched him out of the corner of her eye, happy that her son was entertaining himself quietly, if energetically. The drummer, sitting out this part of the rehearsal, noticed that the boy was having trouble refolding the plane to make it fly farther. He winked at the singers and went to help the seven-year-old improve his aerodynamic design. By the time the singers finished with the piece, the reengineered airplane was soaring across the fellowship hall in long, graceful arcs.

Fellowship Hall, Hillsboro Presbyterian Church Contemporary
Worship, Sunday, September 21, 2009, 9:15 a.m.

Small children ran up the center aisle, clambering to sit close to the youth pastor for the children's sermon. He crouched down on the platform to the children's level, wedging himself in next to a sound monitor. Little pairs of eyes widened as he reached into an alluringly bulging bag.

"I've got several things with me this morning to illustrate the difference between holding on and letting go," the youth pastor said, finally reaching into the bag to pull out an item. "What's this?"

The children responded with delighted shrieks, "A paper airplane!"

"It's a paper airplane, that's right! Paper airplanes are meant to be let go." He cocked his wrist and mimed throwing the airplane at the basketball hoop behind the congregation. When he noticed the children's eager fingers reaching too close, he added, "But not in church, right?" The youth minister tucked the plane safely back into the bag.

Sanctuary, Hillsboro Presbyterian Church Traditional Worship,
Sunday, September 21, 2009, 11:45 a.m.

The youth pastor sat down on the steps leading to the raised chancel area for the children's sermon in the Traditional service. Small children gathered around him, squeezing in between the large wooden pulpit and the lectern. The children—and the adults in the pews—were eagerly waiting to see what his large bulky bag held.

"I've got several things with me this morning to illustrate the difference between holding on and letting go," he said, repeating the words he had spoken earlier in the Contemporary service. "What's this?"

The children's eyes widened and smiles broke out. "A paper airplane!"

"It's a paper airplane, that's right! Paper airplanes are meant to be let go," said the youth pastor. As he raised the airplane up as if to throw it, the children grinned. "But not in church, right?" he added, shaking his head negatively from side to side to imply the correct answer. "Nooooo," said the children, a few shaking their heads in imitation.

In each of these incidents, appropriate use of space defined how children could relate to the paper airplane. Two of the three stories took place in worship space, where airplanes stay grounded. Two of the three stories took place in the fellowship hall, but the use of the space defined the permissibility of the airplane. Different rules for different types of worship changed how people related to the spaces. The disjuncture between appropriate behaviors and times comes from different understandings of worship place and worship space: Is the physical setting a concrete place or is it more of a mental, metaphysical creation in the world?

Initially, incorporating Contemporary music forced many churches to address practical issues of space and place. Most mainline churches hoped to attract new members by making a musical statement of diversity and vitality compatible with America's changing sacred social landscape. A minority of churches were growing so much using Traditional worship that they needed to address capacity issues, but they felt social pressures to offer Contemporary worship instead of duplicating their successful worship formats. Both types of churches wanted their congregations to be able to expand.

Supporting Contemporary and Traditional worship meant creating services that had dramatically different technical needs and contrasting atmospheres. While holding Contemporary worship in sanctuaries initially seemed deviously transgressive, the practical limitations of space and technology proved challenging for many congregations to sustain. Ideally, the worship spaces would complement the music. As a result, adding a Contemporary service frequently resulted in physical changes to the church's space.

Only a certain subset of churches had the desire and resources to negotiate Traditional-Contemporary aesthetic ideals. However, addressing the holistic demographics of those churches did not figure centrally into

180 / (White)Washing Our Sins Away

the rhetoric of the Worship Wars. Worship experts tended to address issues of attendee age, spatial concerns, and theological implications facing *the Church*, without focusing on which racial (White) and economic (middle-class to affluent) American demographics were wrestling with these issues most intensely.[21] While not surprising given the stage of national social conversations around the turn of the millennium, this omission reinforced hegemonic stereotypes of White Christianity, even as the lack of demographic focus also hurt White congregations. Similar to the dynamics that Robin DiAngelo unpacks in *White Fragility*, Worship Wars discourse did not directly engage with the demographic elements of mainline Protestant social relevance concerns. As a result, questions about White culture—which grounded spaces like sanctuaries and fellowship halls—often remained unarticulated. Instead of analyzing the limits of their communities, White American mainline Protestants largely occupied themselves by (re)addressing historically familiar musical controversies within White worship spaces.

When is a worship space church? When is a church a worship space? Perhaps more than ever before in American history, the answers to these questions incorporate our nation's varied, multicultural religious heritage. Whereas Traditional mainline Protestant worship follows Western European Christian notions of spaces and sounds as set apart and sanctified for sacred use alone, Contemporary worship resonates with worshiping communities that have operated outside of institutional norms, temporally sanctifying spaces and sounds, blurring rigid lines between sacred and secular.

Worshipers can affirm their church's diversity without necessarily *personally* participating in it. Reflecting the cultural omnivorism described by sociologists Peterson and Kern,[22] congregants were willing to support their less-preferred style of worship with human and financial capital, even if they did not actually attend those services. Positioning the two styles at opposite ends of the spectrum and then institutionally supporting them both gave congregants a true experience of being tolerant and diverse—even if they valued the *possibility* of experiencing the "other," or someone else experiencing it, more than their own actual experience of it. This feeling, based on genuine support for internal differences, allows mainline Protestants to claim a role in the broader project of American social diversity.

Chapter 7

Social Diversity

Defrosting the Frozen Chosen

By the turn of the millennium, Hillsboro Presbyterian and Spruce Street Baptist Church had been enjoying a unique tradition for a few years. Hillsboro was one of Nashville's oldest White churches; Spruce Street was Nashville's oldest Black church. Each year, the downtown Black church—pastor, musicians, and congregation—would come to lead worship at the suburban White church. The Baptist minister would preach, Baptist musicians would play and sing, and the Black Baptist congregation would join the White Presbyterians in prayer and praise. Then the Presbyterians would provide everyone with a potluck lunch featuring some meal-time entertainment, usually by talented musicians from within their congregation. Then the roles would be reversed and, once a year, the Presbyterians would go to the Baptist church.

In all my years growing up as a Presbyterian, I had never experienced an arrangement quite like this one. Pulpit exchanges where ministers switch congregations for a Sunday are not so uncommon. However, having entire congregations from disparate demographic backgrounds working together in this wholehearted liturgical fashion is unusual, to say the least.[1] While these interactions between the congregations did not go much farther than these shared worship services, participants from both churches reported enjoying this unique arrangement.

I had witnessed one of these exchanges before, in which the Presbyterians went down to Spruce Street. Now, in 2009, the next exchange was coming up in a month and this time it was Hillsboro Presbyterian's

182 / (White)Washing Our Sins Away

turn to host. Since I had been conducting ethnographic fieldwork on the congregation's worship music, the hospitality committee had asked me to come consult on musical programming for the upcoming exchange. I was trying to study the congregation, not influence it, but my overwhelming curiosity convinced me to attend the meeting. And so it was that I sat down with the hospitality committee: a handful of other White women gathered around a table in the church's fellowship hall.

"Since you are an ethnomusicologist, or ethnic music person," the committee chair said, smiling, "we were hoping to get some advice. When Spruce Street comes, we want to have really great music for them this year! Music they will enjoy and feel at home with." The other members of the committee smiled and nodded their heads in agreement. "We were thinking of some African drumming! What do you think? Do you know where we could find some in town?"

I took a big bite of cookie and a sip of coffee to buy myself time to respond. From what I understood, the point of the exchange was for the congregations to share their own worship cultures with each other—and neither Hillsboro nor Spruce Street regularly featured African drumming. I wondered why Hillsboro was not suggesting its chancel choir, praise band, youth band, or some other talented musical grouping from the congregation.

The individuals on the hospitality committee were loving, deeply faithful folk who wanted very much to make the world a better place for everyone. Having been raised in White Presbyterian culture myself, I understood that they were trying to make a considerate, culturally sensitive musical choice. However, as an anthropologist, I could also see that these well-meaning women were not seeing past their own cultural frames to understand how this musical idea could come across as racially charged and offensive. I imagined the Spruce Streeters being deeply insulted and hurt, feeling that the White congregation was projecting a caricature of the Black congregation and its aesthetics . . . but I wanted to learn more about what the hospitality committee was thinking before jumping to conclusions.

"I might be confused," I said. "I thought Spruce Street was coming here to hear all y'all's great music?"

The hospitality committee members looked at each other. One said, "Well, we were talking about it. It's just that their church, with their wonderful lively music, they must think we're so boring."

A few days later, the cicadas were singing on a hot, humid summer afternoon in Nashville, Tennessee. Having just finished serving up lunch in their downtown church's soup kitchen, two older Black women finally took a seat near the window fan. One of the ladies waved me over, patting an empty chair in front of the fan.

"Now, you're from that Hillsboro Presbyterian Church, honey?" one of them asked. "It sure is nice that you come down and help out so often. We don't see much of them outside of that worship sometimes."

It was true. Despite the partnership, hardly anyone from the White suburban church I was studying came downtown to help at the Baptist soup kitchen. That said, the operation *was* running smoothly, and it didn't seem to be like extra hands were desperately needed.

"Thank you so much," I said. "I'm *sort of* from there. I'm an anthropologist researching the congregation, their music particularly. I am Presbyterian myself, but I'm actually from Pennsylvania. I'm just here for the research, so it's important to me that I really get involved in everything this church does so I understand it. And I really do like coming here to help."

The ladies nodded in understanding.

"Well, if you're doing the music there, then I have a question," the other woman began. "We do so enjoy when they come down here."

"Every time Hillsboro comes down here," she continued. "They bring that praise band with the guitars and just a few singers. That's nice and all, but I know they have a big choir. I always wonder why they never bring the choir? . . . Our choir is very small and I would so like to hear their big full choir. Not that the guitar is bad, but I do like a good choir."

The first woman "mmhmm-ed" in agreement.

What I told those ladies in reply was a polite fiction, which I rationalized to myself by saying that I was only an outside researcher. I said that I was not sure why the White church made those musical choices but would happily pass their request along. I wasn't entirely lying, because I did not know the details and I could have been wrong, but I *did* have some ideas about the White church's actions from that recent hospitality committee meeting, and as a lifelong Presbyterian.

Having gotten to know the Presbyterian congregation over years of fieldwork, I knew that this White community truly valued the experience of their partnership with the Black Baptist church, and not just for

184 / (White)Washing Our Sins Away

virtue-signaling optics. When the White church considered its musical options, it was weighing its newer Contemporary worship—featuring a praise band with piano, guitars, drums, and singers—on one side, and its Traditional worship—with a pipe organ and chancel choir—on the other. Although Contemporary music was a departure from centuries of Traditional Presbyterian worship, the White congregation had decided that it was more exciting and engaging (especially for outsiders not used to reserved Presbyterian ways). Why did the White church always bring their praise band? I suspected it was because of a fear that their Tradition would be perceived as bland and lackluster.

White Mainline Protestant Aesthetic Angst

Presbyterians have been worried about their worship music for a long time. In 1914, missionary Donald Fraser was cautioning, "We do not want to super-impose on those sons of Africa our expressionless Scottish characters." Twenty years later, Alexander Hetherwick, a Scottish missionary, raised the question, "Do we Scots missionaries do right by our converts in imposing on them our own quiet, solemn, and expressionless form of worship?"[2] This insecurity did not prevent extensive Presbyterian missions, but it often resurfaces today when White Presbyterians compare their traditional, European-derived Presbyterian music to that of other cultures. By the early twenty-first century, worries of active colonialist cultural imposition may have faded, but congregants at Nashville's Hillsboro Presbyterian still worried that their Black sister church, Spruce Street Baptist, "with their wonderful lively music, must think we're so boring." From Connecticut and Pennsylvania to Indiana and Tennessee, groups of Presbyterians described their own worship with phrases like "maybe people think it's boring, but it's what we do" and "compared to all that, I suppose our music is unexciting." Nevertheless, Presbyterians and other mainline Protestants see their Traditional music as central to their cultural identities.

In part because of this view, diversifying their music became a cultural survival strategy for American mainline Protestants. By the end of the twentieth century, tropes of multicultural America and "hyphenated identity" (including general categories like African American or Asian American and more specific identities like Polish American or Filipino American) rose in the country's cultural discourse. Many mainline Protestants and other upper-middle-class Whites felt a comparative lack of ethnic, regional, and religious identity as the new century began. Ethnomusicologist Mirjana Lausevic's findings that many White Anglo-Saxon Protestants reported "the feeling of being washed out in the vast uniformity of white American society"[3] resonates with cultural theorist Rita Felski's work on middle-class Whites' self-describing as "non-identities" culturally having "nothing to declare."[4] Many White people felt that they were being left behind in an increasingly multicultural United States—a feeling that accompanied mainline Protestants looking with concern at their decreasing membership trends.

This lack of twenty-first-century social prominence frustrated mainline Protestants on multiple levels. First, this position was far from their historically central place in the United States' sacredscape. Second, they had been trying, but struggling, to retain a key social role in diversifying, multicultural American society. Third, their growing lack of cultural capital implied a parallel lack of spiritual impact. While many predominantly White faith communities like Hillsboro *had* been striving to be allies and advocates of diversity, their inclusive aspirations were often ineffective or counterproductive to creating the demographically inclusive congregations they said they wanted.

Mainline Protestant churches had been highly effective in institutionalizing the musical diversity of the Worship Wars binary. Still, as a Presbyterian praise band singer noted, "Our church is diverse in so many ways, but it would be nice if we had some Black people." In the diversity-driven, multicultural landscape of the modern United States, pursuing racial diversity and allyship has become a benchmark of moderate-to-liberal White culture. However, the long histories of systemic racism and social patterns make effectively working toward this goal challenging and painful—White individuals and communities have to confront their past and present behaviors and beliefs.[5] The issue is not just the relationship between Black and White communities (although that relationship is one of the central ones, given the history of the United States), but also a broad, national cultural shift.

In many ways, the music controversies of the Worship Wars provided a familiar set of internal Protestant controversies. In an abstract sense, some of the basic arguments now being applied to Traditional versus Contemporary disputes were the same issues that sixteenth-century Protestant reformers like Martin Luther and John Calvin were wrangling. This time, though, the turn-of-the-millennium Worship Wars offered mainline Protestants a welcome chance to publicly display their newfound tolerance and support of differences. The sign boards in front of many mainline churches around the United States soon advertised their congregations' internal diversity with variations on "Traditional Service, 9 AM; Contemporary Service, 11 AM." These modern Christians were finding institutionalized compromises, unlike their religious ancestors. Thus, mainline Protestants could perceive themselves as triumphing over the polemic dangers of the Worship Wars and their congregations breathed a hard-earned sense of righteous relief.

Debating the merits of pipe organs versus electric guitars had provided welcome tangible flashpoints with concrete deliverables ("Look, now we have two types of worship services!"), but as social theorist Alfred Schutz notes, material culture is "accidental to the social relationship prevailing among the performers."[6] In navigating the Worship Wars, American mainline Protestants were facing deeply embedded cultural patterns and insecurities that were impacting White Christianity's social role in twenty-first-century America.

This chapter explores three main areas of that exploration: expressive behavior, formality, and authority and agency. As mainline Protestant churches incorporated the diversity of Contemporary worship alongside Traditional services, they heard sonic change ushering in the promise of a new era of cultural vitality. However, these sonic changes also fundamentally changed mainline Protestant social structures. As the music changed, so too did congregational cultures begin to shift away from institutions and formality, in arenas from education to expressive behavior. Echoing popular American culture and evangelicalism, long-held bases of spiritual and social authority began to shift. The way that worshipers related to each other and the divine began a transformation.

Perceiving Formality: Ensembles as Social Sites

There's more of an opportunity for people to participate musically in the Contemporary service than in the Traditional service (*pauses*). Well, actually, anybody can invite themselves to the chancel choir, so maybe it's not right to say that, but I think the feeling's still that way, because the music is different.

—Praise band musician

The Choir: Education and Order

Traditional choir structures resemble common twentieth-century social structures in the United States. As sociologist Robert Putnam details, post–World War II suburbia was filled with mostly White leisure institutions like social club lodges, bowling leagues, and garden societies. These groups often had substantial organizational structures: official boards, elected officers, social chairs, and so forth.[7] Mainline church choirs often echo this governmental schema, with presidents, board members, social committees, and the like. On many levels, the internal workings and organization of a Traditional choir mirror that of mainline churches, which until recently had mirrored that of American society as a whole.

The social structures of the choir and the worship service correlate. Hillsboro's Contemporary praise band director noted, "If the people are much more formal in their interactions with other people, other church members, then they're probably going to project that into the worship service—and vice versa."[8] When describing a Traditional choir, worshipers often reference values of Western classical music, musical literacy, and formality: "Traditional choir leaders maybe come off as being a little bit more rigid." "[Having musical notation may be helpful] for some people, if they know how to read music, but most people I know don't. People in the choir maybe." "They've got their own little thing, their little [choir music] book." The material culture of the choir—from assigned music folders kept in assigned slots to uniform robes—demonstrates how choir members are expected to conform to group standards. "The robes are for uniformity and to keep people's minds on what they should be focused on," explains Hillsboro choir director Sherry Kelly, "and that's worship through music, not individuals." A baritone in her choir agrees, "The people in the pews are important to worship, but the choir is more structured, by necessity, where they all function as a unit. Which means that they should have some sort of recognition, in terms of whether I can tell it's a choir." Thus, mainline Protestant church choirs often convey their group identity on multiple visual and sonic levels: members' robes and stoles match, the choir sits and stands as a unit during worship, singers adhere to a printed musical score, and individual voices blend rather than stand out.

Expectations for group behavior vary depending on how formally the choir is administered. In this respect, participation in Traditional choirs echoes debates over participation versus perfection that have dominated

188 / (White)Washing Our Sins Away

discussion of church music as long as churches have had music.[9] Sometimes there are formal bylaws, as in Covenant Presbyterian (PCA) of Nashville's rule books for their choirs, or looser group descriptions, such as: "Music speaks to the heart and permeates the soul. Service through music takes commitment. Come join us and share in that commitment!"[10] Many mainline church choirs have formal auditions, with larger churches having different choirs classed on skill and/or age. In some churches, choirs have paid section leaders (soprano, alto, tenor, and bass) to lead by example and elevate the quality of the ensemble sound. In other churches—and particularly in smaller congregations—Traditional choirs are more interested in attracting new members than vetting for quality. These choirs accept new members without auditions or confirming their ability to read sheet music. Choir members are positioned not as performers, but as public servants, putting the congregation's need before their own. As one soprano explains, "There is an underlying responsibility there to lead. You're part of the worship team if you're in the choir." Director Kelly summarizes this sentiment, saying the choir should be seen "as a group, rather than individuals."

While it is easy to paint Traditional choirs as exclusive and elitist, people who participate in the choirs often perceive the groups as more participatory and egalitarian than Contemporary praise bands. A church choir can become a powerful asset for attracting potential members. Indeed, in mainline churches, the choir often provides an important opportunity for active participation. At Hillsboro Presbyterian, for example, many choir members described the chance to sing as integral to their choosing Hillsboro. One tenor explained, "For me personally, music is extremely important. I've been in choirs since I was fifteen, and it's just something I always look for. Good music is one of the things I'm going to do at a church." A married couple who had been singing at Hillsboro for over fifteen years elaborated:

> HUSBAND: In looking for a church, one of our goals was to find a choir that we could sing in. And we were fairly specific about what we were looking for there. We wanted to find a choir that did quality. Good music in a quality, good way Sunday after Sunday.
>
> WIFE: And was more than just six or ten people.
>
> HUSBAND: Yeah, it had to be more than an ensemble. That was Harpeth [Presbyterian]'s problem and Southminster [Presbyte-

rian]'s problem. They had just these little bitty choirs. But, we wanted to sing in a choir where we could make a difference, too. Where they would know, where they would miss us if we weren't there.

WIFE: So, it wasn't one of these big megachurch choirs that we wanted to be a part of.

HUSBAND: The number of choir members at Brentwood or First Pres, they wouldn't know whether you were there or not. They would never know. It doesn't matter how good your voice is, they have ten other tenors or fifteen other sopranos to make up for it. And Hillsboro was the perfect match.

Many Hillsboro choir members tell a similar story of church choir shopping, comparing Hillsboro's choir with the choirs of neighboring churches before picking their new musical home. One tenor recalls a similar "Goldilocks and the Three Bears"–style story with nothing being quite right for him in other local congregations: he had not appreciated "being mobbed" to join the tiny choir of a nearby Presbyterian church after nearby congregants heard the quality of his voice in the pews during worship. Yet, he had also been uncomfortable with the large size of the choir and the congregation in general at another neighboring Presbyterian church. When he put his young daughter in the nursery, "They barcoded her on the back!" he exclaimed. "To get my child back, I had to have the barcode to get my child back! I thought, you know, this is maybe a little too large, to where we're barcoding our children." Many Traditional choir singers want this sort of balance and to blend into the group sound, without being lost in an impersonal crowd.

Making music as part of a group rather than as an individual is key to Traditional worship. In the choir, there are occasional solos, but most of the music is made as people sing as one of many voices. Each person contributes, but standing out as an individual is not the goal. Rather, vocal sections—soprano, alto, tenor, and bass—blend into a whole.

The Praise Band: Inspiration and Individualism

In contrast to the group nature of a Traditional choir, a Contemporary praise band emphasizes individualism. Each instrument or vocal part is generally the only one of its kind performing that role, so focus is drawn to unique individuals. Clearly executed, specific parts are important, explains Hillsboro's band director, Stephen Nix: "Excuse me, this is an evangelical term, but you don't want to just 'let the Lord have His way.' Could we not sing on top of each other, or not play on top of each other?"

At the same time that Nix wanted distinct vocal parts, the praise band leader also exhorted the members to emphasize their individuality and "really put *yourself* into it!" While Traditional worship music lays out exact vocal and instrumental lines, the comparatively bare-bones chord charts of Contemporary worship encourage individuals to be creative in interpreting their parts. Each musician can display their personality and emotions through the rendition of a musical line, gestures, and facial expressions. Even their clothing choices reflect their personalities, since they are wearing everyday outfits rather than homogenizing ritual dress (like choir robes or concert black).

Contemporary congregants notice and appreciate this projection of personality. When I was playing in the praise band during my field-work, one congregant told me, "Your whole personality comes out, and the recipients can feel it . . . It's a gift." Performing with the praise band allows members to publicly enact and project dimensions of their iden-tities; during worship, a corporate lawyer or a stay-at-home mom can become a celebrated vocalist. By emphasizing individuality and charisma, the praise band lets people plug into various aspects of identity—past, present, and projected.

Individual musicians often use evangelical-style language to describe a personal calling to participate in a Contemporary praise band. In contrast to a Traditional choir's "service" or "leadership," band members describe themselves as being "led," "called," or "blessed" by God. For example:

> PRAISE BAND SINGER #1: Sometimes I just really feel [*chokes up, pauses*] the power of God. I don't really know how to express it [*pauses*]. It makes me smile, it makes me feel happy, and blessed to be in a position to be able to share that with people . . . I would just hope that people would sort of see God through me, or any of us singing, through our music.

> PRAISE BAND SINGER #2: I started on this quest to start enjoy-ing my voice, not just doing what I thought I was *supposed* to be doing. Or whatever. And that kind of led me into the praise band.

PRAISE BAND SINGER #3: I've never seen our director recruit anyone. People will come that are supposed to be there. That's what happens. That's what it felt like for me. I showed up when I was supposed to, you know, for me and for the overall good.

The language in these Contemporary descriptions of fulfillment and divine guidance contrasts with Traditional rhetoric of duty and service.

Spiritual Priorities as a Bridge

Single worship elements can be interpreted in multiple ways: the robed choir processing into the service can be read as "respectful" or "stuffy"; singing expressively in the band can be read as "putting on a show" or "showing religious fervor." A church choir's Western musical literacy may seem an impediment to participation, but on the other hand they often do not limit their membership numbers. The praise band welcomes those who do not necessarily read sheet music, but the structure creates limits on how many musicians they need per part. Within Western Christianity, this ebb and flow between elite perfection and mass participation has been a consistent theme with the pendulum swinging back and forth over historical and social settings. At its extremes, Worship Wars rhetoric tends to support the idea of Contemporary worship encouraging participation and Traditional being more exclusive in adhering to Western classical music's ideals of perfection. These dynamics resonate with the work of ethnomusicologist Tom Turino, when he talks about music as existing along a spectrum from participatory to performative.[11]

Mainline Protestant churches balancing both Traditional and Contemporary musics, however, are choosing a middle path that sees both styles as participatory, supporting social goals of tolerance and diversity. The specific way that participation manifests across the genres may be different, but the underlying value often comes through. At Hillsboro, for example, both the Traditional choir director and Contemporary praise band leader emphasized the importance of working with amateur musicians:

CHOIR DIRECTOR: I have a few trained singers in with some untrained singers. So, what we do is do the very best we can. We prepare it as best we can and always try to give our very best to worship. I know there are choirs around the city that have paid quartets, but I think an all-volunteer choir is better. I think the spirit is better. I think the responsibility, that it's

192 / (White)Washing Our Sins Away

a service that you're not getting paid for, it is part of your service to God and you have a talent and He expects you to use it to His glory. I mean, we don't pay Sunday School teachers, you know.

PRAISE BAND LEADER: Not everyone can be a professional. Spiritualism is not about perfection, it's about experience. And that's where I kind of draw the lines when it comes to music. I never want to take the spirituality out of music. For a lot of people, the experience of being able to express themselves, ever how completely able they are at the moment, is a necessary point of their worship experience. And to give that to people, and to allow that to be a freedom for people is to me what I would consider grace.

For their leaders and members, participating in the choir and band is more about spiritual relationships than goals of perfection. The way that this core value musically manifests may seem incompatible, but talking about the underlying values reveals points of commonality.

For mainline Protestants trying to chart a way forward within American society, it is helpful to perceive Contemporary worship as a continuation of their basic core values. Worshipers may still hear the two musical systems' sounds at odds with each other, but understanding points of commonality rather than only hearing and seeing the differences—and there are many—allows mainline Protestant faith communities to see themselves as tolerantly embracing cultural change.

Authority and Agency

There's enough there to provide adherence to a certain confessional standard, but there's a tremendous amount of freedom in how that's expressed.

—Hillsboro pastor David Kidd

Different social systems operate according to different types of leadership and authority. Musical systems—from jam band collectives to symphony orchestras—all march to their own trap sets and kettle drums (so to speak). Who attains musical authority—who leads and how they have gained

Social Diversity / 193

the legitimacy to do so—is central to understanding how communities negotiate meaning overall.[12] This negotiating meaning is itself central to religious systems, so when music and religion combine, issues of leadership and authority carry more weight. Then, questions of authority do not just move horizontally among humans but also reach up vertically to the divine.

Since music is so central to mainline Protestant worship, changing the musical system impacts authority structures beyond music. When mainline Protestant congregations began incorporating Contemporary worship, adding an amplified praise band seemed like an innocuous aesthetic issue: electric guitars would just be louder, people thought, and praise choruses would be easy to sing. This was true, but incorporating Contemporary music also shifted centuries-old, institutionalized power structures and bases of authority and agency.

In this section, I use the words "authority" and "agency" as specialized terms to explain how Contemporary worship has shifted power within Presbyterian churches. Authority (who selects a worship element) does not always correlate with agency (who enacts a worship element). The power to choose the theology that congregations are singing presents a powerful behind-the-scenes difference between agency and authority in Traditional and Contemporary worship.

In keeping with Presbyterian emphasis on leadership by highly educated clergy (see chapter 2), pastors have historically exercised the primary authority over the content of worship. The central denomination provides guiding materials like lectionaries and hymnals, but the pastor decides on specific sermon topics, prayers, *and the hymns*. Having ministers select hymns based on their theological content stems back to Reformation-era goals of vernacular hymnody as an embodied didactic tool for educated clergy to use alongside biblical exegesis and preaching.

Centuries later, this focus on text still holds. Denominational hymnals providing pastors with a corpus of theologically and musically vetted hymns become important because the vast majority of most Presbyterian seminaries do not provide training in liturgical music. "That never made much sense to me," said one young pastor from Michigan, "because we do sing three hymns a week. Gotta trust in that hymnal!" In Tennessee, Hillsboro pastors David Kidd and Nancy McCurley offered a similar explanation:

> MCCURLEY: Neither one of us can read music, so we're picking it because of the theological richness of the text.

194 / (White)Washing Our Sins Away

KIDD: Or even because we know what it is! "Oh, I know this one."

McCURLEY: We don't really have the kind of training musically to pick out what will move people.

KIDD: I do have a computer program that plays you the music, but it's busted right now.

Clergy gain hands-on experience in hymn selection over the years, and many work closely with their music ministers and choir directors. Yet, overall, the music that a Presbyterian congregation sings in Traditional worship has been selected by the pastor on the basis of the text.

Traditional congregants in the pews may not be aware of this authority (who selects a worship element) because of how agency (who enacts a worship element) flows in their worship services. Between scripture readings, prayers, choral anthems, offertories, and hymns, an array of people implement worship elements, so that no one individual appears to dominate the agency of the service. Providing a printed bulletin with the order of service is standard fare at most mainline Protestant churches (see figure 7.1). This bulletin helps congregants follow the liturgical flow, especially for mainline denominations that do not post the morning's hymn numbers on a sanctuary wall board.

These parts of the service printed in the bulletin—from music to prayers—have been chosen prior to their being played, not spontaneously midservice. Like a classical music program, the bulletin often provides a composer's name along with the song title, grounding the music in a sense of attribution and history. Once worshipers turn to the correct page in the hymnal, they find more background information, including composer, lyricist, dates of creation, name of the tune, and sources of origin. By displaying attributes of ownership and artistic production similar to Western classical music,[13] the bulletin works with the hymnal to link repertoire with people and points of origin beyond the immediate worship service.

In a Traditional format, authority rests with clergy, but agency is spread among clergy, musicians, and laity. As figure 7.2 demonstrates, although the pastor has selected most of the Traditional service elements, certain musicians bear the greatest responsibility for enacting elements of worship. The choir director is one visible music leader. The organist also has agency over nearly half of the elements in the service, such as

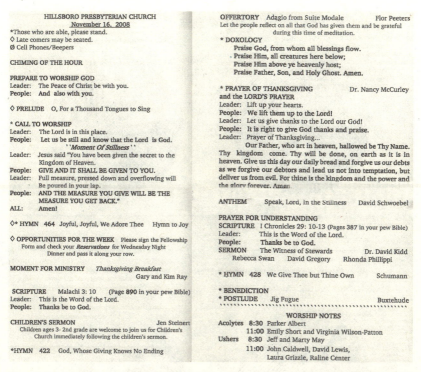

Figure 7.1. Order of service, Hillsboro Presbyterian Church Traditional bulletin. Photo by Deborah Justice.

sounding the opening chords of a hymn for congregational singing or transitioning from the instrumental offertory to the congregationally sung response. The flow of the service tends to alternate agents, giving a sense of shared leadership participation.

Authority and agency work differently in the Contemporary service. Pastoral musical authority decreases; instead, the person who selects the worship element usually enacts it during the service, with the Contemporary band leader playing a dominant role with authority and agency (see figure 7.2). In a typical mainline Protestant Contemporary church bulletin, the specific titles of musical elements in the service are not provided (see figure 7.3). Rather, the order of service is indicated with neutral labels like "Music," "Chorus of Gathering and Adoration," or "Prelude." The flow of the service still alternates agents, but the band leader is more central.

196 / (White)Washing Our Sins Away

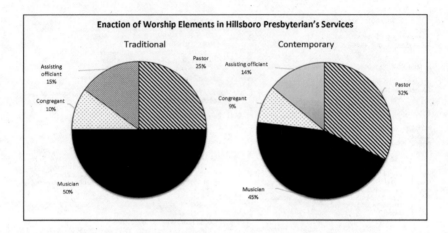

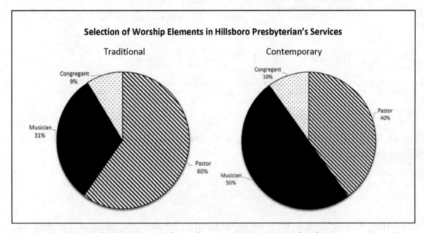

Figure 7.2. Ratio between worship element enaction and selection across Contemporary and Traditional worship at Hillsboro Presbyterian Church. Chart by Deborah Justice.

A major reason for this shift lies in the sources of Contemporary repertoire (see chapter 4). Since Contemporary worship music does *not* come from denominationally vetted sources, like an official hymnal, the praise band leader generally selects the music.

JUSTICE: So, in a Traditional style service, you have the ministers picking hymns—

HILLSBORO PRESBYTERIAN CHURCH
November 16, 2008

Ø Cell Phones/Beepers

PRELUDE

INVOCATION

CHORUS OF GATHERING AND ADORATION

OPPORTUNITIES FOR THE WEEK
Please sign the Fellowship Form and check your
Reservations for Wednesday Night Dinner
and pass it along your pew.

MOMENT FOR MINISTRY *Thanksgiving Breakfast*
Gary and Kim Ray

SACRAMENT OF BAPTISM of Richard Aloysius
Obermeier and Stephanie Irene Obermeier,
children of Steve and Melinda Obermeier, sister Jackie.

MUSIC

SCRIPTURE Malachi 3:10

CHILDREN'S SERMON Jen Steinert
Children ages 3-2nd grade are welcome to join us for
Children's Church immediately following the children's
sermon.

OFFERTORY
Let the people reflect on all that God has given them
and be grateful during this time of meditation.

PRAYER OF THANKSGIVING Dr. Nancy McCurley
and the LORD'S PRAYER...
Our Father, who art in heaven, hallowed be Thy
Name. Thy kingdom come. Thy will be done, on earth as
it is in heaven. Give us this day our daily bread and
forgive us our debts as we forgive our debtors and lead us
not into temptation, but deliver us from evil. For thine is
the kingdom and the power and the glory forever. Amen.

ANTHEM

PRAYER FOR UNDERSTANDING

SCRIPTURE I Chronicles 29: 10-13

SERMON The Witness of Stewards Dr. David Kidd
Rebecca Swan David Gregory Rhonda Phillippi

MUSIC

* BENEDICTION

~~~~~~~~~~~

WORSHIP NOTES

Acolytes	8:30	Parker Albert
	11:00	Emily Short & Virginia Wilson-Patton
Ushers	8:30	Jeff & Marty May
	11:00	John Caldwell, David Lewis,
		Laura Grizzle, Raline Center
Flowers		In honor of Adrienne Martin's 15th birthday.
		Given by her parents, Steve and Ann,
		and brother, Avery.

Figure 7.3. Order of service, Hillsboro Presbyterian Church Contemporary bulletin. Photo by Deborah Justice.

NIX: I say "yikes!" That scares me half to death.

JUSTICE: Why is that?

NIX: Well, I don't pick the sermons. My experience is in music. Their experience is not in music. It scares me because they don't know the limitations of who's playing, of who's doing what. I do! So, that's why it always scares me.

Nix went on to say that he did consider the music's theological content, but that was only one element of his equation. Since he was serving as the primary musical leader (combining the Traditional roles of choir director, organist, and hymn selector), he focused on the technical details of the music and abilities of the musicians who would be enacting it as well as the lyrical content.

198 / (White)Washing Our Sins Away

In sum, Contemporary worship shifts historical patterns of authority and agency in Presbyterian churches. It also prompts similar transformations across other mainline denominations. In the Contemporary service, the clergy's role in shaping worship has decreased, whereas the musical leadership's role has increased. The subtle shift largely results from the Contemporary service's move away from the codified denominational hymnal as the source of congregational repertoire. Without the musical expertise to source Contemporary music themselves, clergy have to work with Contemporary music directors in order to exert theological guidance over the service. One praise band leader described the potential for this relationship to be mutually beneficial:

> When you're a great music director, you know what [music] is good, and you can kind of choose that, and you've learned to work with the clergy. You've learned the styles of your ministers and you know what does work and what doesn't work.

This director's comments speak to the necessity of an ongoing dialogue between the Contemporary music director and the clergy. While these dynamics exist to a certain extent between the choir director and clergy in a Traditional service as well (e.g., coordinating anthems and offertories to fit the theme of each Sunday's message), a Contemporary musical leader has considerably more power in shaping the congregation's experience during worship.

This shift causes Contemporary worship to depart from historical mainline Protestant patterns of highly educated, ordained clergy in leadership positions, instead favoring more evangelical patterns of personality-driven, divinely inspired leadership. As sociologist R. Stephen Warner notes, "Evangelicals do not seek demythologized or symbolic interpretations . . . and thus there is little need for a clergy with esoteric learning to provide them."[14] In Contemporary worship, an unordained band leader may assume responsibility for nearly twice as much of the service as the seminary-educated, ordained pastor. This shift in authority makes musical sense, but holds substantial repercussions for authority structures.

Traditional Authority as Education, Contemporary Authority as Inspiration

Contemporary worship has transformed channels of authority, deemphasizing the historically prominent role of the clergy's institutionalized theological education in selecting music for worship. For many mainline Protestants, Traditional musical authority rests on education. University faculty positions are common credentials among mainline Protestant church music leaders, for example: Marilyn Kaiser (Doctorate in Sacred Music from Union Theological Seminary, working at Bloomington's Trinity Episcopal Church, teaching at the Jacobs School of Music Indiana University), Tom Marshall (Master of Music from University of Michigan, working at Williamsburg Presbyterian Church, teaching at The College of William and Mary), Patrick McCreless (PhD in Music Theory from the Eastman School of Music of the University of Rochester, working at First Presbyterian Church of New Haven, teaching at Yale University), and Dr. Stephen Spinelli (DMA from Northwestern University, working at First Presbyterian of Ithaca, New York, teaching at Cornell University).

Hillsboro Presbyterian's choir director and organist also serve as prime examples. When explaining why the choir director had achieved such success during her years at the church, organist Tim Gmeiner emphasized collegiate ties: "A real solid choral background. Her degree was in choral conducting from Westminster Choir College, which is a big choir school. Plus, she had such a good reputation with Belmont [University]." When Kelly began at Hillsboro, she was also working as a voice professor at Belmont University. Many singers in the church expressed enthusiasm over joining a choir "with a college professor as a director!" Hillsboro members were also delighted that many of Kelly's current and former students "would come and sing in our choir just to work with her some more. We had the cream of the crop, like great sopranos, great tenors just wanting to come and sing." These strong educational ties amplified Kelly's talents as director to bring new singers to her church. People valued her connections to prestigious collegiate music programs, and her educational ties gave her extra authority.

In contrast, the musical leadership in Contemporary services tends to value inspiration and hands-on experience. When Hillsboro Presbyterian's Contemporary service grew enough to require a "director of the band," the hiring committee prioritized a candidate with Christian music industry experience and personal authenticity. A member of the committee summarized the group's opinion:

> We were just really impressed with him. His background, his family was in gospel. He played the piano and sang, and he was a tenor. We were always looking for more parts, and he had the ability to coach vocals. Session musician. Church

200 / (White)Washing Our Sins Away

> music conferences. He just had a lot of good things about him. We just thought, this guy knows the industry, but also probably knows people that we could bring in and enhance things even more.
>
> I think we had about three or four people we brought in and interviewed. Stephen [Nix] came in. And was literally—he had a little bit of the spiked hair. It was blondish—it was like, "Whoa, different." But he was really neat. You could just see in his eyes that he had soul and passion for it. And we just all said, "Yeah, I think he would be really good." We tried him out for a couple of Sundays to see if the feel was there. It was. We said, "Great, let's do this."

The clergy noted that Nix "does not come out of a liturgical background," but this was an asset because the church was looking to hire someone versed in the evangelicalism of Contemporary worship.

Nix's training included a dual bachelor's degree in vocal conducting and music education—and a master's in music pedagogy—but he downplayed his academic credentials to emphasize his extensive hands-on experience. "I didn't want to teach. I wanted to go the commercial realm of music. So, I . . . plugged into what I call 'big church,' you know, the *large* churches, the five- and ten-thousand-member churches kept calling me and I would be working for them whenever they needed that." By age fifteen, he had already gained some experience working as a music director, and quickly gained more by working in over ninety churches and touring with the likes of the Bill Gaither artists, Dolly Parton, and Brian Duncan.

The way that Nix explains his route to the position at Hillsboro demonstrates the personal spirituality of evangelicalism. He references his interactive relationship with God when he says that he felt like a regular Sunday church commitment would give him "some spiritual foundation, something to give back." His coincidental discovery of the post and inclination to apply for it—"I just happened to see it and thought, 'That sounds like something fun'"—echoes anthropologist Tanya Luhrmann's analysis of how evangelical Christians learn to feel and respond to God's voice through every day "coincidences."[15]

Praise band members, congregants, and clergy also talked about the Contemporary band director's networking, natural musical skill, and personal spirituality rather than his educational credentials. Congregants felt that they were "so lucky" and "blessed" to get someone who had been so active as a music director "in several different denominations," as well as noting that he still worked as a freelance songwriter and music coach. "He's just so gifted," raved the clergy in one interview, using descriptive terms that highlight the otherness that transcends experience of virtuosity.[16]

Presbyterians tend not to use heavily evangelical language that might describe leadership as "touched by the hand of the Lord," but congregants and clergy alike described sensing a spontaneous, natural talent and direction in the Contemporary service that seemed less institutionalized than that of the Traditional service. Nix and the band "just look at each other and just know when to connect" explained one woman, "in contrast to Sherry up there in front of the choir." In a 2008 interview, Hillsboro's pastors, David Kidd and Nancy McCurley, also highlighted the Contemporary musical leadership's personal approach in contrast to the Traditional service's greater formality:

> MCCURLEY: If you look at the style, that prompted me to think about the difference between [Contemporary band director] Stephen and [Traditional choir director] Sherry, how Stephen will often introduce a hymn or a song, "Well, the other day, I just happened to be thinking about . . ." or "I was really down . . ."
>
> KIDD: It's great!
>
> MCCURLEY: Very meaningful, very meaningful! But I could never imagine [choir director] Sherry [Kelly] standing up and saying that before an anthem. I just can't imagine that!

McCurley quickly qualified her remarks, emphasizing that Kelly was not falling short or being unfriendly, "it's just that a verbal introduction in the Traditional service would be unusual!" since the two worship styles assume different behaviors from musical leadership.

While Traditional genre expectations kept Kelly from talking about the choir's music during the service, sometimes Nix would use his informal introduction to a Contemporary piece to show God actively at work in the congregation. Although Nix planned the music and the praise band rehearsed the specific pieces, titles or credits were not provided because, as he explained, "They're trying to be 'contemporary' and be less formal. That's basically it." The ambiguous headings create the potential for

202 / (White)Washing Our Sins Away

spontaneity, which is important, because Nix *did* occasionally alter his plans on the spur of the moment.

> I'm like, "Oh, I need to sing this song! This is so great! This works!" Because I tend to be like a little DJ in my head when it comes to songs. I can pull stuff up and play it . . . I've written many songs in response to the sermon on the spot. That's just something I do. I can do that, but I don't do it a whole lot.

During worship, Nix would sometimes introduce a piece of music by explaining that he was making a spontaneous change to his plans, saying things like, "I was planning to play something else, but I feel led to this" or "God is giving me this right now."

Phenomenologists Alfred Schutz and Thomas Luckmann observe that each time a person has an experience, they anticipate the possibility of having a similar future experience.[17] Because Nix only occasionally responded spontaneously to the sermon, participants described the rare times when he did as extremely touching:

> PASTORS KIDD AND MCCURLEY: Amazing. I mean, it is extraordinary. For a while, we were trying to figure out, well, now does he study the text and then come in prepared? But he just hears the sermon and *Boom*! Here comes this thing!

> CONGREGANT IN HER SEVENTIES: A couple of weeks ago, David [Kidd] said something in the sermon, and Stephen changed the music, and I just sat there and cried. I mean, it just made the sermon even stronger for me, what David had preached, because of Stephen singing that song. He'll do that sometimes. I've heard that he even makes up some of the songs.

In another instance a few weeks later, during the worship service, following the sermon, Nix explained that although the pastor had asked him to find a piece of music to respond to the message's theme, he had been unable to find an adequate piece. Instead of giving up, Nix said, he prayed for guidance and was now offering the resultant composition up to God and the congregation. The worshipers responded with overwhelming enthusiasm at this "evidence of God at work." Many were moved to tears. For weeks after, during my fieldwork interviews, the congregation would point to that song as a particularly moving worship experience, repeating themselves to make sure that I understood how significant it was that Nix had served as God's conduit for that song. The overarching Presbyterian frame of worship "decent and in order" ensures that such responses stay in their preassigned times during the service, but congregants felt God moving strongly in these planned opportunities for spontaneity.

Contemporary worshipers understood spontaneity like Nix's as coming from an active God. The opportunity for unscripted responses relates to broad evangelical ideals of worship as human response to a God who is intimately involved in daily human life. In the theological abstract, most mainline Protestants—Traditional or Contemporary—would also agree that God is always active. For those who have "learned to listen" to God, however, as the evangelicalism anthropologist Tanya Luhrmann noted,[18] this level of musical inspiration gives direct evidence of that divine activity. The way that congregants, clergy, and musicians at Hillsboro Presbyterian regularly talked about Contemporary musical leadership's emotion and spontaneity in contrast to Traditional worship leadership demonstrates how keenly worshipers *were* aware of the difference in authority.

Expressive Behavior

Presbyterian Worship or Frostbite Falls?

"You ever watch Rocky and Bullwinkle?" the praise band drummer asked me as we were packing up music gear after the Contemporary service one Sunday morning. Curious, I said that I had seen enough of the moose and squirrel capers to get a general gist of this vintage cartoon series. The drummer explained that he sometimes thought of that cartoon when there seemed to be a disconnect between the praise band and the congregation as he had perceived that morning:

> Since people do sometimes clap or say "Amen," when we play something—like we did today with "Come and See"—where it's so good, so intense, I almost expect them to react to it. I mean, I was *so* into that, man! But when they just sit there, I picture the townspeople in Rocky and Bullwinkle. Frostbite Falls, they call it. The place and people were so cold that when they were really excited about something, you'd just see this

204 / (White)Washing Our Sins Away

> stoic crowd and one would hold up a sign that said, "Yay." So
> when the people just sit there, I think [*deadpan, stoically*], "Yay."

We talked some more about how the Hillsboro congregants rarely responded
to worship with overt enthusiasm or emotional display. I asked him why
he chose to participate in a church with such reserve and lack of crowd
response. He quickly clarified that, while he would appreciate a little bit
more enthusiasm, "so many churches—like that televangelist Joel Osteen
fella" went too far. After a certain point, the drummer felt that the congregational response became more of a crowd-based, big audience response
to a performance than sincere worshipful behavior.

"I think our people feel a lot more than they show," he said, "although
sometimes I just have to laugh to myself and say, 'Yay.'"

The Frozen Chosen

When Presbyterians compare their worship music to other Christian
traditions, they often use the metaphor of Presbyterians as the "frozen
chosen." (I can attest to this, having grown up Presbyterian myself!) This
label plays off two historical characteristics of Presbyterianism: first, the
theological doctrine of predestination—that an omniscient, omnipotent
God has preordained the course of human lives such that some are "chosen" by God for salvation; and second, the "decent and in order" decorum
of Presbyterian worship. While most Presbyterians have liberalized away
from strict predestination theologies, they remain relatively reserved on
the scales of worship expression measured by sociologists (e.g., clapping,
dancing, ecstatic expression).[19]

If Contemporary worship was supposed to loosen up Presbyterian
worship, the faith culture's overarching behavioral norms have largely
prevailed. As one congregant who had attended a variety of Presbyterian
churches for years compared Presbyterian worship to her previous young
adult experience in a Free Will Baptist congregation:

> People don't really get into it here and *sing* as a body. And, I
> think maybe in the early [Contemporary] service they tend to
> sing a little bit more, but I guess Presbyterians are not known
> for really belting it out [*laughs*].
>
> In the [Free Will Baptist] church where I come from, they
> had a man who led the singing. He would really encourage

you to sing out. You know, "Let's sing that one over again. Come on you can do better than that!" Really lead you and encourage you to sing out those praises to God . . . Why not have someone who would be directing the congregation to sing out? To sing their praises to God and be able to feel that freedom to do that. I think that would be worthwhile, but I don't know whether that's a Presbyterian thing or not [*laughs*].

Many of the Traditional congregants expressed views similar to an older Indiana woman who said, "I feel like they try to get a *little* more [*pauses, then mischievously*] 'lively' in the Contemporary service." "Lively" is relative, however. As a teenager who played guitar with Hillsboro Presbyterian's praise band explained:

I guess the whole congregation is kind of strict . . . We *are* very Presbyterian. Like on the youth mission trip to Waco, Texas, we went to a Baptist church there and it kind of amazed me how much the congregation is involved there, you know, responding to the preacher's word and stuff. So, I guess the congregation is strictly Presbyterian because we don't get involved with the service as much.

In my fieldwork, I observed only slightly more movement in mainline Contemporary services, usually by congregants swaying slightly from side to side with the music or, very occasionally, clapping along to a song. This economy of expression notwithstanding, congregants frequently described worshiping with Contemporary music as freeing. "I had a little bit of trouble at first," explained one man from Indiana. "But then, I thought there was a lot more liberation, once I got over my misgivings about doing things that are, you know, catchy." While self-identifying as "frozen chosen" still happens across both Contemporary and Traditional Presbyterian worship services, adding Contemporary worship has added a caveat. As one congregant joked, they're now "frozen chosen, albeit slightly defrosted."

Potential for Participation

Many congregants explained that Contemporary worship facilitated this defrosting by creating the *potential* for more free expression and movement. Even though they associated Contemporary music with more expressive

206 / (White)Washing Our Sins Away

worship behaviors from neighboring evangelical faith communities, when it came to implementing Contemporary worship in their own churches, many mainline Protestants continued their historically predominant reserved behaviors. My interview with a Contemporary congregant (we'll call her Jill) from Hillsboro Presbyterian explores these themes.

When I arrived at Jill's home for our interview one sunny morning, not only had she laid out coffee and pastries on china, she had also loaded up her CD player. Hitting play, Jill started swaying with the music.

> JILL: What I *love* is this jazzy piano with St. Olaf! And the reason I say it's sort of worshipful, it's the words, they're singing about Jesus. That's what I *love* about Contemporary worship with Stephen [Nix at Hillsboro Presbyterian], it's so *personal*. But, also, in all honesty [*dancing around the table*], I love to move in worship! As far as frozen Presbyterians, I'm not a frozen one! See, you can kind of [*dances*] . . . Then you can put your arms up!

> JUSTICE: Do you normally put your arms up during worship?

> JILL: [*Stops moving, looks vaguely horrified*] No! It's completely different! The reason I say it's "sort of worshipful," and I feel a little guilty, even if it wasn't for all that "God and Jesus" in the words, [is that] I'd still be moving! [*Laughs*] That's the little iffy thing! Like, are you praising the Lord, or are you just wanting to move around?! Anyway, I love the combination of the words—you're praising the Lord—but you're moving!

> JUSTICE: Why don't you do it during church?

> JILL: Why don't I put my arms up and move around? Well, I'm not so . . . [*pauses*] . . . well, I just don't want to probably draw attention to myself. I mean, we're there for the *Lord*, really we are, as a community. So that would be inappropriate . . . and I am almost seventy! I don't want to make a fool of myself! I really don't! [*Laughs loudly*] So, I am restrained. Now, if that type of worship was what I wanted, I would go to a charismatic church where you raise your hands. But that's not the focus for me. I'll bob my head or tap my toe on Sundays.

Although Jill insists that she is not a "frozen chosen" Presbyterian, like many mainline Protestants, she does have strong ideas about appropriate expressive behavior during worship. Bobbing her head or tapping her toe are fine. Dancing would be inappropriate in a church service, but dancing around her living room to "sort of worshipful" music is fun and good.

This phenomenon of Presbyterians being more musically "defrosted" outside of church illustrates their relationship to broader Christian worship culture and the Contemporary music industry. In *God Rock, Inc.: The Business of Niche Music*, ethnomusicologist Andrew Mall writes that "attending a worship service and attending a concert are two very distinct experiences with entirely separate sets of expectations and objectives."[20] As a result, different types of Contemporary music have arisen to meet these contrasting public and private needs. This is important because Mall, building on work by ethnomusicologists Monique Ingalls[21] and Thomas Turino,[22] draws a distinction between Contemporary music in participatory contexts (in "congregational song," we sing *together*) and presentational contexts (in which artists sing *to* us). Mall elaborates:

> Christian music scholars have tended to distinguish . . . music that enables you to connect to God both in public moments (at a church's worship service) and in private ones (a solo devotional at home with your morning coffee), reveals theological lessons and truths, and enables religious reflection; and . . . music that entertains you, gets you to dance, or distracts you from banal daily chores and activities.[23]

Jill illustrates this division: using one type of music for free movement at home and another type of music for more subdued movements in church. This follows broader cultural patterns that promote one type of interaction with Christian music in the private sphere, and a different type of interaction in communal worship.

Jill attends the Contemporary service but still imposes behavioral restrictions on herself in church. At the same time, she recognizes that it is her own sense of restraint that is guiding her (in)action. Most worshipers in her church are similarly restrained. Another Contemporary congregant in her fifties explained, "Singing is like praying to me, except really excited! It's an opportunity to be over the top and not be embarrassed. It's like 'Thank you, Thank you, Thank you God! You're so wonderful!! Wonderful!!' And you know you can just sing and everybody's doing it." She only felt

208 / (White)Washing Our Sins Away

comfortable being expressive because "everybody's doing it." It was her perceived context for her actions—singing heartily, swaying gently side to side, and occasionally clapping—that rendered them "over the top."

Another Presbyterian woman, raised in Kentucky and living in Tennessee—we'll call her Lynn—offered a typical explanation of how Contemporary worship was encouraging her to be tolerant of decreasing cultural formality in herself and others:

> LYNN: I think it's far more eclectic, casual in the Contemporary service. I still am not able to do that real well. Like, I can't do the jeans. But that's just my own thing.
>
> JUSTICE: Why wouldn't you want to wear jeans?
>
> LYNN: It's just the tradition I was raised is very—[*considers*] that's where you go to honor God. To honor God, you look your best. That's kind of my mindset still. Now, it's not like it was. I went *years* before I wore pants to church and now I don't wear dresses, ever, if I can help it! So, that's just my own tradition.
>
> JUSTICE: So, what function, then, do you feel like dress has in church?
>
> LYNN: It really doesn't have any. It really doesn't matter to me what anybody around me is wearing.
>
> JUSTICE: But what about for you?
>
> LYNN: I don't go out and buy a new Easter dress anymore like I used to. I finally quit that. Actually, I wear the same things to church that I wear to work. I don't really have separate wardrobes. Can't afford to have separate wardrobes. But I still will not, I just won't, I don't wear jeans to church. Now, I wear cropped pants now to church, which is kind of a big step. Cropped pants. And flip flops. Dressier flip flops. And that's because my feet always hurt.
>
> JUSTICE: Now, why would you want dressier flip-flops, or to dress up? What is the meaning behind it for you?

Social Diversity / 209

LYNN: In the sixties, it was kind of like, it was the same thing as when you went to the doctor. We *still* talk about this; my friends and I talk about this and here we are in our midfifties! When you went to the doctor, you dressed up. When you rode on an airplane, *oh my gosh!* You wore your Sunday best. So, it comes from that. Why ever it was, I don't know. It was just the time, the culture at the time.

JUSTICE: So, it doesn't have any theological applications?

LYNN: You know, it is a tad about the respect. Respecting the house of God. And that may be something my parents taught me. Because everybody did it back then. You had to have a big old Easter hat, you know.

JUSTICE: Oh, I remember as a little girl, having new Easter dresses.

LYNN: [*Smiles*] Oh absolutely, and ruffly socks and patent leather shoes! You just did it, and it's kind of hard to break out of that.

I had to nod in agreement, because I remember Easter in the early 1980s being the first time each year that my childhood self was finally allowed to wear white frilly ankle socks and white patent leather Mary Janes.

A desire to break away from old routines kept for their own sake and from White Anglo-Saxon Protestant (WASP) hegemonic midcentury mindsets came to dominate the discourse of incorporating Contemporary worship behavior in many mainline Protestant churches. Individual congregants, like Lynn, were working to balance internal self-restraint and restriction with external tolerance-signaling declarations that "it doesn't really matter to me what anybody around me does."

Like Lynn, most mainline congregants were careful not to actually say the "opposing" music was *bad*, just that they didn't like it for themselves. They tended to express themselves in a first-person, feeling-based language. Consider these comments from a mix of Traditional and Contemporary worshipers expressing their opinions about their less-preferred musical style:

That organ stuff doesn't turn me on. I don't relate to it.

It's just too draggy, weighted. It's just so heavy feeling. I don't think that feels good to me.

It's not my style.

I would never choose to turn on and listen to the music done in the Traditional service.

I guess that appeals to other people, but [*shudders/shakes shoulders*] I just don't like it as well [*laughs*]!

Even Hillsboro's Traditional choir director was quick to clarify that her judgment of Contemporary music and everything with it (including instrumentation) is not based on the music's inherent evil: "It's not that choruses and everything are *bad*. I don't mean to say that."

Rather than making universally applicable truth claims (e.g., "organs are bad, guitars are evil"), worshipers tended to express themselves through individually centered aesthetic preferences. Ethnomusicologist Kiri Miller calls this tactfully withholding judgment a way to "make space for pluralist tolerance."[24] Pluralistic tolerance, in turn, makes space for "emotives," or emotion-heavy statements that alter the state of their own speakers.[25] As a result, many people feel better about themselves when they express their strong views in a tolerant, subjective way. For example, "I guess that appeals to other people" (I am aware that other people have different opinions than I do), "but I just don't like it as well" (I feel safe to assert my own opinion) or "I know it's a *thing*" (I am aware that other people like it), "but that organ stuff doesn't turn *me* on" (my opinion). By qualifying the judgment-heavy statement as only reflecting their own subjective stance, worshipers can both truthfully express their opinions and experience themselves as tolerant of others.

Congregants feel free to support the "other" style of worship in large part because they are not compelled to experience it. Worshipers describe the *possibility* of visiting either service as empowering and symbolizing diversity: "Sherry is incredibly talented . . . I may be missing a lot at the Traditional service." Keeping the experience of such musical diversity optional—and thereby largely unrealized—renders it enriching rather than threatening. More musicians and congregants value the (unrealized) opportunity to participate in the internal Other rather than actually experience the Other. They also greatly value the few worshipers who do choose to interact with the internal Other.

Defrosting

I think that in the more Traditional service, the more formal liturgy and more formal clothes and things like that have a kind of intervening quality. In the Contemporary service there's a move away from that, basically a statement that that [formality] gets in the way; it's a distraction, get that out of there.

It's all about the church and church culture, and that this or that's required or this or that enhances or facilitates one's relationship with God.

—Hillsboro pastor David Kidd

When church cultures can change over time, the ways that people relate to each other and the divine changes, too. One elderly Hillsboro elder chuckled as he explained that he had "been worshiping in a Traditional style for his entire life, and that's been a while!" He pointed to his white hair and laughed. "Doing something new is a nice, healthy change. I genuinely like the difference and the greater degree of informality [in the Contemporary service]." For this man and many other congregants, Contemporary worship created a new space for imperfection and authenticity through informality. Another septuagenarian explained:

I used to prefer the Traditional because I grew up that way. However, I'm ancient—I'm seventy-three! [*Laughs*] . . . but I got to the point where I really enjoy the Contemporary service. I like the idea that if that guy wants to say something, I don't remember his name, but if the pastor asks a question when he's preaching, this guy will answer it. So, who cares?! And I like it because it is not so formal that you can't express a feeling or say Amen if you want to or that sort of thing.

This "defrosted," or even "thawed," openness resonates with America's increasingly informal society but contrasts centuries of Presbyterian and

212 / (White)Washing Our Sins Away

White mainline Protestant religious heritage and identity. Mainline congregations and individuals often had some degrees of conflicted self-perception about how they could best use potentially advantageous tools of Contemporary worship. Mainline churches tended to mitigate stark differences between Contemporary and Traditional, but the genres still registered as contrasting enough to be useful. By understanding Contemporary as providing such a strong contrast to Traditional, congregants and congregations were able to experience themselves in a new light. Another septuagenarian explained:

> And I've gotten so that I like the music. I used to think, "Oh they're just trying to use this *modern* music!" But, no, it's really got a message in it. But I also like the choir and the formality of the other service, even though it's not really very formal here at Hillsboro. I mean, I worked at [neighboring] Westminster [Presbyterian] for a year, I was on staff there, and their service is very, very, very conservative [*corrects himself*], no, not conservative, Traditional. I mean, they follow the letter of the law in the Book of Order on how you're supposed to do a worship service. It's a beautiful service and I enjoy it, but so many times when you get this very extreme order of worship it's almost like, well, what if God wants to do something a little different in the service? Or, God doesn't *really* care if you make a mistake or if the speaker system goes "whoo" or something. It's more like we're worshiping that way because that's what we're "supposed to" do.

Concepts of how worship is "supposed to" be have continued to strongly influence mainline Protestant worship.

Yet, even as Presbyterians have been defrosting and the mainline has been expanding its tolerance for expression and emotion in worship, certain other types of diversity have remained elusive. The social changes that accompanied Contemporary music have been pushing up against existing cultural patterns, but those patterns are deeply entrenched. As Beverly Tatum writes in the 2017 introduction to the twentieth-anniversary edition of her classic *Why Are All the Black Kids Sitting Together in the Cafeteria?*:

> Twenty years after I wrote these chapters [in 1997], how we see ourselves and each other is still being shaped by racial

Social Diversity / 213

categories and the stereotypes attached to them. The patterns of behavior I described then still ring true because our social context still reinforces racial hierarchies, and still limits our opportunities for genuinely mutual, equitable, and affirming relationships in the neighborhoods, in classrooms, or in the workplace.[26]

Tatum's list does not include "houses of worship," but as mainline Protestant demographics in the 2020s continue to suggest, social context indeed still reinforces racial hierarchies, and still limits opportunities for relationships. The Reverend Dr. Martin Luther King Jr's label of Sunday morning as "the most segregated hour in America" has continued to ring true into the twenty-first century.

When mainline Protestant churches adopted the Worship Wars framework of Traditional versus Contemporary worship, they were not expecting a musical panacea that would suddenly find their pews (and folding chairs) overflowing with people of every type. Yet these churches did hope to expand their diversity, to better serve their own congregants and others. Faith communities began intense journeys of reorganization and introspection. Initially, they often did not fully understand the multivalent impacts of musical changes. However, these churches very quickly learned that adding guitars, amplification, and lighting also led to shifts in how they thought about their own worship traditions. Shifts in music created ripples resulting in broader changes in mainline agency and authority structures. Many of these changes were departures from existing cultural and theological principles, but an undercurrent of necessity was driving musical choices. Churches that successfully navigated the social tensions of the Worship Wars had to face all of these implications without schism. As middle Tennessee's executive presbyter Phil Leftwich had explained, "It's usually the anxiety that drives the anger and conflict. It's not the anger that drives it; it's anxiety that drives it." His comments from 2009 continue to be relevant to White mainline Protestantism's general understanding of itself within multicultural postmillennial America.

Conclusion

Music, Faith, and Reconfiguring American Protestant Identities

A Typical Sunday Morning Worship Service, Hillsboro Presbyterian Church

Five minutes before the service was supposed to begin, a few people had gathered, but the worship space was still largely empty. Only after the prelude had begun did people really start filling the space. As worshipers entered, ushers handed out paper bulletins that outlined the order of service. Parents calmed their children and people found places for themselves in rows of seating facing the front of the worship space. Musicians were playing an opening piece to welcome everyone and create atmosphere. The worshipers listened to the music, but did not sing along with it. Most sat in silence, reading the bulletin or praying, but some talked softly among themselves.

The congregants grew quiet as candles were lit on a table in the front of the worship space and the ministers proceeded to their seats. As the prelude music ended, the head minister stood to face the gathered people, greeted them, and invited them to worship.

Except for the seated keyboard player leading the music, those who were physically able rose to sing the opening song of praise and gathering. The congregation was nearly all White, but the majority of them had white hair, as well. While the service featured music during this part of worship each Sunday, the exact musical selection varied from week to week. Words were provided so congregants could sing along. They sang mostly in unison, but the musicians leading worship had rehearsed the

216 / (White)Washing Our Sins Away

piece and sang distinct harmonic parts. No one moved much during the singing, at most some of the musicians and congregants subtly shifted their weight from foot to foot or swayed slightly.

Everyone sat down when the music ended, except for the pastor who announced upcoming events in the life of the congregation, service possibilities, and fellowship activities. Then, as indicated in the bulletin, everyone else stood up again to sing. This time, the song's lyrics specifically supported the theme of the coming sermon. After the singing finished, the associate pastor invited the congregation to take their seats. She read a passage of scripture and led the worshipers in a prayer.

At the close of the prayer, four ushers walked from the back of the assembled congregation to a table in the front. As the pastor encouraged the congregation to reflect on the gifts that God had given them, music started, and the ushers began passing the collection plates down each row of congregants. From the keyboard, the lead musician visually noted the ushers' progress and tailored the length of the musical piece in response.

Following the offertory, the assistant pastor stood in front of the congregation and prayed. The other participants remained silent until the opening phrase of the Lord's Prayer, "as Jesus taught us to pray, saying . . ." The congregation joined in a unison recitation of this ritual text.

Next, the musicians played while the congregation listened in a time of reflection. The exact content of this part of the service varied from week to week, but the music's title or lyrics always echoed the sermon's theme. Congregations received the music with a range of responses, from applause to silence. This week, a murmur of approval ran through the congregation and a few people firmly, quietly said, "Amen."

Introducing the sermon, the head pastor read a scripture passage, prayed that the sermon would reveal divine wisdom to the listeners, and began to preach. Aside from laughing at the pastor's jokes or the very affirmative "Amen," the worshipers sat silently to listen.

Musicians led the congregation in a final song that lyrically built upon the sermon's message. As the worshipers sang, the altar candles were extinguished and the pastors walked back down the center aisle to the rear of the worship space. The congregation continued facing the front of the room as the music ended. Speaking from behind the people, the pastor intoned a benediction, closing with, "And now, beloved . . . go out into the world, and fear nothing." A moment of silence hovered over the congregation, but the stillness was soon dispelled by a jubilant postlude. Music swelled and conversation erupted as worshipers greeted each other,

Conclusion / 217

laughed, and shook hands with the pastors before spilling out into the hallway.

Contrasts, Continuities, and Constructs of Difference

The preceding narrative could describe *either* Traditional or Contemporary worship at Hillsboro Presbyterian on any given Sunday. This description is very different from the depiction of the services in the interlude between chapters 3 and 4, but it is no less accurate. In this book's interlude, I highlighted contrasts between the services to illustrate how congregants chose to experience Contemporary and Traditional as *very* different. Here, however, I highlight the continuities between Hillsboro's two services. This description shows how congregants could chose to experience the two worship styles as very similar. None of the actual musical or social elements change, and neither descriptive technique is more truthful or accurate, but—like a useable past—the narratives and perspectives they represent serve different aims.

A reductionist description like mine here is helpful in describing continuities: similar structures, using similar media, similar worship elements with similar functions. At Hillsboro and most other mainline Protestant congregations, Traditional and Contemporary worship services tend to follow a preset structure of music and speech each week. The music is chosen to facilitate congregational participation in group song. Congregational expressive behavior does not differ drastically between the services; in both, the worshipers sit and stand quietly in rows without much interpersonal interaction. The worshipers sing and pray at set times, the clergy and musicians adhere to planned worship elements, and spontaneous interjections or participation from anyone occurs rarely, if ever. All of this happens in sonic spaces that have been designed or rearranged with worship in mind.

In short, the worship styles share substantial overarching commonalities—but these similarities become clearest when these worship styles are compared to possibilities from other major religious traditions: trance, animal sacrifice, fasting, dancing, daylong ritual services, exorcism, possession, snake handling, extemporaneous prayer, spontaneous musical expression, and similar elements. Given what they could be doing to communicate with the divine, mainline Protestants have Traditional and Contemporary worship conforming to sociologist Mark Chaves's general

218 / (White)Washing Our Sins Away

description of American churchgoing: "Whatever else happens at collective events in congregations, worship in the United States mainly involves people getting together to sing and listen to somebody talk."[1]

So how and why would mainline Protestants—and many other American Christians—chose to hear the differences between Traditional and Contemporary? Human beings have a unique ability to construct our experience. As phenomenology demonstrates, two people can perceive the same stimuli as either very similar or very different. On varying levels of consciousness and awareness, we choose to assign value to what we perceive as creating meaning and order in the world around us. This happens both in the world at large and in worship.[2]

Choosing to Hear Useable Difference

While turn-of-the-millennium mainline Protestants could have been hearing similarities across Traditional and Contemporary worship, most were hearing dissonance. Presbyterians and other mainline Protestants adopted Worship Wars rhetoric to accentuate differences across intersectional sonic, social, and sacred spheres. For these worshipers, Traditional and Contemporary had different answers to many questions from cultural heritage and institutional history; what to play, what to sing, and how to sing; how to relate to neighboring Christian groups and the limits of congregational unity; and negotiations of agency, authority, and behavioral norms.

Yet, in a historically unprecedented approach, many churches tried to support both Traditional *and* Contemporary worship. Churches wanted to have their cake and eat it, too; Traditional and Contemporary were similar enough to manage under one steeple, yet different enough to raise fears of congregational strife or schism. Issues of guitars versus organs amplified into more abstract contrasts of musical immanence versus musical transcendence (see chapter 4). The holistic musical negotiations brought threats of serious congregational conflict. What was—and still is—at stake for mainline Protestants in terms of music, power, and diversity?

When churches devoted time, energy, and resources to successfully navigating the divisive threats of the Worship Wars, they could rightfully celebrate themselves as resilient, tolerant, and diverse faith communities. Taking risks in order to keep faith communities vibrant mattered for mainline Protestants beyond local-level institutional survival; active congregations demonstrated the continued cultural relevance of mainline Protestantism in America. Although the membership remained predominantly older and White, these communities enjoyed understanding themselves as willing to bend and change.

Multiple factors—from cultural hegemony and demographics to economics and theology—combined to make the Traditional-Contemporary dichotomy subconsciously and overtly appealing to mainline Protestants. This branch of Christianity had historically enjoyed cultural prominence, but over the last half of the twentieth century, American institutional affiliation with Christianity in general had been decreasing. Cultural shifts and new patterns of living and working had Americans renegotiating their relationships with institutions, from bridge clubs and bowling leagues to scout troops and churches.[3] By the turn of the millennium, mainline Protestants had suffered particularly sharp membership losses, which contrasted painfully with their previous cultural hegemonic power. Remaining mainline Protestant membership continued to conform to the group's traditionally well-educated, affluent, theologically moderate, predominantly White norms, but the composition of the United States was moving in a more diverse direction. If mainline churches wanted to retain their current position within American culture (much less regain their former prominence), these institutions would need to diversify along with broader national demographics.

Many mainline Protestant congregations and denominations had long been working toward goals of diversification. Yet they only met with modest levels of success and the mainline remained predominantly White.

When individuals and congregations have tried to move forward, they have often found themselves hampered by historically ingrained patterns of behavior. As sociologist Michael Emerson observes, rather than resulting in a socially preeminent postracial Church, efforts to create openness often had unintended effects: "In the aggregate, multiracial congregations are doing exactly what pastors of color tell me they fear—that they will serve merely as a tool into white assimilation."[4] In *Redisciplining the White Church: From Cheap Diversity to True Solidarity*, Pastor David Swanson explains:

> It's not that white Christians haven't tried to bridge this gap of experience and trust. Sociologists define a multiracial church as one in which no one racial group makes up more than 80 percent of the congregation. Between 1998 and 2012, Protestant churches saw these diverse congregations rise from 3

220 / (White)Washing Our Sins Away

percent to 12 percent. Yet . . . statistics don't tell the full story of white Christianity's segregation from the rest of the body of Christ. In fact, sociologists have found that many multiracial churches with a significant percentage of white people end up perpetuating white cultural assumptions.[5]

Even progressive congregations have struggled to move beyond cultural assumptions. Common turn-of-the-millennium mainline strategies to increase diversity in mainline churches, from the architectural innovations discussed in chapter 6 to incorporating multilingual hymnody and songs and hiring worship leaders of color,[6] have often fallen flat. One representative example from Hillsboro Presbyterian sticks in my memory.[7]

During fieldwork in 2009, I had invited a Black Baptist ethnomusicologist colleague to come observe Hillsboro's congregational exchange with Spruce Street Baptist Church (the oldest African American church in Nashville). As we were walking across the parking lot, an older White woman came over to say hello. Turning to my colleague, she warmly said, "Oh, I am so glad to have you visiting here today. I just love your choir!"

My colleague didn't miss a beat. She replied, "Well, thank you ma'am, I'm glad to be here. But I would be surprised if you've heard my choir. I'm from Florida. I'm just visiting this morning to do some musical research with my colleague."

Instantly, the Hillsboro congregant realized her mistake and looked mortified. She had laid bare the assumption that the only Black people visiting Hillsboro that morning would be members of the Black sister church. Since no Black people normally worshiped in the Presbyterian congregation, her assumption was not illogical. Even though the historically White church had a relationship with the historically Black church, congregational diversity did not result.

The worshipers in their pews were not providing mainline Protestants with much racial diversity, but the musical tensions of the Worship Wars gave mainline Protestants—and other White Christians—the opportunity to feel relevant and diverse. With demographics and membership numbers in mind, turn-of-the-millennium mainline Protestants knew they had to take steps quickly. They looked to their religious neighbors for strategies and inspiration. American evangelicals, their closest cousins, were not substantially more racially diverse, but they were doing somewhat better

Conclusion / 221

on the membership front (including having younger members on average than mainline Protestants).[8] Evangelicals had also been more culturally flexible, experimenting with and adopting popular musics into their worship. Mainline Protestants hoped that a simple change of playlist might help their situation. Initially, many congregations thought, "Why not add some guitars and drums if they would make such a big difference?"

Mainline Protestants soon discovered, however, that adding the drums, guitars, and evangelical music of Contemporary worship held further implications—some expected and some less anticipated. Churches hoped that adding Contemporary worship would give them a useable musical diversity. Contemporary music existed against Traditional music in the dichotomy of the Worship Wars. Since the rhetoric of these aesthetic conflicts positioned Traditional and Contemporary as incompatible opposites, congregations successfully balancing both styles rightfully felt a sense of accomplishment. These churches experienced themselves as projecting diversity and tolerance in the face of potential conflict and schism. The musical diversity did not directly address racial diversity, but it did help White mainline Protestants feel like they were proactively taking steps to negotiate their changing position with the United States' social and sacred landscape.

When mainline Protestants began highlighting the "useable differences" between Traditional and Contemporary worship as a diversity strategy, extramusical sacred and social contrasts came along with the sonic contrasts. Contemporary music brought increased evangelical influence. As they became protective of their own traditions changing, mainline Protestants became aware of how Contemporary music was applying a new "cultural tool kit"—or repertoire of shared ideas and behaviors that organize and interpret reality[9]—to mainline worship practices and culture. In their study *Divided by Faith*, sociologists Michael Emerson and Christian Smith found that White evangelicals had developed a cultural tool kit with three main tools linked by theology: freewill individualism, relationalism, and antistructuralism.[10] Building on this work, sociologist Robert P. Jones notes that as mainline churches incorporated more Contemporary music and other evangelical source materials, "the cultural tool kits of white mainline Protestants increasingly contain[ed] the individualist tools of their white evangelical cousins."[11] Mainline Protestants had been emphasizing musical changes, but interrelated changes in other areas also had far-reaching echoes.

222 / (White)Washing Our Sins Away

Moving Forward

By the 2020s, the flames of the Worship Wars have largely died down throughout White Christian America. Although some churches are still negotiating the now-familiar issues of organs versus guitars and hymns versus praise choruses, an entire generation has passed since the Worship Wars began. Two generations have passed since the Contemporary worship movement got its start in the 1960s and '70s. Incendiary levels of musical tension between Contemporary and Traditional musical styles have occurred, but such intense levels of conflict have largely burnt themselves out.

While some congregations have remained strong and vibrant, overall, mainline Protestant churches have continued to lose members. They have also remained predominantly White. Evangelicals have fared only marginally better in terms of membership numbers and racial diversity, although during the presidency of Donald Trump, White evangelicalism gained political and social influence as the more visible face of American Christianity. The moderates and liberals of the mainline were becoming concerned about how shifting narratives about race in America were conflating Whiteness and conservativism. As Robert P. Jones writes in *White Too Long*, "Increasing anxieties around the perceived decline of white identity and white Christian culture are driving right-wing extremism both at home and abroad."[12] Overall, American churches have slightly racially diversified, but very few congregations are multiracial. Religious "nones"—people who may have strong beliefs but prefer not to formally affiliate with organized religion—are growing rapidly.

Yet, as the 2015 Pew Religious Landscape Survey reports, 14.7 percent of Americans still identify as mainline Protestant. Such Christians remain a significant group in the nation's religious life. Although they are still negotiating their future, these historical American congregations and their musical traditions continue. Concluding *The End of White Christian America*, Robert P. Jones writes about the trajectory of previously hegemonic Christian groups, and specifically mainline Protestants:

> Confronted with the psychic discomfort that results from a lack of cultural confidence and security, the greatest threat to White Christian America's descendants is the siren song of nostalgia . . . but nostalgia is not only unfaithful to the past, it also threatens the present . . . With regard to White Chris-

tian America's mainline descendants, the culture has moved in the direction of their more socially liberal public agenda but without their banner at the head of the parade. . . . They risk apathy if they succumb to wistfulness for a powerful past—or perhaps worse, to a kind of autopilot press release activism that mistakes being busy for making real change in the world.[13]

Following the contentious, politically active summer of 2020, national conversations around antiracism and allyship have expanded dialogues to new levels. The election of Joseph Biden, a liberal Catholic, as the forty-sixth president of the United States has set the stage for a potential new era of activism in line with mainline Protestantism's historically socially liberal agenda. The social pause and distancing of the COVID-19 pandemic has given much of American society a chance to renegotiate how we relate to others.

Utilizing the Traditional-Contemporary dichotomy of the Worship Wars helped mainline Protestants navigate their turn-of-the-millennium identity within America's rapidly shifting social and religious climate. As illustrated in the beginning of this chapter, people could have selectively heard newer worship musics as continuations of ever-evolving worship traditions. Instead, people learned to hear differences within a certain value structure and to play those differences off against each other. Through this tension, mainline Protestants did begin to experience new levels of sonic diversity; perhaps these changes will pave the way for new levels of social diversity as well. To find their way forward, mainline Protestants will have to recognize that they are now one of many religious voices in a shifting, changing diverse America. Only time will tell if mainline Protestants will choose to hear contrasts or continuities—and how those strategies will serve them—as the twenty-first century unfolds.

Notes

Introduction: Academia, Presbyterians, and Me

1. Belsie, "New Nationalism on the Rise"; Frank, "One Nation, Indescribable"; Powell, "Rethinking Who They Are."
2. Marti, *Worship across the Racial Divide.*
3. Merriam, "Ethnomusicology."
4. Hood, "Training and Research Methods in Ethnomusicology."
5. About William and Mary, "History and Traditions."
6. Campbell, "An Address on Colleges, Delivered in the City of Wheeling, Va., 1854."
7. Brill, *Religion and the Rise of the University.*
8. Minor, "Body Ritual among the Nacirema."
9. Kelman, *Shout to the Lord*, xiii.
10. Coined by ethnomusicologist Christopher Small, the concept of "musicking" is a verb that holistically, succinctly combines sonic and social aspects of making music. Small, *Musicking.*
11. Hollinger, "After Cloven Tongues of Fire," 23.
12. Kendi, *How to Be an Antiracist*, 9.

Chapter 1. Using Sound to Reconfigure Mainline Protestant Sacred and Social Identity

1. Case, "One of Syracuse's Oldest Churches Closes on Easter."
2. "U.S. Census Bureau QuickFacts"; "Pew Religious Landscape Study."
3. Jones, *End of White Christian America*, 1.
4. "Pew Religious Landscape Study."
5. Hout, Greeley, and Wilde, "Demographic Imperative in Religious Change in the United States."

225

226 / Notes to Chapter 1

6. "Pew Religious Landscape Study."

7. In the United States, Presbyterians fall into three main denominations: the liberal Presbyterian Church (U.S.A.), the moderate Evangelical Presbyterian Church, and the conservative Presbyterian Church in America.

8. A 2008 survey conducted by the Presbyterian Church (U.S.A.) revealed typical demographics. Racially, 96 percent of members self-identified as White. Sixty-six percent of Presbyterians had earned at least bachelor's degree, with 30 percent also holding a higher degree. Just half of Presbyterians reported being employed; median age of members is sixty years and two out of every five were retired. Yet, median household income in 2007 was still over $80,000. Thirty-eight percent of Presbyterians reported 2007 income over $100,000, while only 6 percent reported earning less than $20,000. While outliers and exceptions exist, in sum, these figures summarize the PC(USA) as having a financially secure, well-educated, mature, White membership. Other mainline Protestants in the United States are similarly well situated. See Research Services, Presbyterian Church (U.S.A.), "Religious and Demographic Profile of Presbyterians, 2008," 11–14.

9. Finke and Stark, *Churching of America, 1776–2005.*

10. Roof and McKinney, *American Mainline Religion,* 6.

11. Scherer, "Mainline."

12. Wuthnow and Evans, *Quiet Hand of God,* 27.

13. Wuthnow and Evans, 7.

14. Rommen, *Mek Some Noise: Gospel Music and the Ethics of Style in Trinidad.*

15. Spittler, "Are Pentacostals and Charismatics Fundamentalists? A Review of American Uses of These Categories"; Turner, *Bill Bright and Campus Crusade for Christ.*

16. Ingalls, "Awesome in the Place: Sound, Space, and Identity in North American Evangelical Worship," 7.

17. Coote, "Hymns That Keep on Going," 30.

18. Etymology and definitions from *Oxford English Dictionary Online* and *Merriam-Webster Online.* According to the research tool Google Books Ngram that chronologically tracks the frequency of words in published books, http://ngrams.googlelabs.com/

19. Keightley, "Reconsidering Rock," 131.

20. Miller, *Traveling Home,* 171.

21. "Mainstream," www.urbandictionary.com.

22. Wuthnow and Evans, *Quiet Hand of God,* 5.

23. Grossman, "Most Religious Groups in USA Have Lost Ground, Survey Finds."

24. Ammerman, *Congregation and Community.*

25. Baum and Singh, "Organizational Niches and the Dynamics of Organizational Mortality."

Notes to Chapter 1 / 227

26. Wuthnow, *Producing the Sacred*.

27. Ammerman, *Congregation and Community*.

28. Ammerman, 36.

29. Wilford, *Sacred Subdivisions: The Postmodern Transformation of American Evangelicalism*.

30. Jones, *End of White Christian America*.

31. Cf. Cimino and Lattin, *Shopping for Faith*; Roof, *Spiritual Marketplace*; Warren, *Purpose-Driven Church*.

32. "Definition of a Megachurch from Hartford Institute for Religion Research."

33. Loveland and Wheeler, *From Meetinghouse to Megachurch*, 115.

34. "American Congregations at the Beginning of the 21st Century: National Congregations Study," 3.

35. Jones, *White Too Long: The Legacy of White Supremacy in American Churches*, 97.

36. Ammerman, *Congregation and Community*, 131.

37. Ammerman, 36.

38. Ellingson, *Megachurch and the Mainline*, 45.

39. Greater Good, "Diversity Definition | What Is Diversity."

40. Swanson, *Rediscipling the White Church*, 30.

41. Wuthnow and Evans, *Quiet Hand of God*.

42. Marcum, interview with Deborah Justice.

43. Ingalls, *Singing the Congregation*, 1.

44. Turner, *Bill Bright and Campus Crusade for Christ*, 6.

45. Nix, interview with Deborah Justice.

46. Thorngate, "New Harmonies: Music and Identity at Four Congregations."

47. Goffman, *Frame Analysis*.

48. Ingalls, "Awesome in the Place: Sound, Space, and Identity in North American Evangelical Worship"; Roof, *Spiritual Marketplace*.

49. "Should You Make Your Preferences Clear?"

50. Randel, "Canons in the Musicological Toolbox," 19.

51. Weber, *Economy and Society*.

52. Niebuhr, *Social Sources of Denominationalism*.

53. Schneider, *Religion in Twentieth Century America*.

54. Douglas, "Social Preconditions of Enthusiasm and Heterodoxy."

55. Turner, *Ritual Process*.

56. Turner, "Liminality and Communitas."

57. Ellwood, *Alternative Altars*.

58. Alberoni, *Movement and Institution*.

59. Warner, *New Wine in Old Wineskins*, 46.

60. Levine, *Highbrow/Lowbrow*.

61. Asad, *Genealogies of Religion*.

228 / Notes to Chapter 1

62. Dueck, "Binding and Loosing in Song: Conflict, Identity, and Canadian Mennonite Music," 248.

63. Chaves, *Congregations in America*, 140.

64. Ingalls, *Singing the Congregation*, 1.

65. Ruth, "Eruption of the Worship Wars: The Coming of Conflict," 3.

66. In the last ten years, the burgeoning field of congregational music studies has generated significant scholarship on the Worship Wars, often vis-à-vis evangelicalism. See, among others, Dueck, "Binding and Loosing in Song: Conflict, Identity, and Canadian Mennonite Music"; Ingalls, *Singing the Congregation*; Ingalls, "Awesome in the Place: Sound, Space, and Identity in North American Evangelical Worship"; Justice, "A Cosmopolitan Dichotomy: Mainline Protestantism and Contemporary versus Traditional Worship Music"; Justice, "Sonic Change, Social Change, Sacred Change: Music and the Reconfiguration of American Christianity"; Nekola, "Between This World and the Next: The Musical 'Worship Wars' and Evangelical Ideology in the United States, 1960–2005"; Ruth, "Eruption of the Worship Wars: The Coming of Conflict."

67. Dueck, "Binding and Loosing in Song: Conflict, Identity, and Canadian Mennonite Music," 230.

68. Loveland and Wheeler quoted in Ellingson, *Megachurch and the Mainline*, 66.

69. Ellingson, *Megachurch and the Mainline*.

70. Towns, *Putting an End to Worship Wars*.

71. Long, *Beyond the Worship Wars*.

72. Byars, *Future of Protestant Worship*.

73. Johnson, "Singing Down Walls of Race, Ethnicity, and Tradition in an African American Megachurch."

74. Jones, *Flaming?*

75. Costen, *In Spirit and in Truth*, xv.

76. Butler, "Musical Style and Experience in a Brooklyn Pentecostal Church: An 'Insider's' Perspective."

77. No I Has Heard, "Worship Wars and the Black Church."

78. Chapman, "Worship in Black and White," 27.

79. Corbitt, *Sound of the Harvest: Music's Mission in Church and Culture*.

80. Makujina, *Measuring the Music: Another Look at the Contemporary Christian Music Debate*.

81. Makujina; Smith, *Let Those Who Have Ears Hear*; Smith, *Oh, Be Careful Little Ears*; Towns, *Putting an End to Worship Wars*.

82. "Taking off the White Mask"; Nekola, "'More than Just a Music.'"

83. Corbitt, *Sound of the Harvest: Music's Mission in Church and Culture*; Dawn, *Reaching Out without Dumbing Down*; Hustad, *True Worship: Reclaiming the Wonder and Majesty*; Langford, *Transitions in Worship: Moving from Traditional to Contemporary*; Tilley, *Inventing Catholic Tradition*.

Notes to Chapter 2 / 229

84. Hustad, *True Worship: Reclaiming the Wonder and Majesty*, 84.

85. Dawn, *Reaching Out without Dumbing Down*, 112–13.

86. Nekola, "Between This World and the Next: The Musical 'Worship Wars' and Evangelical Ideology in the United States, 1960–2005," 2–3.

87. Ingalls, *Singing the Congregation*, 6.

88. "Focus on 'Worship Wars' Hides the Real Issues Regarding Connection to God."

89. Wuthnow, *Quiet Hand of God*, 7.

90. Swanson, *Redisciplining the White Church*, 32.

Chapter 2. "The Least Puzzling or Flamboyant of Christians"

1. The Presbyterian Presence: The Twentieth-Century Experience, a series edited by Milton J. Coalter, John M. Mulder, and Louis B. Weeks: *The Presbyterian Predicament: Six Perspectives*, *The Mainstream Protestant "Decline": The Presbyterian Pattern*, *The Confessional Mosaic: Presbyterians and Twentieth-Century Theology*, *The Diversity of Discipleship: Presbyterians and Twentieth-Century Christian Witness*, *The Organizational Revolution: Presbyterians and American Denominationalism*, *The Pluralistic Vision: Presbyterians and Mainstream Protestant Education and Leadership*, and *The Re-Forming Tradition: Presbyterians and Mainstream Protestantism, 1990–1992*, published by Westminster John Knox Press.

2. Joshi, *White Christian Privilege*, 64–68.

3. Matthew 28:19–20, New International Version.

4. Tisby, *Color of Compromise*, 29.

5. Jones, *White Too Long*, 6.

6. Jones, 6.

7. Jennings, *After Whiteness*, 120.

8. Joshi, *White Christian Privilege*, 6.

9. Jennings, *After Whiteness*, 64.

10. Bauman and Briggs, *Voices of Modernity*, 307.

11. Dueck and Reily, Introduction, 2.

12. Marcus, *Ethnography through Thick and Thin*, 42.

13. Cannell, *Anthropology of Christianity*.

14. Henderson, Dance Discourse in the Music and Lives of Presbyterian Mvano Women in Southern Malawi and A Paradigm of Africanisation: Music of Mvano Women of the Church of Central Africa Presbyterian, Malawi.

15. Kisliuk, *Seize the Dance!*, 149.

16. Keane, *Christian Moderns*, 30.

17. Henderson, Dance Discourse in the Music and Lives of Presbyterian Mvano Women in Southern Malawi, 51; cf. Kartomi, "Processes and Results of Musical Culture Contact," 6.

230 / Notes to Chapter 2

18. Roy's field recordings reside in the Archives of Traditional Music at Indiana University, as well as in the Boulton/Roy Collection in the Harvard Loeb Music Library. Roy's research culminated in the 1998 publication, with Ragheb Moftah and Margit Tóth, of *The Coptic Orthodox Liturgy of St. Basil: With Complete Musical Transcription.* ·

19. For eighteen years, Indiana University doctor of ethnomusicology Henderson "lived and worked in Malawi as an overseas staff person (missionary) of the Presbyterian Church in Canada." Henderson, "Dance Discourse," 13.

20. Titon, " 'Tuned Up with the Grace of God,' " 323.

21. Titon, 320.

22. Miller, *Traveling Home*, 38.

23. Jackson, *White and Negro Spirituals*; Jackson, *White Spirituals in the Southern Uplands*; Montell, *Singing the Glory Down*; Titon, *Powerhouse for God.*

24. Jackson, *White and Negro Spirituals*; Jackson, *White Spirituals in the Southern Uplands*; Jackson, *Story of the Sacred Harp, 1844–1944*; Marini, "Rehearsal for Revival."

25. Mall, *God Rock, Inc.*, 14.

26. Cannell, *Anthropology of Christianity*, 1.

27. Nettl, *Study of Ethnomusicology*, 230.

28. Mall, *God Rock, Inc.*, 22.

29. Brettell, *When They Read What We Write*, 14.

30. Robbins, "Afterword: On Limits, Ruptures, Meaning, and Meaninglessness," 220.

31. Asad, *Genealogies of Religion.*

32. Sahlins, "Sadness of Sweetness."

33. Cannell, *Anthropology of Christianity*, 8.

34. Marini, *Sacred Song in America: Religion, Music, and Public Culture*, ix.

35. Bohlman, "Introduction: Music in American Religious Experience," 10–11.

36. Dueck and Reily, Introduction, 4.

37. Lieberman, Helm, and Palisca, "Should Ethnomusicology Be Abolished?"

38. Laugrand and Oosten, *Inuit Shamanism and Christianity.*

39. Cf. Nettl, *Heartland Excursions.*

40. Randel, "Canons in the Musicological Toolbox," 20.

41. Marini, *Sacred Song in America: Religion, Music, and Public Culture*, ix.

42. Ellingson, *Megachurch and the Mainline*, 8.

43. McGann, *Precious Fountain*, xix.

44. Bohlman, Blumhofer, and Chow, *Music in American Religious Experience*, vi.

45. Ingalls, *Singing the Congregation*, 10.

46. Jones, *End of White Christian America*, 229. Jones is quoting Berger, *Sacred Canopy*, 67.

47. Jones, 231.

Chapter 3. Telling the Story of a Useable Past

1. Tilley, *Inventing Catholic Tradition*, 29.
2. Anderson, *Imagined Communities*.
3. Hobsbawm and Ranger, *Invention of Tradition*.
4. Turner, "Liminality and Communitas."
5. Wegner, *Imaginary Communities*.
6. Wegner, xvi.
7. Hoffman, *Art of Public Prayer*.
8. Cohen, *Making of a Reform Jewish Cantor*, 25.
9. Zamora, *Usable Past*, ix.
10. Jones, *White Too Long*, 6.
11. Jones, 23–24.
12. Noll, " 'Christian America' and 'Christian Canada,' " 362.
13. *History of the Presbyterian Church*.
14. Walker, "Church History," 340.
15. Walker.
16. Walker.
17. Gore, *History of the Cumberland Presbyterian Church in Kentucky to 1988*.
18. Walker, "Church History," 341.
19. A minority of Cumberland Presbyterians chose to retain their own denominational identity and remain separate from the Presbyterian Church U.S.A. The Cumberland Presbyterian Church continues today as an independent denomination with around fifty thousand members.
20. Moorhead, "Presbyterians and Slavery."
21. "2016ResolutionofRepentance.Pdf."
22. Jones, *White Too Long* Jones and *End of White Christian America*; Joshi, *White Christian Privilege*; Kendi, *Stamped from the Beginning*; Tisby, *Color of Compromise*.
23. Jones, *White Too Long*, 48.
24. Kidd and McCurley, interview with Deborah Justice.
25. Walker, "Church History."
26. Walker, 340.
27. Kidd and McCurley, interview with Deborah Justice.
28. Cf. Wilford, *Sacred Subdivisions*.
29. Jones, interview with Deborah Justice.
30. Kidd and McCurley, interview with Deborah Justice.
31. In 1954, $80,000 would be $787,700 in 2021.
32. Walker, "Church History," 339.
33. Most recently available US Census data is from 1940, which listed a Black cook among the household. Census data from 1950, which would have included the larger Singing Hills property, will not be available until April 2022.

232 / Notes to Chapter 4

Given other available data from Nashville estates at the time, the servants were likely Black.

34. Walker, "Church History," 339–340.

35. Walker, 340.

36. Walker, 2.

37. Leftwich, interview with Deborah Justice.

38. Tatum, *Why Are All the Black Kids Sitting Together in the Cafeteria?*, 8.

39. Claman, Butler, and Boyatt, *Acting on Your Faith*.

40. Cf. Dawn, *Reaching Out without Dumbing Down*; Hustad, *True Worship*; Langford, *Transitions in Worship*.

41. Langford, *Transitions in Worship*, 10.

42. Ingalls, *Singing the Congregation*; Lim and Ruth, *Lovin' on Jesus: A Concise History of Contemporary Worship*; Mall, *God Rock, Inc.*

43. McKay and Crawford, *William Billings of Boston*, 10.

44. McKay and Crawford, 15.

45. Noyes, "Group," 464.

46. Position Description for Contemporary Service Music, 2000. Hillsboro Presbyterian Church Archives.

47. Chaves, *Congregations in America*, 161.

48. Rommen, *Mek Some Noise*.

Interlude

1. Music by John Hughes, 1907; lyrics by William Williams, 1745.

2. Music and lyrics by Tim Hughes. ©ThankYou Music, 2001.

3. Music and lyrics by Tony Wood, Chad Cates, Todd Smith, and James Smith. ©New Spring, Inc., Row J Seat 9 Songs, Upper Cates Music, Nkembo Music/Administered by Bug Music, Curb Songs and Okapi One Music/Administered by Curb Songs, 2005. Popularized on Selah's *Bless the Broken Road* in 2006 with Nicole C. Mullen.

4. Music and lyrics by Godfrey Birtill. ©ThankYou Music, 2000.

Chapter 4. Sonic Diversity: Deciding When to Hear Harmony

1. Lim and Ruth, *Lovin' on Jesus*.

2. Chaves, *Congregations in America*, 136.

3. Chaves, 139.

4. Hustad, *True Worship*, 139.

5. Hamilton, "Triumph of the Praise Songs: How Guitars Beat Out the Organ in the Worship Wars."

Notes to Chapter 4 / 233

6. Cf. Kraft, "Organ/Guitar Preference Reflects View of God"; Kraft, "Organ/Guitar Question a Matter of Context"; Long, *Beyond the Worship Wars*; Towns, *Putting an End to Worship Wars*; York, *America's Worship Wars*.

7. Keane, *Christian Moderns*, 247.

8. Dawn, *Reaching Out without Dumbing Down*, 98.

9. Langford, *Transitions in Worship*, 58.

10. Hustad, *True Worship*, 207.

11. Jeffrey J. Noonan, *Guitar in America*.

12. Hustad, *True Worship*, 207.

13. Lim and Ruth, *Lovin' on Jesus*; Ingalls, *Singing the Congregation*; Mall, *God Rock, Inc.*; Nekola, "Between This World and the Next"; Park, Ruth, and Rethmeier, *Worshiping with the Anaheim Vineyard*; Stowe, *No Sympathy for the Devil*.

14. Cf. Makujina, *Measuring the Music*; Smith, *Oh, Be Careful Little Ears*.

15. Nekola, " 'More than Just a Music,' " 412.

16. Ingalls, *Singing the Congregation*, 9.

17. Ingalls, "Sound of Heaven on Earth."

18. Interview with Deborah Justice, June 5, 2008.

19. "Hymn."

20. Presbyterian Hymnal Committee, "A Statement on Language."

21. Holzapfel, "Singing from the Right Songbook"; Blumhofer, *Singing the Lord's Song in a Strange Land*; Marini, "Hymnody and History."

22. Rommen, *Mek Some Noise*.

23. Miller, *Traveling Home*.

24. Etherington, *Protestant Worship*, 91.

25. Burkholder, Grout, and Palisca, *History of Western Music*, 247; Fisher, "Music and Religious Change."

26. Temperley, "Hymn."

27. Marini, "Hymnody and History," 145.

28. Marcum, *Hymns We Like to Sing*.

29. "God of the Sparrow" was written by Jaroslav Vajda in 1983. Five of the six verses feature questions about "the creature," similar to verse 1: "God of the sparrow/ God of the whale/ God of the swirling stars/ How does the creature say Awe/ How does the creature say Praise."

30. Mall, *God Rock, Inc.*; Stowe, *No Sympathy for the Devil*; Wagner, *Music, Branding and Consumer Culture in Church*.

31. Busman, "(Re)Sounding Passion"; Ingalls, *Singing the Congregation*; Ingalls, "Awesome in the Place"; Mall, *God Rock, Inc.*; Nekola, "Between This World and the Next"; Lim and Ruth, *Lovin' on Jesus*.

32. Ingalls, *Singing the Congregation*, 10.

33. McCracken, "Hipster Faith."

34. McCracken.

35. Miller, *Traveling Home*, 203.

234 / Notes to Chapter 5

36. Ingalls, *Singing the Congregation*; Mall, *God Rock, Inc.*; Nekola, "Between This World and the Next"; Nekola, "'More than Just a Music'"; Wagner, *Music, Branding and Consumer Culture in Church*.

37. Ingalls, *Singing the Congregation*, 11.

38. Lim and Ruth, *Lovin' on Jesus*.

39. Dawn, *Reaching Out without Dumbing Down*; Hustad, *True Worship*; Langford, *Transitions in Worship*.

40. Frame, *Contemporary Worship Music*, 8.

41. Langford, *Transitions in Worship*, 30.

42. McCurley, interview with Deborah Justice.

43. Keane, *Christian Moderns*, 2.

44. Loveland and Wheeler, *From Meetinghouse to Megachurch*, 257.

45. Dawn, *Reaching Out without Dumbing Down*; Hustad, *True Worship*.

46. During my fieldwork, the nine most-often sung songs in Hillsboro's Contemporary service were "Breathe," "Draw Me Close," "Outrageous Grace," "I Surrender All," "I Give You My Heart," "Holy, Holy, Holy," "Here I Am to Worship," "God of Wonders," and "All My Life."

47. Bebbington, *Evangelicalism in Modern Britain*; Dayton and Johnston, *Variety of American Evangelicalism*; Eskridge, "Defining Evangelicalism."

48. Gray, "'When in Our Music God Is Glorified.'"

49. Slobin, *Subcultural Sounds*.

50. Putnam, *Bowling Alone*.

51. Wilford, *Sacred Subdivisions*.

52. Music and lyrics by Martin Smith, ©1994 Curious? Records.

53. Music by Conrad Kocher, 1838. Lyrics by Folliott Sandford Pierpoint, 1864.

54. Cannell, *Anthropology of Christianity*, 43.

55. Robinson, "Yoga, the Manger, and the Grumpy Old Fart."

Chapter 5. "We're Only Medium Contemporary": Creating Identity Boundaries

1. Warner, *New Wine in Old Wineskins*, 291–292.

2. Thorngate, "New Harmonies."

3. Finke and Stark, *Churching of America*.

4. Lorton, "Christian Music's Authenticity Problem"; Powers, "Mumford & Sons Preaches to Masses."

5. Noonan, *Guitar in America*.

6. Busman, "(Re)Sounding Passion."

7. General Assembly Mission Council, "Presbyterian Distinctives."

8. Cf. Bealle, *Public Worship, Private Faith*; Miller, *Traveling Home*.

Notes to Chapter 6 / 235

9. "Glory to God."

10. McCormick, "Presbyterian Hymnody and Hymnals, USA."

11. Marini, *Sacred Song in America*.

12. Langford, *Transitions in Worship*, 28.

13. Words and music by Charles Austin Miles, 1913.

14. Finke and Stark, *Churching of America*.

15. Hicks, "Hymns Movement"; "Red Mountain Music."

16. Benedict, "Observations on the New Hymns Movement."

17. Cf. Driscoll et al., *Listening to the Beliefs of Emerging Churches*; Gibbs and Bolger, *Emerging Churches*; Kimball, *Emerging Church*; Kimball, Crowder, and Morgenthaler, *Emerging Worship*.

18. Typically, Sundays following major holidays (Christmas and Easter) and during the summer when many families are on vacation see fewer congregants in the pews.

19. Hamilton, "Triumph of the Praise Songs | Christianity Today"; Ingalls, "Awesome in the Place."

20. Rommen, *Mek Some Noise*, 2.

21. Hoffman, *Art of Public Prayer*.

Chapter 6. Spatial Diversity:
Making Places for Traditional and Contemporary Worship

1. Written by John Thompson of El Shaddai fame and bluegrass giant Earl Scruggs's son Randy. John W. Thompson and Randy Scruggs, 1982 Full Armor Publishing Company (administered by peermusic), CCLI Song Number 24140.

2. Eskridge, *God's Forever Family*; Ingalls, *Singing the Congregation*; Mall, *God Rock, Inc.*; Stowe, *No Sympathy for the Devil*; Turner, *Bill Bright and Campus Crusade for Christ*.

3. Jones, *End of White Christian America*, 7.

4. Park, Ruth, and Rethmeier, *Worshiping with the Anaheim Vineyard*, 7.

5. Loveland and Wheeler, *From Meetinghouse to Megachurch*, 5.

6. Eskridge, *God's Forever Family*; Justice, "Religion Reinserted"; Justice, "Church in the Cinema"; Stowe, *No Sympathy for the Devil*.

7. Mall, *God Rock, Inc.*; Wagner, "Branding, Music, and Religion."

8. Justice, "Multi-site Mediated Worship."

9. Bohlman, Blumhofer, and Chow, *Music in American Religious Experience*; Finke and Scheitle, "Understanding Schisms"; Lewis and Lewis, *Sacred Schisms*.

10. Mather, *Magnalia Christi Americana*, 264.

11. Jennings, *After Whiteness*; Jones, *White Too Long*; Joshi, *White Christian Privilege*; Kendi, *Stamped from the Beginning*; Tisby, *Color of Compromise*.

12. "Pew Religious Landscape Study."

236 / Notes to Chapter 7

13. Peterson and Kern, "Changing Highbrow Taste."
14. Lewis and Lewis, *Sacred Schisms*, 1.
15. Ross, *Evangelical versus Liturgical?*
16. Hamilton, "Triumph of the Praise Songs | Christianity Today."
17. Kapp, *Annual Well-Church Assessment.*
18. Loveland and Wheeler, *From Meetinghouse to Megachurch*, 109.
19. Loveland and Wheeler, 110.
20. Luke 10:38–42, New International Version.
21. Dawn, *Reaching Out without Dumbing Down*; Frame, *Contemporary Worship Music*; Hustad, *True Worship*; Langford, *Transitions in Worship.*
22. Peterson and Kern, "Changing Highbrow Taste."

Chapter 7. Social Diversity: Defrosting the Frozen Chosen

1. See Justice and Hadley, "Collaborative Fieldwork."
2. Quoted in Henderson, "Dance Discourse in the Music and Lives of Presbyterian Mvano Women in Southern Malawi," 15.
3. Lausevic, *Balkan Fascination.*
4. Felski, "Nothing to Declare."
5. Jones, *White Too Long*; Jones, *End of White Christian America*; DiAngelo and Dyson, *White Fragility*; Swanson, *Redisciplining the White Church.*
6. Schutz, *Collected Papers*, 177.
7. Putnam, *Bowling Alone.*
8. Nix, interview with Deborah Justice, June 5, 2008.
9. Brown, *Good Taste, Bad Taste, and Christian Taste*; Kock, "Between the Altar and the Choir-Loft."
10. Hillsboro Presbyterian Church, "Hillsboro Presbyterian Church Welcome Packet."
11. Turino, *Music as Social Life.*
12. Cohen, *Making of a Reform Jewish Cantor.*
13. Nettl, "Mozart and the Ethnomusicological Study of Western Culture."
14. Warner, *New Wine in Old Wineskins*, 291.
15. Luhrmann, *When God Talks Back.*
16. VanderHamm, "Virtuosity, Ravi Shankar, and the Valuation of Skill."
17. Schutz and Luckmann, "Everyday Life-World and the Natural Attitude," 11.
18. Luhrmann, *When God Talks Back.*
19. Chaves, *Congregations in America.*
20. Mall, *God Rock, Inc.*, 22.
21. Ingalls, *Singing the Congregation*, 5.
22. Turino, *Music as Social Life.*

Notes to Conclusion / 237

23. Mall, *God Rock, Inc.*, 19.
24. *Traveling Home*, 197.
25. Reddy, "Against Constructionism."
26. Tatum, *Why Are All the Black Kids Sitting Together in the Cafeteria?*, 72.

Conclusion: Music, Faith, and Reconfiguring American Protestant Identities

1. Chaves, *Congregations in America*, 133.
2. Berger, *Stance*; Justice, "Cosmopolitan Dichotomy"; Justice and Hadley, "Collaborative Fieldwork."
3. Putnam, *Bowling Alone*; Wilford, *Sacred Subdivisions*.
4. Quoted in Zylstra, "Surprise Change in How Multiethnic Churches Affect Race Views."
5. Swanson, *Redisciplining the White Church*, 27.
6. Emerson and Smith, *Divided by Faith*; Shelton and Emerson, *Blacks and Whites in Christian America*.
7. See Justice and Hadley, "Collaborative Fieldwork."
8. "Pew Religious Landscape Study."
9. Swindler, "Culture in Action"
10. Emerson and Smith, *Divided by Faith*.
11. Jones, *White Too Long*, 99.
12. Jones, *White Too Long*, 106.
13. Jones, *End of White Christian America*, 230.

Bibliography

#8. Interview with Deborah Justice, July 3, 2008.

"2016ResolutionofRepentance.Pdf." http://www.cumberland.org/gao/assembly/2016ResolutionOfRepentance.pdf. Accessed January 24, 2021.

About William and Mary. "History and Traditions." https://www.wm.edu/about/history/index.php. Accessed July 16, 2020.

Alberoni, Francesco. *Movement and Institution*. Translated by Patricia C. Arden Delmoro. New York: Columbia University Press, 1984.

"American Congregations at the Beginning of the 21st Century: National Congregations Study." https://sites.duke.edu/ncsweb/files/2019/03/NCSII_report_final.pdf 2012.

Ammerman, Nancy. *Congregation and Community*. New Brunswick, NJ: Rutgers University Press, 1997.

Anderson, Benedict. *Imagined Communities*. London: Verso, 1983.

Anderson, Carol. *White Rage*. Rpt. ed. New York: Bloomsbury Adult, 2017.

Asad, Talal. *Genealogies of Religion: Discipline and Reasons of Power in Christianity and Islam*. Baltimore, MD: Johns Hopkins University Press, 1993.

Baum, Joel, and Jitendra V. Singh. "Organizational Niches and the Dynamics of Organizational Mortality." *American Journal of Sociology*, no. 100 (1994): 346–380.

Bauman, Richard, and Charles L. Briggs. *Voices of Modernity: Language Ideologies and the Politics of Inequality*. New York: Cambridge University Press, 2003.

Bealle, John. *Public Worship, Private Faith: Sacred Harp and American Folksong*. Atlanta: University of Georgia Press, 1997.

Bebbington, David W. *Evangelicalism in Modern Britain: A History from the 1730s to the 1980s*. New ed. London: Routledge, 1989.

Belsie, Laurent. "A New Nationalism on the Rise." *Christian Science Monitor*, June 11, 2002.

Benedict, Bruce. "Observations on the New Hymns Movement." *Cardiphonia* (blog), 2012. http://cardiphonia.org/2012/01/17/observations-on-the-new-hymns-movement/.

240 / Bibliography

Berger, Harris M. *Stance: Ideas about Emotion, Style, and Meaning for the Study of Expressive Culture.* Middletown, CT: Wesleyan University Press, 2010.

Berger, Peter L. *The Sacred Canopy: Elements of a Sociological Theory of Religion.* New York: Anchor, 1967.

Blumhofer, Edith. *Singing the Lord's Song in a Strange Land: Hymnody in the History of North American Protestantism.* Birmingham: University Alabama Press, 2004.

Bohlman, Philip, Edith Blumhofer, and Maria Chow, eds. *Music in American Religious Experience.* Oxford: Oxford University Press, 2006.

Bohlman, Philip V. "Introduction: Music in American Religious Experience." In *Music in American Religious Experience*, edited by Philip Bohlman, Edith Blumhofer, and Maria Chow, 3–22. Oxford: Oxford University Press, 2006.

Brettell, Caroline B. *When They Read What We Write: The Politics of Ethnography.* New York: Bergin & Garvey, 1996.

Brill, Earl H. *Religion and the Rise of the University: A Study of the Secularization of American Higher Education, 1870–1910.* Ann Arbor, MI: University Microfilms, 1970.

Brown, Frank Burch. *Good Taste, Bad Taste, and Christian Taste: Aesthetics in Religious Life.* Oxford: Oxford University Press, 2003.

Burkholder, J. Peter, Donald Jay Grout, and Claude V. Palisca. *A History of Western Music.* Eighth Edition. New York: W. W. Norton, 2009.

Busman, Joshua. "(Re)Sounding Passion: Listening to American Evangelical Worship Music, 1997–2015." PhD dissertation, University of North Carolina at Chapel Hill, 2015.

Byars, Ronald P. *The Future of Protestant Worship: Beyond the Worship Wars.* 1st ed. Nashville, TN: Westminster John Knox Press, 2002.

Campbell, Alexander. "An Address on Colleges, Delivered in the City of Wheeling, Va., 1854, Being One of a Series of Lectures in Behalf of the Erection of a New Church Edifice in That City." *Millennial Harbinger* 4, no. 2 (1854): 61.

Cannell, Fenella. *The Anthropology of Christianity.* Durham, NC: Duke University Press, 2006.

Cannon, Ben. Interview with Deborah Justice, September 22, 2008.

Case, Dick. "One of Syracuse's Oldest Churches Closes on Easter." Syracuse.com, February 23, 2012. https://www.syracuse.com/opinion/2012/02/one_of_syracuses_oldest_church.html.

Chapman, Reynolds. "Worship in Black and White." *Christianity Today*, 2011.

Chaves, Mark. *Congregations in America.* Cambridge: Harvard University Press, 2004.

"Church History," n.d.

Cimino, Richard, and Don Lattin. *Shopping for Faith: American Religion in the New Millennium.* 1st ed. San Francisco: Jossey-Bass, 2002.

Bibliography / 241

Claman, Victor N., David E. Butler, and Jessica A. Boyatt. *Acting on Your Faith: Congregations Making a Difference—A Guide to Success in Service and Social Action*. Boston: Insights, 1994.

Cohen, Judah. *The Making of a Reform Jewish Cantor: Musical Authority, Cultural Investment*. Bloomington: Indiana University Press, 2009.

Coote, Robert. "The Hymns That Keep on Going." *Christianity Today*, 2011.

Corbitt, J. Nathan. *The Sound of the Harvest: Music's Mission in Church and Culture*. Grand Rapids, MI: Baker Books, 1998.

Costen, Melva Wilson. *In Spirit and in Truth: The Music of African American Worship*. Louisville, KY: Westminster John Knox Press, 2004.

Dawn, Marva J. *Reaching Out without Dumbing Down: A Theology of Worship for This Urgent Time*. Grand Rapids, MI: Wm. B. Eerdmans, 1995.

Dayton, Donald W., and Robert K. Johnston, eds. *The Variety of American Evangelicalism*. Knoxville: University of Tennessee Press, 2001.

"The Definition of a Megachurch from Hartford Institute for Religion Research." http://hirr.hartsem.edu/megachurch/definition.html. Accessed December 5, 2020.

DiAngelo, Robin, and Michael Eric Dyson. *White Fragility: Why It's So Hard for White People to Talk about Racism*. Rpt. ed. Boston: Beacon Press, 2018.

Douglas, Mary. "Social Preconditions of Enthusiasm and Heterodoxy." In *Forms of Symbolic Action*, edited by Robert F. Spencer, 69–79. Seattle: University of Washington Press, 1969.

Driscoll, Mark, John Burke, Dan Kimball, Doug Pagitt, and Karen Ward. *Listening to the Beliefs of Emerging Churches: Five Perspectives*. Grand Rapids, MI: Zondervan, 2007.

Dueck, Jonathan. "Binding and Loosing in Song: Conflict, Identity, and Canadian Mennonite Music." *Ethnomusicology* 55, no. 2 (2011): 229–254.

Dueck, Jonathan, and Suzel Reily. Introduction. In *The Oxford Handbook of Music and World Christianities*, edited by Jonathan Dueck and Suzel Riley, 1–32. New York: Oxford University Press, 2016.

Ellingson, Stephen. *The Megachurch and the Mainline: Remaking Religious Tradition in the Twenty-First Century*. Chicago: University of Chicago Press, 2007.

Ellwood, Robert S. *Alternative Altars: Unconventional and Eastern Spirituality in America*. Chicago: University of Chicago Press, 1979.

Emerson, Michael O., and Christian Smith. *Divided by Faith: Evangelical Religion and the Problem of Race in America*. Oxford: Oxford University Press, 2012.

Eskridge, Larry. "Defining Evangelicalism." Institute for the Study of American Evangelicals, 2011. http://isae.wheaton.edu/defining-evangelicalism/defining-the-term-in-contemporary-times/.

———. *God's Forever Family: The Jesus People Movement in America*. 1st ed. New York: Oxford University Press, 2013.

242 / Bibliography

Etherington, C. L. *Protestant Worship: Its History and Practice*. New York: Holt, Rinehart, and Winston, 1962.

Felski, Rita. "Nothing to Declare: Identity, Shame, and the Lower Middle Class." *PMLA* 115, no. 1 (January 1, 2000): 33–45. https://doi.org/10.2307/463229.

Finke, Roger, and Christopher P. Scheitle. "Understanding Schisms: Theoretical Explanations for Their Origins." In *Sacred Schisms: How Religions Divide*, 1st ed., edited by James R. Lewis and Sarah M. Lewis, 11–34. Cambridge: Cambridge University Press, 2009.

Finke, Roger, and Rodney Stark. *The Churching of America, 1776–2005: Winners and Losers in Our Religious Economy*. New Brunswick: Rutgers University Press, 2005.

Fisher, Alexander J. "Music and Religious Change." In *The Cambridge History of Christianity*, 6:386–405. Cambridge: Cambridge University Press, 2007.

"Focus on 'Worship Wars' Hides the Real Issues Regarding Connection to God." The Barna Group, 2002. http://www.barna.org/barna-update/article/5-barna-update/85-focus-on-qworship-warsq-hides-the-real-issues-regarding-connection-to-god.

Frame, John M. *Contemporary Worship Music: A Biblical Defense*. Phillipsburg, NJ: P & R, 1997.

Frank, John. "One Nation, Indescribable; More People Describe Their Ancestry as 'American,' Census Finds." *Roanoke (Va.) Times and World News*, July 4, 2002.

General Assembly Mission Council. "Presbyterian Distinctives—Presbyterian 101—Ministries and Programs—GAMC." Presbyterian Church (USA). http://gamc.pcusa.org/ministries/101/distinctives/. Accessed March 23, 2010.

Gibbs, Eddie, and Ryan K. Bolger. *Emerging Churches: Creating Christian Community in Postmodern Cultures*. Grand Rapids, MI: Baker Academic, 2005.

"Glory to God (Purple Pew Edition, Presbyterian) Hardback: PC USA Store." http://www.pcusastore.com/Products/0664503136/glory-to-god-purple-pew-edition-presbyterian.aspx. Accessed May 2, 2015.

Gmeiner, Tim. Interview with Deborah Justice, September 10, 2008.

Goffman, Erving. *Frame Analysis: An Essay on the Organization of Experience*. Boston: Northeastern University Press, 1986.

Gore, Matthew H. *The History of the Cumberland Presbyterian Church in Kentucky to 1988*. Memphis, TN: Joint Heritage Committee, 2000.

Gray, Judith. " 'When in Our Music God Is Glorified': Singing and Singing about Singing in a Congregational Church." In *Music in American Religious Experience*, edited by Philip Bohlman, Edith Blumhofer, and Maria Chow, 195–214. Oxford: Oxford University Press, 2006.

Greater Good. "Diversity Definition | What Is Diversity." https://greatergood.berkeley.edu/topic/diversity/definition. Accessed July 20, 2020.

Grossman, Cathy Lynn. "Most Religious Groups in USA Have Lost Ground, Survey Finds." *USA Today*, March 9, 2009.

Bibliography / 243

Hall, Lesli. Interview with Deborah Justice, August 26, 2008.

Hamilton, Michael. "The Triumph of the Praise Songs | Christianity Today | A Magazine of Evangelical Conviction." *Christianity Today*, July 12, 1999. http://www.christianitytoday.com/ct/1999/july12/9t8028.html.

———. "The Triumph of the Praise Songs: How Guitars Beat Out the Organ in the Worship Wars." *Christianity Today*, July 12, 1999. http://www.christianity today.com/ct/1999/july12/9t8028.html.

Henderson, Clara. "Dance Discourse in the Music and Lives of Presbyterian Mvano Women in Southern Malawi." PhD dissertation, Indiana University, 2009.

———. "A Paradigm of Africanisation: Music of Mvano Women of the Church of Central Africa Presbyterian, Malawi." MA thesis, Indiana University, 1995.

Hillsboro Presbyterian Church. "Hillsboro Presbyterian Church Welcome Packet," 2008.

The History of the Presbyterian Church. South Deerfield, MI: Channing Bete, 2000.

Hobsbawm, Eric J., and Terence O. Ranger. *The Invention of Tradition*. Cambridge: Cambridge University Press, 1992.

Hoffman, Lawrence A. *The Art of Public Prayer: Not for Clergy Only*. 2nd ed. Woodstock, VT: Skylight Paths, 1999.

Hollinger, David. "After Cloven Tongues of Fire: Ecumenical Protestantism and the Modern American Encounter with Diversity." *Journal of American History*, 98, no. 1 (2011): 21–48.

Holzapfel, Otto. "Singing from the Right Songbook: Ethnic Identity and Language Transformation in German American Hymnals." In *Music in American Religious Experience*, edited by Philip Bohlman, Edith Blumhofer, and Maria Chow, 175–194. Oxford: Oxford University Press, 2006.

Hong, Angie. "Don't Hire People of Color as Worship Leaders and Expect Them to Change Your Church." *Faith and Leadership*. https://faithandleadership. com/angie-hong-creating-diverse-congregation-requires-more-diverse-wor-ship. Accessed May 15, 2021.

Hood, Mantle. "Training and Research Methods in Ethnomusicology." *Ethnomusicology Newsletter*, no. 11 (n.d.): 2–8.

Hout, Michael, Andrew Greeley, and Melissa J. Wilde. "The Demographic Imperative in Religious Change in the United States." *American Journal of Sociology* 107, no. 2 (September 2001): 468–500. https://doi.org/10.1086/324189.

Hustad, Don. *True Worship: Reclaiming the Wonder and Majesty*. Wheaton, IL: H. Shaw, 1998.

"Hymn." In *Oxford Dictionary of Music Online*. Oxford: Oxford University Press, 2007.

"The Hymns Movement." Zac Hicks. http://www.zachicks.com/the-hymns-move-ment/. Accessed May 6, 2021.

244 / Bibliography

Ingalls, Monique. "Awesome in the Place: Sound, Space, and Identity in North American Evangelical Worship." PhD dissertation, University of Pennsylvania, 2008.

———. "The Sound of Heaven on Earth: Spiritual Journeys, Eschatological Songs, and Community Formation in Evangelical Conference Worship." Los Angeles, 2010.

Ingalls, Monique M. *Singing the Congregation: How Contemporary Worship Music Forms Evangelical Community.* New York: Oxford University Press, 2018.

Jackson, George Pullen. *The Story of the Sacred Harp, 1844–1944.* Nashville, TN: Vanderbilt University Press, 1944.

———. *White and Negro Spirituals: Their Life Span and Kinship.* New York: J.J. Augustin, 1943.

———. *White Spirituals in the Southern Uplands.* Mineola, NY: Dover, 1966.

Jennings, Willie James. *After Whiteness: An Education in Belonging.* Illus. ed. Grand Rapids, MI: Eerdmans, 2020.

Johnson, Birgitta J. "Singing Down Walls of Race, Ethnicity, and Tradition in an African American Megachurch." *Liturgy* 33, no. 3 (2018): 37–45.

Jones, Alisha Lola. *Flaming? The Peculiar Theopolitics of Fire and Desire in Black Male Gospel Performance.* New York: Oxford University Press, 2020.

Jones, Robert P. *The End of White Christian America.* New York: Simon & Schuster, 2016.

———. *White Too Long: The Legacy of White Supremacy in American Churches.* New York: Simon & Schuster, 2020.

Jones, Todd. Interview with Deborah Justice, January 15, 2009.

Joshi, Khyati Y. *White Christian Privilege: The Illusion of Religious Equality in America.* New York: New York University Press, 2020.

Justice, Deborah. "Church in the Cinema: Using Music and Media to Embrace Transnational Evangelicalism." Eskisehir, Turkey, 2012.

———. "A Cosmopolitan Dichotomy: Mainline Protestantism and Contemporary versus Traditional Worship Music." In *The Oxford Handbook of World Christianities,* edited by Jonathan Dueck and Suzel Reily, 487–512. Oxford: Oxford University Press, 2016.

———. "Multi-Site Mediated Worship: Why Simulcast Sermons Need Live Local Praise Bands." In *Media and Religion: The Global View,* edited by Stewart Hoover, 63–82. Berlin: De Gruyter, 2021.

———. "Religion Reinserted: When Church and Cinema Blur Boundaries through Media-Savvy Evangelicalism." *Journal of Religion, Media, and Digital Culture* 3, no. 4 (2014): 84–119.

———. "Sonic Change, Social Change, Sacred Change: Music and the Reconfiguration of American Christianity." PhD dissertation, Indiana University, 2012.

Justice, Deborah, and Fredara Hadley. "Collaborative Fieldwork, 'Stance,' and Ethnography." *Yearbook for Traditional Music* 47 (2015): 64–81.

Bibliography / 245

Kapp, Deborah. *The Annual Well-Church Assessment*. Louisville, KY: Research Services, Presbyterian Church (U.S.A.), 2008.

Kartomi, Margaret J. "The Processes and Results of Musical Culture Contact: A Discussion of Terminology and Concepts." *Ethnomusicology* 25, no. 2 (1981): 227–249.

Keane, Webb. *Christian Moderns*. Los Angeles: University of California Press, 2007.

Keightley, Keir. "Reconsidering Rock." In *The Cambridge Companion to Pop and Rock*, edited by Will Straw, Simon Frith, and John Street, 131. New York: Cambridge University Press, 2001.

Kelly, Sherry. Interview with Deborah Justice, March 12, 2008.

———. Interview with Deborah Justice, June 25, 2008.

Kelman, Ari Y. *Shout to the Lord: Making Worship Music in Evangelical Americana*. New York: New York University Press, 2018.

Kendi, Ibram X. *How to Be an Antiracist*. London: One World, 2019.

———. *Stamped from the Beginning: The Definitive History of Racist Ideas in America*. Rpt. ed. Queens, NY: Bold Type Books, 2017.

Kidd, David, and Nancy McCurley. Interview with Deborah Justice, March 13, 2008.

Kimball, Dan. *The Emerging Church: Vintage Christianity for New Generations*. Grand Rapids, MI: Zondervan/Youth Specialties, 2003.

Kimball, Dan, David Crowder, and Sally Morgenthaler. *Emerging Worship: Creating Worship Gatherings for New Generations*. Grand Rapids, MI: Zondervan/ Youth Specialties, 2004.

Kisliuk, Michelle. *Seize the Dance! BaAka Musical Life and the Ethnography of Performance*. Oxford: Oxford University Press, 2000.

Kock, Gerald. "Between the Altar and the Choir-Loft: Church Music—Liturgy or Art?" In *Music and the Experience of God*, edited by Mary Collins, David Noel Power, and Mellonee Victoria Burnim, 11–19. London: T&T Clark, 1989.

Kraft, Chuck. "Organ/Guitar Preference Reflects View of God." *Worship Leader*, 1993.

———. "Organ/Guitar Question a Matter of Context." *Worship Leader*, 1993.

Langford, Andy. *Transitions in Worship: Moving from Traditional to Contemporary*. Nashville, TN: Abingdon Press, 1999.

Laugrand, Frederic B., and Jarich G. Oosten. *Inuit Shamanism and Christianity: Transitions and Transformations in the Twentieth Century*. Montreal: McGill-Queen's University Press, 2009.

Lausevic, Mirjana. *Balkan Fascination: Creating an Alternative Music Culture in America*. Oxford: Oxford University Press, 2007.

Leftwich, Phil. Interview with Deborah Justice, January 8, 2009.

Levine, Lawrence. *Highbrow/Lowbrow: The Emergence of Cultural Hierarchy in America*. Cambridge: Harvard University Press, 1990.

Lewis, James R., and Sarah M. Lewis. *Sacred Schisms: How Religions Divide*. 1st ed. Cambridge: Cambridge University Press, 2009.

246 / Bibliography

Lieberman, Frederic, E. Eugene Helm, and Claude Palisca. "Should Ethnomusicology Be Abolished?" *Journal of the College Music Society* 17, no. 2 (1977): 198–206.

Lim, Swee Hong, and Lester Ruth. *Lovin' on Jesus: A Concise History of Contemporary Worship.* Nashville, TN: Abingdon, 2017.

Long, Thomas G. *Beyond the Worship Wars: Building Vital and Faithful Worship.* Herndon, VA: Alban Institute, 2001.

Lorton, Zach. "Christian Music's Authenticity Problem (or How I Learned to Stop Consuming and Actually Engage)." *Rogue* (blog), August 20, 2013. https://www.patheos.com/blogs/geekgoesrogue/2013/08/christian-musics-authenticity-problem-or-how-i-learned-to-stop-consuming-and-actually-engage/.

"Love Divine, All Loves Excelling." Hymnary.org. https://hymnary.org/text/love_divine_all_love_excelling_joy_of_he. Accessed May 11, 2021.

Loveland, Anne C., and Otis B. Wheeler. *From Meetinghouse to Megachurch: A Material and Cultural History.* St. Louis: University of Missouri Press, 2003.

Luhrmann, T. M. *When God Talks Back: Understanding the American Evangelical Relationship with God.* New York: Knopf, 2012.

Makujina, John. *Measuring the Music: Another Look at the Contemporary Christian Music Debate.* Salem, OH: Schmul, 2000.

Mall, Andrew. *God Rock, Inc.: The Business of Niche Music.* Oakland: University of California Press, 2021.

Marcum, Jack. *Hymns We Like to Sing.* Louisville, KY: General Assembly Council of the Presbyterian Church (USA), 2009.

Marcus, George E. *Ethnography through Thick and Thin.* Princeton, NJ: Princeton University Press, 1998.

Marini, Stephen A. "Hymnody and History: Early American Evangelical Hymns as Sacred Music." In *Music in American Religious Experience*, edited by Philip Bohlman, Edith Blumhofer, and Maria Chow, 123–154. Oxford: Oxford University Press, 2006.

———. "Rehearsal for Revival : Sacred Singing and the Great Awakening in America." In *Sacred Sound: Music in Religious Thought and Practice*, edited by Joyce Irwin, 71–91. Chicago: Scholars Press, 1983.

———. *Sacred Song in America: Religion, Music, and Public Culture.* Chicago: University of Illinois Press, 2003.

Marti, Gerardo. *Worship across the Racial Divide: Religious Music and the Multiracial Congregation.* Oxford: Oxford University Press, 2012.

McCalla, Lynne, and Kerry McCalla. Interview with Deborah Justice, September 13, 2008.

McCormick, David. "Presbyterian Hymnody and Hymnals, USA." In *The Canterbury Dictionary of Hymnology.* London: Canterbury Press, 2014. https://hymnology.hymnsam.co.uk/p/presbyterian-hymnody-and-hymnals,-usa?q=Presbyterian.

Bibliography / 247

McCracken, Brett. "Hipster Faith." *Christianity Today*, 2010. http://www.christianitytoday.com/ct/2010/september/9.24.html?start=2.

McCurley, Nancy. Interview with Deborah Justice, March 9, 2009.

McGann, Mary. *A Precious Fountain: Music in the Worship of an African American Catholic Community*. Collegeville, MN: Liturgical Press, 2004.

McKay, David Phares, and Richard Crawford. *William Billings of Boston: Eighteenth Century Composer*. Princeton, NJ: Princeton University Press, 1975.

Merriam, Alan. "Ethnomusicology: Discussion and History of the Field." *Ethnomusicology* 4, no. 3 (1960): 107–114.

Metzl, Jonathan M. *Dying of Whiteness: How the Politics of Racial Resentment Is Killing America's Heartland*. Illus. ed. New York: Basic Books, 2020.

Miller, Kiri. *Traveling Home: Sacred Harp Singing and American Pluralism*. Chicago: University of Illinois Press, 2010.

Minor, Horace. "Body Ritual among the Nacirema." *American Anthropologist* 58, no. 3 (1956): 503–507.

Montell, William Lynwood. *Singing the Glory Down: Amateur Gospel Music in South Central Kentucky, 1900–1990*. Lexington: University Press of Kentucky, 1991.

Moorhead, James. "Presbyterians and Slavery." https://slavery.princeton.edu/stories/presbyterians-and-slavery. Accessed January 24, 2021.

Nekola, Anna. "'More than Just a Music': Conservative Christian Anti-Rock Discourse and the U.S. Culture Wars." *Popular Music* 32, no. 3 (2013): 407–426.

Nekola, Anna E. "Between This World and the Next: The Musical 'Worship Wars' and Evangelical Ideology in the United States, 1960–2005." PhD dissertation, University of Wisconsin–Madison, 2009.

Nettl, Bruno. *Heartland Excursions: Ethnomusicological Reflections on Schools of Music*. Chicago: University of Illinois Press, 1995.

———. "Mozart and the Ethnomusicological Study of Western Culture (an Essay in Four Movements)." *Yearbook for Traditional Music* 21 (January 1, 1989): 1–16. https://doi.org/10.2307/767764.

———. *The Study of Ethnomusicology: Thirty-One Issues and Concepts*. Chicago: University of Illinois Press, 2005.

Niebuhr, H. Richard. *The Social Sources of Denominationalism*. New York: Henry Holt, 1929.

Nix, Stephen. Interview with Deborah Justice, June 5, 2008.

———. Interview with Deborah Justice, March 19, 2009.

No I Has Heard. "The Worship Wars and the Black Church," January 10, 2016. https://noihasseen.wordpress.com/2016/01/10/the-worship-wars-and-the-black-church/.

Noll, Mark A. "'Christian America' and 'Christian Canada.'" In *The Cambridge History of Christianity*, edited by Sheridan Gilley and Brian Stanley, 8:359–380. Cambridge: Cambridge University Press, 2006.

248 / Bibliography

Noonan, Jeffrey J. *The Guitar in America: Victorian Era to Jazz Age*. Jackson: University Press of Mississippi, 2007.

Noyes, Dorothy. "Group." *Journal of American Folklore* 108, no. 430 (1995): 449–378.

Park, Andy, Lester Ruth, and Cindy Rethmeier. *Worshiping with the Anaheim Vineyard: The Emergence of Contemporary Worship*. Grand Rapids, MI: Eerdmans, 2016.

Peterson, Richard A., and Roger M. Kern. "Changing Highbrow Taste: From Snob to Omnivore." *American Sociological Review* 61, no. 5 (1996): 900–907.

"Pew Religious Landscape Study," 2015. https://www.pewforum.org/2015/05/12/chapter-1-the-changing-religious-composition-of-the-u-s/.

Powell, Michael. "Rethinking Who They Are: Census Shows People Are Declining to Report Their Heritage." *Washington Post*, May 25, 2002.

Powers, Ann. "Mumford & Sons Preaches to Masses." NPR.org, September 12, 2012. https://www.npr.org/sections/therecord/2012/09/27/161883725/mumford-sons-preaches-to-masses.

Presbyterian Hymnal Committee. "A Statement on Language." The Presbyterian Hymnal Project. http://presbyterianhymnal.org/committeeStatements.html. Accessed December 17, 2010.

Putnam, Robert D. *Bowling Alone: The Collapse and Revival of American Community*. New York: Touchstone Books by Simon & Schuster, 2001.

Randel, Don Michael. "The Canons in the Musicological Toolbox." In *Disciplining Music: Musicology and Its Canons*, edited by Katherine Bergeron and Philip V. Bohlman, 9–22. Chicago: University of Chicago Press, 1992.

"Red Mountain Music." http://www.redmountainmusic.com/. Accessed May 6, 2021.

Reddy, William. "Against Constructionism: The Historical Ethnography of Emotions." *Current Anthropology* 38, no. 3 (1997): 327–351.

Research Services, Presbyterian Church (U.S.A.). "Religious and Demographic Profile of Presbyterians, 2008: Findings from the Initial Survey of the 2009–2011 Presbyterian Panel." Louisville, KY, 2009.

Robbins, Joel. "Afterword: On Limits, Ruptures, Meaning, and Meaninglessness." In *The Limits of Meaning: Case Studies in the Anthropology of Christianity*, edited by Matthew Engelke and Matt Tomlinson, 211–224. New York: Berghahn Books, 2006.

Robinson, Scott. "Yoga, the Manger, and the Grumpy Old Fart." *Elephant Journal*, December 19, 2010. http://www.elephantjournal.com/2010/12/yoga-the-manger-and-the-grumpy-old-fart/.

Rommen, Timothy. *Mek Some Noise: Gospel Music and the Ethics of Style in Trinidad*. Berkeley: University of California Press, 2007.

Roof, Wade Clark. *Spiritual Marketplace: Baby Boomers and the Remaking of American Religion*. Princeton, NJ: Princeton University Press, 2001.

Roof, Wade Clark, and William McKinney. *American Mainline Religion: Its Changing Shape and Future*. New Brunswick, NJ: Rutgers University Press, 1990.

Bibliography / 249

Ross, Melanie. *Evangelical versus Liturgical? Defying a Dichotomy.* Grand Rapids, MI: Wm. B. Eerdmans, 2014.

Ruth, Lester. "The Eruption of the Worship Wars: The Coming of Conflict." *Liturgy* 32, no. 1 (2017): 3–6.

Sahlins, Marshall. "The Sadness of Sweetness: The Native Anthropology of Western Cosmology." *Current Anthropology* 37 (1996): 395–428.

Scherer, Ross P. "Mainline." In *Encyclopedia of Religion and Society*, edited by William H. Swatos and Peter Kivisto, 280–282. New York: Rowman AltaMira, 1998.

Schneider, Herbert Wallace. *Religion in Twentieth-Century America.* Cambridge: Harvard University Press, 1952.

Schutz, A. *Collected Papers, Vol. 2: Studies in Social Theory.* 1st ed. New York: Springer, 1976.

Schutz, Alfred, and Thomas Luckmann. "The Everyday Life-World and the Natural Attitude." In *Structures of the Life-World, Vol. 1*, 1st ed., 3–20. Chicago: Northwestern University Press, 1973.

Shelton, Jason E., and Michael Oluf Emerson. *Blacks and Whites in Christian America: How Racial Discrimination Shapes Religious Convictions.* New York: New York University Press, 2012.

"Should You Make Your Preferences Clear? Study Suggests Yes." *Cornell Chronicle.* https://news.cornell.edu/stories/2021/03/should-you-make-your-preferences-clear-study-suggests-yes. Accessed April 29, 2021.

Slobin, Mark. *Subcultural Sounds: Micromusics of the West.* Middletown, CT: Wesleyan University Press, 1993.

Small, Christopher. *Musicking: The Meanings of Performing and Listening.* 1st ed. Hanover, NH: Wesleyan University Press, 1998.

Smith, Kimberly. *Let Those Who Have Ears Hear.* Enumclaw, WA: Winepress, 2001.

Smith, Kimberly, with Lee Smith. *Oh, Be Careful Little Ears.* Enumclaw, WA: Winepress, 1997.

Spittler, Russell P. "Are Pentecostals and Charismatics Fundamentalists? A Review of American Uses of These Categories." In *Charismatic Christianity as a Global Culture*, edited by Karla Poewe, 103–118. Columbia: University of South Carolina Press, 1994.

Stowe, David W. *No Sympathy for the Devil: Christian Pop Music and the Transformation of American Evangelicalism.* Chapel Hill: University of North Carolina Press, 2011.

Swanson, David W. *Rediscipling the White Church: From Cheap Diversity to True Solidarity.* Downers Grove, IL: IVP, 2020.

"Taking Off the White Mask: It's Time to Recognise the Black Roots of Western Popular Music." *Lovepost*, February 25, 2021. https://www.thelovepost.global/decolonise-your-mind/articles/taking-white-mask-it%E2%80%99s-time-recognise-black-roots-western-popular.

250 / Bibliography

Tatum, Beverly Daniel. *Why Are All the Black Kids Sitting Together in the Cafeteria? And Other Conversations about Race*. Rev. ed. New York: Basic Books, 2017.

Temperley, Nicholas. "Hymn." *Grove Music Online*, edited by Warren Anderson, n.d. Accessed December 13, 2010.

Thorngate, Steve. "New Harmonies: Music and Identity at Four Congregations." *Christian Century (Online Edition)*, 2011. http://www.christiancentury.org/article/2011-11/new-harmonies?print.

Tilley, Terrence W. *Inventing Catholic Tradition*. Maryknoll, NY: Orbis Books, 2003.

Tisby, Jemar. *The Color of Compromise: The Truth about the American Church's Complicity in Racism*. Grand Rapids, MI: Zondervan Reflective, 2020.

Titon, Jeff Todd. *Powerhouse for God: Speech, Chant, and Song in an Appalachian Baptist Church*. Austin: University of Texas Press, 1988.

———. "'Tuned Up with the Grace of God': Music and Experience among Old Regular Baptists." In *Music in American Religious Experience*, edited by Philip Bohlman, Edith Blumhofer, and Maria Chow, 311–334. Oxford: Oxford University Press, 2006.

Towns, Elmer L. *Putting an End to Worship Wars*. Nashville, TN: Broadman & Holman, 1997.

Turino, Thomas. *Music as Social Life: The Politics of Participation*. Chicago: University of Chicago Press, 2008.

Turner, John G. *Bill Bright and Campus Crusade for Christ*. Chapel Hill: University of North Carolina Press, 2008.

Turner, Victor. "Liminality and Communitas." In *The Ritual Process: Structure and Anti-Structure*, 94–130. Chicago: Aldine, 1995.

———. *The Ritual Process: Structure and Anti-Structure*. New Brunswick: Aldine Transaction, 2007.

"U.S. Census Bureau QuickFacts: United States." https://www.census.gov/quickfacts/fact/table/US/PST045219. Accessed May 4, 2021.

VanderHamm, David. "Virtuosity, Ravi Shankar, and the Valuation of Skill." Memorial University, Newfoundland, Canada, 2018.

Wagner, Tom. "Branding, Music, and Religion: Standardization and Adaptation in the Experience of the 'Hillsong Sound.'" In *Religion as Brands: New Perspectives on the Marketization of Religion and Spirituality*. London: Ashgate, 2013.

———. *Music, Branding and Consumer Culture in Church: Hillsong in Focus*. 1st ed. New York: Routledge, 2020.

Walker, Aaron. "Church History." In *Church Cookbook*, 2nd ed., 339–344. Gallatin, TN: Elkins Enterprises, 1982.

Warner, R. Stephen. *New Wine in Old Wineskins: Evangelicals and Liberals in a Small-Town Church*. Berkeley: University of California Press, 1990.

Warren, Rick. *The Purpose-Driven Church: Growth without Compromising Your Message and Mission*. 3rd printing. Grand Rapids, MI: Zondervan, 1995.

Bibliography / 251

Weber, Max. *Economy and Society: An Outline of Interpretive Sociology.* Edited by Guenther Roth and Claus Wittich. Berkeley: University of California Press, 1922.

Wegner, Phillip E. *Imaginary Communities: Utopia, the Nation, and the Spatial Histories of Modernity.* Berkeley: University of California Press, 2002.

Wilford, Justin. *Sacred Subdivisions: The Postmodern Transformation of American Evangelicalism.* New York: New York University Press, 2012.

Wuthnow, Robert. *Producing the Sacred: An Essay on Public Religion.* Chicago: University of Illinois Press, 1994.

Wuthnow, Robert, and John H. Evans, eds. *The Quiet Hand of God: Faith-Based Activism and the Public Role of Mainline Protestantism.* Berkeley: University of California Press, 2002.

York, Terry W. *America's Worship Wars.* Herndon, VA: Hendrickson, 2003.

Zamora, Lois Parkinson. *The Usable Past: The Imagination of History in Recent Fiction of the Americas.* Cambridge: Cambridge University Press, 1997.

Zylstra, Sarah Eekhoff. "Surprise Change in How Multiethnic Churches Affect Race Views." ChristianityToday.com, December 2, 2015. https://www.christianitytoday.com/ct/2015/december-web-only/surprise-shift-in-how-multiethnic-churches-affect-race-view.html.

Index

a cappella singing, 124
Africa: cultures, 184, 47–48; diaspora, 33, 50; Christianity, 47–48; music, 91, 182; slavery in the United States, 63–64
African American. *See* Black Christians, Black churches
Architecture: historic, 164; sacred, 164, 168–169; Traditional versus Contemporary, 172–173
Ammerman, Nancy, 24
amplified sound 102–103, 175, 193, 213
Anderson, Benedict, 59
Applause, 93. *See also* clapping
"As the Deer," 111
audience, 204. *See also* performance
authenticity, 61, 200, 211

band director. *See* band leader
band leader, 90–93, 104–105, 128, 173, 190–192, 195–198
Baptists, 20, 109, 181–184, 204–205, 220
Belmont University, 199
Black: Americans, 71, 212–213; Christians, 33, 133, 220; churches, 160, 220; worship, 33, 133, 135–136
blended worship, 33, 117, 146–151

bluegrass, 132, 134, 139
Bohlman, Philip, 51–52
"Breathe," 122, 234

Calvinism, 108, 133, 185
Catholicism, 21
Chaves, Mark 80, 96, 217
choir, 121, 87–90, 124, 164, 175–176, 181–184, 186–189, 191, 220
choir director, 87, 124, 128, 191, 194, 199–201
chorus. *See* praise and worship
Christianity Today, 21
clapping, 204–205. *See also* applause
clergy. *See* pastor
colonialism, 44–46, 50
concert, 207. *See also* performance
congregations: demographics, 20, 27, 41, 54, 68, 73, 81; histories, 57–60; useable past of, 59–60
commercialism, 111, 125, 141. *See also* consumerism
consumerism, 24. *See also* commercialism
Contemporary: as capitalized genre label, 37; as non-chronological term, 112–114
Cumberland Presbyterian Church, 61–66

254 / Index

dancing, 204, 206–207
destination church, 23–24. *See also*
    niche church
disidentification, 21
diversity: as a value, 129, 183,
    191–192; demographic, 27–29, 55,
    55, 129, 132, 151–152, 169, 180,
    185–186, 220–223; opportunity for,
    17–18, 180, 210, 212–213
drums, 78, 91, 96–98, 105, 170, 221
Dueck, Jonathan, 30, 32, 47

emotion, 100, 116, 125, 128, 136, 190,
    203, 204, 210, 212
ethnicity. *See* race
ethnography. *See* fieldwork
ethnomusicology, 1, 5, 10, 50–52
evangelical, 17, 21–22, 25, 29, 53–55,
    102, 108, 111, 114, 116, 126,
    132–138, 151–152, 163, 190, 198,
    200–203, 221–222

feedback interview, 143–146
fellowship hall, 90–94, 160, 162–163,
    169–180
fieldwork: ethical concerns within,
    46–49, 51, 182–184; technique,
    36–37, 116, 144, 220
financial resources, 159, 161–162
folk, 45–47
folk music, 101, 121, 132–135
frozen chosen, 204–207

"God of the Sparrow," 110, 233
gospel music, 135–136, 142
guitar, 95, 97–98, 101–106, 193
guitarist, 78, 103, 105

hand-raising, 125
heritage, 80–81, 107–109, 132–137,
    218
hymnals, 85–86, 107–110, 121,
    123–125, 135–136, 193–198

hymns: defined, 106–107; retuned
    138, 143, 152; within Presbyterian
    heritage, 107–109; newly composed,
    109; as repetitious, 117–120

imagined communities, 58
immanence, 32, 38, 104, 126–129, 152
Ingalls, Monique, 21, 31, 35, 53, 103,
    111, 207
instruments. *See* guitar; keyboard;
    mandolin; organ; piano

Jones, Robert P. 54, 59, 221–222
Johnson, Birgitta, 33

Kendi, Ibram, 10
keyboard, 90, 104–105, 157, 16, 172,
    215

Lancaster County Bible Church. *See*
    Lives Changed by Christ
"Landa Jesu," 91–93
lighting, 157, 170, 173–174
Lives Changed by Christ (LCBC), 155
"Love Divine, All Loves Excelling,"
    138–140
Luhrmann, Tanya, 200, 203

mainline: decline, 15, 19–21, 222;
    Protestantism, definition of, 20–21;
    history of term, 22; relation to
    mainstream, 22–23
Mall, Andrew, 50, 207
Mandolin, 134
Marti, Gerardo, 4
media: global flows, 111, 143;
    mainstream channels 126
megachurch, 111, 113, 143, 157, 162,
    170
Mennonites, 8, 124
Microphones, 93, 141, 142, 173
Miller, Kiri, 22, 210
money. *See* financial resources

Index / 255

Mumford and Sons, 132, 133, 134
music industry, 98, 111, 157, 199–200, 207

Nacirema, 8, 49–50
Nashville: demographics of, 72–73; history of, 61
Nekola, Anna, 34
niche church, 24, 29, 66

organ, 84–90, 172–173, 97–101, 104–105
organist, 194–195, 199
"Outrageous Grace," 93

parochial school, 67
pastor: attire, 85, 90; and musical authority, 193–198
performance, 22, 170–175, 204
pew, 99, 150, 156, 160, 164, 175
Pew Religious Landscape Study, 222
piano, 87–88, 90, 98, 104–106, 142
pipe organ. See organ
postlude 94, 104, 216
praise and worship, 76, 79, 106, 110–111, 119
praise band, 78–79, 90–94, 104–105, 140–146, 164, 173, 186–191, 193, 203–205
praise chorus, 17, 21, 106–107, 111, 113–114, 119, 193
praise team. See praise band
prayer, 85–93, 127–128, 216–217
preaching. See sermon
prelude 84, 90, 105, 195, 215
Presbyterian Church in America (PCA), 168, 188
Presbyterian Church (USA): demographic norms 73; history, 61–66
psalms, 108, 135
Putnam, Robert B. 25, 116, 187

race, 18, 27, 98, 222
racism, 44, 59–60, 66, 67, 158, 185
recording, 46, 111, 126
recordings. See fieldwork
rehearsal, 88, 93, 178, 201, 215
repetition: in Contemporary worship, 119; in Traditional music, 120; lyrical, 117–120
robes: choir, 87–88, 156, 187, 190; clergy, 85, 164, 187
Rommen, Timothy, 21, 94

sanctuary: as haven, 159–160; as architectural space, 83–90, 155, 156, 159–160, 163–165, 175, 178
schism, 38, 63, 66, 157–158
Schuller, Robert 156
Scots-Irish, 60–61
Scotland, 60
screens 91, 121, 124–125, 157, 164
segregation, 28, 39, 44, 158, 220
sermon, 78, 91, 93, 99, 171, 193, 197, 202, 216
singing technique, 141–142
Slobin, Mark, 7
Spruce Street Baptist, 181–184, 220
Suburbs, 24–25, 68–71, 167, 187

Tatum, Nancy, 71, 212–213
technology 96, 125, 170, 174, 179
teenagers, 205
Tisby, Jamar, 44
Titon, Jeff Todd, 49
Tomlin, Chris, 104, 143
transcendence, 32, 38, 104, 125–129, 152, 173, 218

useable past, 59, 63, 219

Whiteness: as American demographic, 2, 4, 71–72, 112, 167, 222; and American Christianity, 4, 10, 17–20, 28, 33, 44, 59, 73, 158, 180, 219–

256 / Index

Whiteness *(continued)*
221; as identity, 2, 43, 134–135,
181–185; and academia, 5, 6, 8, 46,
48–49, 54

Wilford, Justin, 24, 116
Worship wars: definition of, 31–36;
history, 17, 29
Wuthnow, Robert, 22, 24, 36